Dear Wealth Seeker:

Would you like to make an extra $50,000 to $100,000 a year for life?

Because of your interest in Making Money. I want to work with you on a personal basis to help you reach your financial goals.

My name is Robert Allen. I'm the author of two of the largest selling financial books in history; both #1 New York Times best sellers—read my millions of people in the past 20 years.

My current best-selling audio program from Nightingale/Conant is entitled Multiple Streams of Income: How to Generate a Lifetime of Unlimited Wealth.

103,000 people attended my $500 weekend investment seminars in the 80's.

20,000 people attended my $5,000 week long Wealth Training in the 90's.

Thousands of them are now financially free.

I'm now in the process of finishing my latest book in which I reveal many little known financial techniques and strategies for earning 18%, 36% and as high as 50% on your money. All guaranteed by the government! Plus 6 other ways of earning as much as $1,000 a day right from your own home.

Every time I write a new best seller I do a challenge to prove that the new techniques can be profitably applied by anyone.

When I wrote my first book I said:

"Send me to any city in America, take away my wallet, Give me $100 for living expenses and in 72 hours I will buy you an excellent property, all with none of my own money."

The Los Angeles Times took me up on my challenge. They flew me to San Francisco with an L.A. times Reporter. In 57 hours I had purchased 7 properties worth $722,000. Today those assets are worth almost triple that amount.

For my next #1 best seller, I did the St. Louis Challenge. I said:

"Send me to any unemployment line. Let me select someone who is broke, out of work, discouraged. Let me teach him in two day's time the secrets of wealth. And in 90 days he'll be back on his feet, with $5,000 cash in the bank, never to set foot in an unemployment line again..."

I selected a young couple from the unemployment lines of St. Louis, Missouri. Ninety days later they had earned $5,000 using one of my techniques.

In the next 12 months they had earned over $100,000. To celebrate, I took them on Good Morning America with me.

To publicize my next book, I accepted an invitation to appear on the Regis Philbin Show. From the studio audience, I selected a woman named Pat Watson.

90 days later, Pat and I were back on the show with an incredible story to tell. Starting from scratch, using my system, she had earned over $20,000.

I've been working on my latest book for the past 8 years. I'm, now, ready for my next challenge. I call it the Multiple Streams of Income Challenge.

"Send me a group of people who want to become financially independent. Let me teach them my strategies for Creating Wealth. In 90 days, they will have developed multiple streams of income. Eventually these streams of income will give them the freedom to do what ever they want for the rest of their lives."

What's the bottom line? I need success stories. I'm looking for a group of people who are willing to follow my advice and make money with my strategies

Interested?

I'm in the process of selecting a group of people to work with me on a personal basis. We go into depth in three areas.

#1 Real Estate (Nothing Down and Foreclosures)

#2 Info-Preneuring (Information and Internet)

#3 Financial (Stock Market and Asset Protection)

Our Goals are simple:

#1 Buy an excellent piece of Real Estate at a bargain price.

#2 Start on the road to make a $1,000 a day on the Internet.

#3 Make money in the Stock Market. Set up your Financial Fortress with Corporations, Limited Partnerships and Trusts.

Read the Road to Wealth. If your intuition tells you that it's appropriate to work with me, give my office a call at **1-801-852-8700. Or visit my website at www.multiplestreamsofincome.com**

Good Luck

Robert G Allen

ROAD TO WEALTH

Previously published as "The Challenge"

ROBERT ALLEN

ROAD TO WEALTH

CONTENTS

10   **Contents**

GIVE A MAN A FISH AND YOU FEED HIM FOR A DAY. TEACH
A MAN TO FISH AND YOU FEED HIM FOR A LIFETIME.—Lao Tzu

1

TEACH A MAN TO FISH

"Excuse me. You're an average American. How are you doing financially? Are you making enough money?"

"I'm doing OK."

"Would you like to do better than OK?"

"Sure, I'd like to be doing better! Who wouldn't want to get out of the rat race, travel, play a little golf, buy nice things for the family, be self-reliant, have some extra cash in the bank? But let's face it; it's not realistic. How many people ever make it in America? One percent?"

"Oh, so the American dream doesn't work anymore?"

"Maybe a hundred years ago. But today? It's all a matter of luck."

"What if I could show you that it's not just luck?"

"I'll believe it when I see it."

"Somehow, I had a feeling you were going to say that. Feel free to be skeptical. That's healthy. But try not to be negative just for the sake of being negative. In other words, don't shut the door. Leave it open a crack. Because I'm going to prove that the American dream is alive and well and that anyone—including you—can make it happen."

"Yeah? How?"

"Let's start with a challenge: Send me to any unemployment line. Let me select someone who is broke, out of work and discouraged. Let me teach him in two days the secrets of wealth. And in ninety days he'll be back on his feet, with five thousand dollars cash in the bank, never to set foot in an unemployment line again."

"But why pick an unemployed person? I'm an average American. What's the matter with me? I'll volunteer."

"I'm sure you would. But I want to prove that ANYONE can make it in America. And I'm willing to bet everything to prove it."

"Sounds kind of risky. You're rich. Why don't you just stay home and count your money or, better yet, distribute it to the poor?"

"Believe it or not, I've thought of that. But if I redistributed my entire net worth to every man, woman and child on this planet, it wouldn't be more than a penny or two apiece. There's a better way. Wealth consists of much more than money. Maybe I could make a lasting impact by giving them my two cents' worth instead—my advice, my knowledge, my experience."

The more I thought about that challenge, the more I was compelled to try it. Artists are compelled to paint. Musicians have to play. Entertainers must entertain. And I have a compelling urge to help people remove the barriers that stand between them and their dreams. If people from an unemployment line could actually turn their lives around in a few short months, what message would this send to the rest of the country? Wouldn't it prove that success has nothing to do with luck or status or social connections? Wouldn't it prove the American dream is for everyone?

This book is the true story of how I went to the unemployment lines of St. Louis, Missouri, and under the watchful eye of former St. Louis Mayor John Poelker, selected not one, but three individuals. First, there was Mary Bonenberger, an unemployed mother of two and wife of a Baptist minister struggling to make ends meet. Then, I recruited Philip Moore, a young black man born in the ghettos of St. Louis, with no skills, only a high school education, and no job to help support his wife and son. And finally, Nora Jean Boles came aboard, a single parent in her middle forties, behind in her mortgage payments, no job in sight. No hope.

"So what happened? Did they make it?"

"Come see for yourself. But don't forget that this book is not just about three unemployed people from St. Louis. It's about you. It's about your dreams and your goals. With this in mind, I have provided special self-help lists and guidelines throughout the book to give you even more powerful knowledge and motivation on your exciting adventure in success. But I'm getting ahead of myself. First, let's go to St. Louis."

WHEN YOU AIN'T GOT NOTHIN' YOU AIN'T GOT NOTHIN' TO LOSE.
—Bob Dylan

2

NOTHING TO LOSE AND EVERYTHING TO GAIN

1. _____

From all outward appearances, it was going to be just another ordinary day in St. Louis, Missouri. On Leduc Street, in a predominantly black neighborhood in the central west end of the city, all was normal. People coming and going. A few cars passing. The sound of a lawn mower. A dog barking. Some older children playing in the street. Nothing out of the ordinary.

But just after one o'clock the tranquillity of the afternoon was pierced as an old 1978 Buick screeched around the corner and slammed to a halt in front of a small two-story brown brick duplex—one of several on that street all sporting flat roofs and white trim. Out of the car jumped a heavyset black man dressed in a T-shirt and sandals. He hurried up the walk, bounded up the front steps and impatiently rang the doorbell to the upper flat. In his hand he clutched a single yellow sheet of paper.

In the tiny upstairs apartment Philip Moore was just sitting down to a lunch that his wife, Karen, had made before she left for her part-time job as a medical records clerk at the hospital. At the sound of the doorbell, he went to the door.

"Phil," said the man excitedly. "I got something for you. You ain't gonna believe it!"

Philip was a bit put off to see that it was just Ron. A big guy, six feet three inches tall and not an ounce shy of 300 pounds, Ron was a regular visitor to the Moore residence, much to Karen's dismay. It had been that way ever since Ron had been fired from his last job. Actually, the last time that either Ron or Philip had worked was at the same job: Popeyes Chicken—more than a year before. Ron had been the manager, and Philip was in line to be the assistant manager making minimum wage and doing all of the dirty work. But the boss was a tough man to please, and Philip had quit in an indignant huff. Ron had been fired about a week later.

"Hey, Phil," he said. "I got some good news. Look at this."

"What is it?"

"I've been over to the unemployment office. And there's this guy over there handing out this paper. It says, 'Financial Independence can be yours.' Man, this is for you! You're always talkin' about owin' your own business and stuff like that."

"Let me see that."

Philip's eyes pored over the single paragraph in the center of the yellow sheet of paper.

UNEMPLOYED? . . .

Financial independence can be yours. We will provide intensive training for self-starters who are willing to work and learn. You must have a car and be available for at least 90 days. No selling or travel. Information and an interview can be obtained at a meeting to be held tomorrow morning at 9:00 A.M., Tuesday, June 5, 1984, in the Palladium Room, Cheshire Inn and Lodge, 6300 Clayton Road, corner of Forest Park, St. Louis. The meeting will begin sharply at 9:00 A.M.—don't be late. You must be currently unemployed to qualify. You'll kick yourself if you miss this.

This employment opportunity has been reviewed by the Missouri Division of Employment Security.

"Where'd you get this?" Philip asked.

"I told you, man. There was this guy at the unemployment office handin' 'em out to everyone that came in the door. I went up to him and he says he's working for a guy named Robert Allen who's written some famous books on real estate."

Philip was more than a bit skeptical, but he invited his friend to come in. "I don't know about this," he said, still puzzled by the yellow paper as they sat down in the living room.

"Well, all I know is the guy handin' out the fliers said it was a chance to make some money in real estate. And I know you've been talkin' about getting into real estate. So I thought this would be right up your alley."

"Yeah. Real estate. That's a great job. I'd like that job."

"Well this isn't exactly a job. The guy at the unemployment office said that this Robert Allen is going to pick some people off the unemployment line and teach 'em how to get rich. Like how to invest and stuff like that."

"Sure. And what's he gonna get out of it?"

"The guy told me it's kinda like a challenge. You know, to see if it can be done. I don't know. I still think it sounds like somethin' worth checkin' out. Want to go to the Cheshire tomorrow and see what's goin' on?"

"Right. Right. OK. Pick me up tomorrow morning and we'll check it out."

After Ron left, Philip returned to his desk in the little room he liked to refer to as his office, which was, in reality, nothing more than a storage room with a window. He set the yellow flier to one side of his desk and picked up the weekend classifieds to continue the process of job hunting. He'd been calling all morning with not much luck. There just didn't seem to be many opportunities for a twenty-four-year-old unemployed black male with few skills and only a high school education. Fry cook. Janitor. Car wash attendant. Handyman. Part-time laborer. Kitchen help. Ice cream salesman. Mostly minimum-wage stuff. Not much future. But he needed a job, so he kept on making calls.

"Sorry, that position has been filled."

"Sorry, we were looking for someone with a little more experience."

"Sorry, we were looking for someone a little older."

"Sorry, we were looking for someone a little younger."

After each rejection, he'd lean back in his chair and survey the bulletin board on the wall in front of his desk, where he had tacked up several newspaper clippings and magazine articles to remind him of some of his goals. In one corner was an article from *Success* magazine about owning your own business—something he'd always wanted to do. A newspaper clipping carried the headline: "When Starting a Business You Can Have Fun or Money But Not Both." Nearby was another clipping: "Rehab Apartments Underway in Hyde Park Neighborhood." He had always been interested in real estate and planned to take a course to get a real estate license as soon as he could scrape up the fifty-four dollars tuition.

Could Robert Allen teach him what he needed to know?

He glanced up to the mounted pictures of some of his heroes, wondering what they would do in his place.

Martin Luther King. ("I think he was a great man.")

Jesse Jackson. ("I like his style. So much energy. He's not afraid of anything.")

Malcolm X. ("He was a doer, self-taught, a family man. The media portrayed him as a strong-willed and hateful man. But he wasn't.")

Frederick Douglass. ("I first read about him in the fifth grade. Before that I didn't even know that black people had a history. He was a pioneer. A good role model for me.")

He tried to return to his telephone prospecting but had a hard time concentrating. He kept looking at his bulletin board and then at the bright yellow flier on his desk. The words kept popping into his mind.

Financial independence can be yours.

"Sure, that's what I want," he thought. "But that's crazy. You've got to have money for that. I don't even have a job!"

You must be currently unemployed to qualify.

"Why does he want unemployed people? What's the angle? Unemployed people don't have any money."

... intensive training for self-starters ... willing to work and learn.

"I don't believe it. Probably a scam. But the flier says it's been checked out by the Missouri Division of Employment Security."

You'll kick yourself if you miss this.

"OK, I'll just go over there and check it out. If I see it's not for me, I can always leave."

Financial independence can be yours.

That was the sentence that pounded over and over in Philip's mind like a rolling surf. That's what he really wanted. He didn't want a dead-end job. He wanted to be his own boss. To be free. Not to take orders from anyone. To be in control. To call his own shots.

But it was more than that. Financial independence was not having to worry about pink slips or the plant closing down. Or being on unemployment. Or having to beg for a job.

And it was having some security for his family. Being a millionaire never really crossed his mind. He just wanted to have fewer money worries. Maybe a few nicer things for the people he cared about most in his life. A decent car. A wedding band for Karen. Maybe some new furniture. A trip. A vacation. Those were things he and Karen always wanted but could never afford.

When Karen came home that evening, he didn't tell her about the flier. Why get her hopes up with such a longshot? Sure, I'm willing to work. Willing to learn. But they're never going to choose me anyway. I'm black. No education. No experience. But that night as Philip lay in bed, his hands behind his head and Karen lying asleep beside him, a rare, quiet confidence began to grow in him. Again he thought about all the good things he wanted for his wife and son, he thought about his own ideals, goals and dreams. Usually, when he had thoughts like that, he would get up and wander through the house, too restless to go back to sleep. On this night, however, he slept soundly, peacefully.

2.

Nora Jean Boles sat bolt upright, startled by a jangling sound that seemed to come from far away ... light years away. The jangling intensified until it filled her head, jarring her into abrupt consciousness.

She reached out and turned off her alarm. It was seven o'clock. Monday morning.

"But if this is Monday," she thought, "why is the sun shining? Mondays I work at the donut shop. The sun is never up by the time I have to go to work at the donut shop. It's always dark."

On a normal Monday, she would have been up at 4:00 A.M. to be at work at 5:00. From five till noon, selling donuts and coffee. Seven hours a day. Three days a week at four dollars an hour. That was twenty-eight dollars a day. Eighty-four bucks a week, cash money. Cash because she wouldn't have to report it to the I.R.S.—or to the unemployment office. If the unemployment office found out, it would surely cut her benefits. And that would be disastrous. The fifty-five-dollar unemployment check wasn't much, but it made the difference between sinking and swimming.

On the weekends she had another part-time job, bartending at the local Elks Club. Three nights of seven-hour shifts—another hundred dollars a week, counting tips. Cash money under the table so no one would find out.

She hated sneaking around like that. It was dishonest. It bothered her, but she pushed it to the back of her mind. You do what you have to do when you're desperate. Three daughters to feed and heat bills to pay and the payments on the house, which were already a few months behind. Then there was that four-thousand-dollar bill for her unexpected gall bladder operation last year. And the attorney fees still unpaid from the divorce. Bills. Bills. Bills.

Yes, she needed that fifty-five dollars each week. She needed every cent.

And then she remembered.

The letter.

"That's why the sun is shining and I'm not at work at the donut shop this morning. The letter."

The letter lay on her dresser. She had received it on Friday. All weekend she had stewed about it. It had sounded so stern—telling her to report to the unemployment office immediately or face losing her benefits.

She had no choice but to go ... part-time job or not.

She arose and showered, dressing quickly. She stood in the bathroom applying her makeup. The face in the mirror looked back at her. High cheekbones, dark brown eyes set wide—the only hints that her mother was a full-blooded Cherokee. A narrow nose. Pointed chin. Her Irish father's contribution. Her dark brown hair was streaked with gray. Too many wrinkles about the eyes and mouth for a forty-four-year-old face.

She woke the two girls. Jennifer was fourteen. Sylvia, her youngest, was twelve. Her three older girls were on their own now. Margaret, eighteen, was married with two children. Cristine, twenty-one, and Marvena, twenty-seven, lived by themselves. Jeffrey, her beautiful little boy, would have been nineteen. The years never diminish an ache like that. You just learn to cope.

After breakfast she said good-bye to her girls and got in her battered Plymouth Arrow, and made the twenty-minute drive to the Crestwood Plaza unemployment office in southwest St. Louis. It was a few minutes before nine o'clock when she hurried through the door. Above the door was a large sign. The Missouri Department of Employment Security.

"Employment Security," she thought. "Those two words don't seem to go together anymore. I never had a job that was secure. Fired or laid off from every one."

Inside, a well-dressed young man was handing out yellow fliers. She took one, then checked in with the receptionist and found a seat in the waiting area. About thirty of the fifty chairs were filled with other people. Many of them were reading the same yellow flier. Some had already finished reading and had discarded the fliers on the floor or on a vacant chair.

She looked down at the flier in her hand, her eyes devouring the words.

Financial independence can be yours . . . intensive training for a few self-starters . . . willing to work and learn . . . no selling or travel . . . meeting . . . tomorrow morning . . . must be unemployed to qualify . . . kick yourself if you miss . . .

She finished the flier, her heart pounding. Only a couple of months ago a seminar had come to town, a free seminar on real estate investing. What was it? "Nothing Down." She remembered the free part and the nothing down because that's about all the money she had. She went to the seminar, and the speaker mentioned something about his boss—who was he?—Robert Allen, an investor who had perfected some sort of system for investing in real estate with little or no money down. The speaker said that this Robert Allen would teach anyone off an unemployment line how to become wealthy. Starting with absolutely nothing.

After the ninety-minute free lecture she had sought out some of the people in charge to tell them she was the person Robert Allen was looking for. She was unemployed. They were nice, but they were too busy signing up people for the $445 seminar they were selling. She, too, wanted to sign up for the seminar, and for once she even had the money, but it was already earmarked for buying a used car. She stood in line weighing her choices.

"Should I buy the car? I need a car. But I sure would like to take this seminar. It's all the money I've got."

The car won the battle. She stepped out of line and went home, troubled.

Could the yellow flier the young man had just given her at the unemployment office have something to do with Robert Allen? She decided to find out.

"Hello. Can you tell me more about this?" she asked.

"Sure. My name is Tom Painter. I work for Robert Allen."

"He's here!" she thought. "He's right here in St. Louis. Of all of the unemployment lines in America, he's picked my line." She couldn't believe it. Who says opportunity doesn't knock twice?

"I'd like to be the one you select," she said.

Tom smiled. "Ma'am, that's what a lot of people have told me today. I'm sure that you'll have as good a chance as anyone."

"I'll be there. You tell Mr. Allen I'll be there."

She literally flew home. Her little 1978 blue stick-shift Plymouth Arrow barely touched the ground. "He could have come to any city in the United States ... to any unemployment line," she thought. "And he came to my city and to my unemployment line on the very day that I happened to be there. It's my lucky day."

It sure hadn't started out lucky. She remembered the letter that warned her of losing her benefits. She remembered the dread that had filled her on her trip that morning to the unemployment office. But after she read the flier and met with the unemployment counselor, all plump and patronizing, who informed her that she was on probation, she remembered looking back at him as if to say, "I don't need your money anymore. You just wait and see. I'm going into real estate. I'm going to be financially independent."

3.

Mary Bonenberger was busy getting ready to leave for work. Her husband, Steve, would be driving her. As they were walking out the door, their baby-sitter, Cheryl, announced that she was quitting the next week—going to work at McDonald's. On any other morning, that might not have caused such a stir. But on this day, for Mary, it was the final straw.

Today marked her first full week of work at the Hertz rental counter at the St. Louis International airport. Next week she would be traveling to Chicago for two full weeks of training at company headquarters. She had agonized over this trip—leaving her family, her husband. But Steve had encouraged her. "It'll be good for you," he reasoned. "You've been looking for a job, a career. Something to challenge you, give you a sense of fulfillment. Maybe this is it. And you know we need the money."

Yes, they needed the money. They both knew that they could not make it on his salary as a minister. There were just too many budget-busters. Only last week the insurance company had refused to pay Mary's maternity bill. They only paid for sick babies, and Kyle, her son was a "well baby"—nine pounds four ounces well. That was a fifteen-hundred-dollar shock. And there were other little things— car payments, house bills, bills and more bills. The bottom line was, they just didn't make enough money. She would have to go to work to make up the difference.

After two or three interviews she had landed a great job with Hertz. Six dollars an hour. Relatively easy work. Just shuffling keys, cars and commuters. There was only one problem. She hated every minute of it. But the pay was great—golden handcuffs.

As Steve drove her to work that morning, Mary felt as though everything was closing in on her. What kind of mother would leave her three-year-old daughter and newborn son with a teenage baby-sitter for two whole weeks—especially to train for a job she didn't enjoy? She was torn. What about the money? What about her dreams of independence? What about her husband's career? What about the children? When she couldn't stand it anymore, she broke down and cried. Steve knew what was troubling her and tried to comfort her. He could arrange his schedule to take care of the kids, they would find another baby-sitter, an even better one. None of that seemed to work. Finally, he said, "Well, honey, if you hate the job so much, maybe you should quit."

Although it was what she would have expected him to say, she knew it wasn't what he expected her to do. But when Steve pulled the car up in front of the Hertz office, she didn't care anymore. She asked him to wait. She opened the door, marched right in to her supervisor and quit. Told him that she would return her uniform as soon as she could go home and take if off. And walked out.

That was the beginning of the most serious argument in the six years of their marriage. When Mary came back to the car and announced that she had quit, Steve's face just went blank.

"I don't believe it," he said. "Forget the fact that we need the money. You're the one who really wanted the job. I can't believe that you're walking away from it!"

"But I hated that job," Mary countered. "And you're the one who just told me I should quit. You love your job. I'll just find something else—a job I like."

It wasn't that easy, although she spent three or four hours a day at it. Nothing was right. Mary wasn't going to accept just a minimum-wage job—that would be demeaning. There wouldn't be enough money left over after baby-sitting costs to make it worthwhile. She'd just rather stay home with her kids and be poor.

As the days dragged into weeks, Mary began to regret her decision to quit the Hertz job. The reality of the cold, hard world began to make itself felt as she now went from interview to interview with no luck. She began to question herself, until almost two months had passed and she finally accepted the fact that any job would do. Any minimum-wage job. Hang the independence. Hang the fulfillment. She'd just have to wait for some future time in her life. For now, they needed the extra money.

It was on a Sunday evening, June 3, as they were sitting reading the classified ads, that a flicker of hope began. Steve saw the ad first.

"Hey, honey. How about this?" He read the ad in the upper right-hand corner of the *St. Louis Post-Dispatch* page 9E.

FINANCIAL INDEPENDENCE can be yours. Will provide intensive training for self-starters willing to learn and work. Must have car and be available for ninety days. No selling or travel. No investment. Information & interview, 9 A.M., Tues., June 5, Palladium Room at Cheshire Inn & Lodge, 6300 Clayton Rd., corner of Forest Park, St. Louis. Must be currently unemployed to qualify. You'll kick yourself if you miss this.

He read the ad with mock seriousness, and Mary began to laugh.

"Probably some door-to-door scheme or something like that," she said.

But then Steve said, "You know it might be worth checking out. You never can tell."

The idea of financial independence was foreign to Mary, really. Never crossed her mind before. Steve was definitely more interested in that kind of thing than she was. Sure, it would be nice to be free of money worries. But the lure of financial freedom was not as strong as her desire for a truly fulfilling job. Then she read the last line of the ad again: *You'll kick yourself if you miss this.*

She just couldn't bear the thought of missing something. "I wonder why they said that," she thought. "If a thing sounds too good to be true it usually is. But I wonder if this opportunity is different." Finally, she rationalized by saying to herself that Tuesday was her interview day anyway. She already had one interview set up in that part of town at 11:00. It couldn't hurt to run over to the Cheshire Inn and check it out.

She made a mental note of the place and the time. She knew the Cheshire Inn. It was in Clayton, a nice suburb of St. Louis. It was worth a look. But all the next day she did not think about it once. That night she tucked her children in early. She had three interviews set up for the next day. One of them had to pan out, she thought.

4.

Later that evening, long after Philip Moore had fallen asleep, Nora Jean Boles had finished ironing her blouse and setting out her nicest hat for the meeting the next morning, and Mary Bonenberger had checked her sleeping children before retiring to bed, I was still awake in the Presidential Suite on the fourth floor of the Daniele Hotel in Clayton, Missouri.

Robert Allen, the famous author, lecturer, investor and millionaire, was scared to death.

Tom Painter wasn't the only one who had passed out yellow fliers that day. I had gone to the unemployment office on King's Highway—with a camera crew. The manager of that unemployment office had been fully briefed on the Challenge and had granted permission to film me as I passed out the fliers to everyone who entered the office. George Rasmussen, the film director, hovered nearby, taking still pictures with his Pentax. Dr. Blaine Lee, the consultant, stood to one side, taking in the scene. After they read the fliers, a few people in the large waiting room looked up from their chairs. There seemed to be so much hostility in their eyes.

A man in his early thirties came up to me.

"What's this all about?" he asked. The antagonism in his voice was unmistakable as he explained that he had been laid off at the Chrysler plant more than a year earlier. There had been nothing for him ever since. He listened to my explanation about the Challenge and passed it off with a bitter sneer.

The reaction from others was similar. This was not at all what I had expected. I had hoped to see some light of hope in at least one person. Some enthusiasm. Some desire. And I had not seen it. Not even a glimmer.

Back at the hotel, through all of the meetings with my associates that filled the night—the brainstorming, the planning, the logistics—I could not rid myself of the vision of those faces. They haunted me as I realized my Challenge might have been a hollow boast. Now my neck was on the line.

I lay in bed awake long after all the others had retired to their various rooms. For the very first time I seriously entertained the thought of failing. If someone accepted my Challenge, and I couldn't prove what I promised on that flier, it seemed as though I had not much to gain—and everything to lose.

THE SECRET OF SUCCESS IN LIFE IS FOR A MAN TO BE READY FOR HIS OPPORTUNITY WHEN IT COMES.—Benjamin Disraeli

3

LOOKING FOR A FEW "GO-GETTERS"

1. _____

Dr. Lee looked at his watch. It was 9:07 A.M.

"Where are all the people?" he fretted.

From his vantage point, standing on a raised platform at the far end of the Palladium Room of the Cheshire Inn, he counted no more than forty people scattered sparsely in chairs throughout the long, narrow room.

In the front row sat a well-dressed black gentleman. Behind him, two rough-looking young men sat together. In the middle, in the second row, were two older women. One wore a hat. On the right side was a hippie-looking fellow with long hair tied back in a pony tail. Just then, two shabbily dressed couples—obviously from the same family—entered the room and took seats at the rear. One of the women bottle-fed a newborn baby. Dr. Lee felt a surge of compassion. His own wife was pregnant with their eighth child. He surveyed the whole scene, realizing that from this group he would have to help choose three people for the Challenge. He shook his head, ever so slightly. After a few more minutes, he stepped up to the podium to address the sparse group, which he now estimated at between fifty and sixty people. The quiet, almost morguelike silence made him acutely conscious of his own growling stomach.

"Ladies and gentlemen," he said, "thank you for coming. My name is Dr. Blaine Lee. I'm an educational adviser working with Bob Allen on an exciting project."

This failed to raise a ripple from his audience.

"Would you please look at the material you received as you came in the door this morning."

Mary Bonenberger, sitting in the audience, scanned the sheet of paper in front of her.

Dear Applicant:

Thank you for your interest in this career opportunity. As a college graduate, Robert Allen found himself in the same situation as many of you—no job or credit rating and little money. But he did possess determination and a will to succeed. By the time he was in his early thirties he had become a millionaire by investing in real estate. Then, he shared his knowledge in two bestselling books: *Creating Wealth* and *Nothing Down: A Proven Program* that shows you how to buy real estate with little or no money down.

In promoting *Nothing Down*, he said:

"Send me to any city in America. Take away my wallet. Give me $100 for living expenses. And in 72 hours I'll buy an excellent piece of real estate using none of my own money."

The *Los Angeles Times* challenged him to do just that. In January of 1981, they flew him with a reporter to San Francisco and within the allotted time he had purchased six houses worth a half a million dollars—all with less than $100 in his pocket. The headline in the *Times* read:

Boastful Investor Accepts *Times* Challenge—And Wins!
But still, many didn't believe, prompting him to say:

"Send me to any unemployment line. Let me choose someone who is out of work and discouraged. Let me teach this person in two days the secrets of wealth. And in 90 days, he'll be back on his feet with $5,000 cash in the bank, never to set foot in an unemployment line again."

To prove this, Mr. Allen plans to select three individuals from the unemployment lines of St. Louis. If you think that you could fill the position and are presently unemployed, with a poor credit rating and deep in debt, you are eligible.

"So this really is a once-in-a-lifetime opportunity," Mary thought. She could hardly wait to tell her husband.

Dr. Lee spoke again. "We will be selecting three of you here in this room this morning for the Challenge. If you are interested, please remain to fill out an application. If not, Mr. Allen would like you to have a set of tapes as appreciation for your time."

As soon as he finished, about a third of the people got up, collected their tapes and left.

"Are there any questions?" Dr. Lee asked the remaining forty-two people.

No one spoke. No hands were raised. The room remained silent. Dr. Lee went on to explain that he would be reviewing the applications and would post a list of those selected for further interviews outside the Palladium Room before 11:00 A.M. Then he came to the rear of the room, where I had been watching the proceedings.

"What do you think?" he asked me hesitatingly. "I'm worried. There aren't enough people."

"I was worried myself until I had a chance to visit with some of them," I replied.

Tom Painter joined us. He was only twenty-four years old but wise beyond his years. As the official detail man of the Challenge team, he had been at the Cheshire Inn before seven that morning to make sure that things were in order. Expecting a large crowd, he had the room set up for two hundred people and was more than a bit unnerved when so few showed up. He sighed a breath of relief when Nora Jean Boles arrived at about ten to nine. She looked pretty in her dress and hat. Secretly, he hoped that she would be one of the participants.

"There sure aren't many people," Tom said as he joined our discussion. "But that lady I told you about is here."

"Yes," I said, "the one with the hat. I met her this morning. She told me about her dream to start a multimillion-dollar resort on some land for sale near her home. Sometimes people live in a dream world. Is she a doer or a dreamer?"

"I'll review her application," answered Dr. Lee.

Dr. Lee's specific assignment, which he took very seriously, had been to design a screening process that would weed out the dreamers from the doers—the go-getters who would surmount any obstacle to get the job done.

"I'm really miffed," Dr. Lee said. "I must have met fifteen people at the unemployment office yesterday who promised they'd be here."

I pointed out a couple of likely candidates I had met that morning. One was an All-American high school basketball player sitting near the front with his fiancée. He had shown a lot of initiative by buying my book and staying up all night to read it. Sitting near him was another young black fellow who was short on experience but long on enthusiasm. I felt I could work with him.

"We don't want to pick the All-American boy," Dr. Lee advised. "Picking the strongest person defeats the purpose of the Challenge."

"Make up your mind," I joked. "First, you're worried that we don't have enough people to choose from, and then you tell me not to pick the strongest one."

We all laughed. It was about 9:45.

Dr. Lee returned to the podium to announce that I would collect the completed applications at the rear of the room.

I looked each person squarely in the eye as, one by one, they handed in their applications. If the person returned my gaze with a look of desire and determination, I placed the application in my right hand. These were the ones whose names would be posted on the list at 11:00 A.M. When all applications were turned in, we counted twenty applications for further consideration. I left my assistants to narrow this group down to six or eight for my interviews that evening.

As I drove back to the hotel, I was reminded of a song from one of the Rocky movies.

> It's the eye of the tiger,
> It's the thrill of the fight;
> Rising up to the challenge of our rival.

And the last known survivor stalks his prey in the night;
And he's watching us all with the eye of the tiger.

"The eye of the tiger," I thought to myself. "That's what I'm looking for."

2. _____

Back in the Palladium Room, Dr. Lee was preparing to address the seventeen people who had returned at eleven o'clock for further interviews.

Philip Moore, sitting in this group, surveyed his competition, calculating the odds in his mind. There are six other black men. Got to be a least one black in the final three. One out of seven. There are two older women. One with a hat. A couple of white men. One has a German accent. A hippie. Then he noticed the young woman sitting next to him. Sharp features. Dark hair. Quite attractive. Not exactly beautiful. But a strength in her face that makes her stand out.

"Hi," he said. "What do you think about all of this?"

Mary Bonenberger smiled. "I think it's great. I called my husband, and he's even more excited than I am."

"Yeah. My wife can't believe it either. Think we'll make it?"

They were interrupted by Dr. Lee speaking from the front of the room.

"Thanks for coming back," he said as he passed out some more forms.

"Unfortunately, we can select only three of you. Quite frankly, some of you are too strong. We are looking for someone who has some big hurdles to overcome but who still has the will to succeed. This is not going to be a joyride. It's going to be one of the toughest things you will ever do. Any questions? No? OK. Please review the materials, fill out the next application, and when you're done, I'll interview each of you in turn."

Nora Jean Boles studied the new materials.

CHALLENGE OVERVIEW, PART II

If you are selected for the Challenge, you will be asked to overcome personal doubt and fear, the criticism of friends, and some self-defeating habits. You will be asked to set goals, learn new skills and become independent. There will be no nine-to-five job, with a time clock and an employee benefits plan. This will require you to be responsible for yourself. Are you willing to do that? You will be given two days of intensive training at no charge to you. Then, you will be on your own for ninety days. You will have books and other materials to refer to, and the use of a telephone hot line for consultations as needed. But the work will be up to you. There is no guarantee of success but if you follow the system, you should be able to end up with new skills, a new vocation and money in the bank.

Throughout the 90 days a film crew will record what happens to you. Later, a documentary film will be made of the entire experience so that others can be motivated by observing your failures and successes. Whether or not you are selected, your being here is evidence that you are willing to pay a price to improve your situation. We sincerely wish you the best in dealing with your personal and financial challenges.

Nora finished reading and began filling out the new form. By the time she and the others had finished their face-to-face interviews with Dr. Lee, it was past two o'clock. The sheet listing the final selections was to be posted at four.

Mary Bonenberger waited patiently in her car. If her name was on that list, she'd be expected to return for one final interview with Robert Allen. That would conflict with her daughter's birthday party, scheduled for seven that evening. Katie was turning three, and all of the extended family was coming over for a family celebration. She tried not to worry about it. If she made the final cut, she'd just have to call and tell everyone to come early. She hoped they'd understand.

At four o'clock, Tom Painter posted the new sheet. It consisted of eight names.

> Caldwell Jones
> Philip Moore
> Richard Dabney
> Abdul Shakir
> Jamal Coley
> Robert Russell
> Mary Bonenberger
> Nora Jean Boles

Mary saw her name and ran to a pay phone to call Steve. Philip gave a shout of excitement. Nora's name was there also.

Nora jumped in her car. Her fingers trembled as she fumbled with the keys to the ignition. "Oh, God," she prayed under her breath. "I want this."

Speeding down the freeway, she went over a strategy in her mind. It was down to eight people. She qualified in almost every respect. Unemployed. Discouraged—boy, was she discouraged! She had her beat-up car for transportation. But the two part-time jobs worried her. They probably won't object to a weekend part-time job. But I'd better quit the donut shop.

She pulled in the driveway to her house and went straight inside to call the owner of the donut shop.

"Hello, Phyllis? This is Nora Jean. I'm sorry, but I'm going to have to quit my job."

"What's come up?"

"I can't really explain right now. I've just got this other opportunity."

Nora hung up the phone. She'd really done it now—burned her bridges. How was she going to make ends meet? She tried not to think of that.

She'd worry about it after the interview.

3.

While Blaine Lee was narrowing the field to eight, I had gone on an eye-opening tour of the city with Bob Coombs, a successful local investor. Coombs had driven me into north St. Louis to show me the racially mixed neighborhoods where I was able to soak up the flavor of the real estate market—the prices, the customs, the declining areas, those on the upswing.

I learned that St. Louis proper had a population of almost half a million—50 percent black—with over two million in the surrounding metropolitan area. The inner city had undergone major urban flight in the sixties and early seventies, losing almost a third of its population—more than any other city in America.

But recently there had been a considerable renaissance in many neighborhoods. Yuppies were homesteading in droves. The pendulum had begun to swing in the other direction.

As we drove, we caught several glimpses of the mighty Mississippi River, which flows serenely through the city. I learned that St. Louis was not only the nation's busiest inland river port but also boasted the headquarters of Anheuser-Busch, the nation's largest brewer of beer, as well as being the site of several major automobile assembly factories for General Motors and Chrysler.

Coombs brought me back to the hotel around 4:30 P.M., just as Dr. Lee and Tom Painter returned with the names for the final interviews that evening. I quickly perused the sheet of names.

"I see Nora Boles made the cut," I said, looking at Dr. Lee questioningly.

"She's a tank, Bob. She won't break any speed records, but she's a survivor. I'd be disappointed if she wasn't one of the final three."

I looked at Tom for his reaction.

"I agree," he said, smiling.

"That settles it, then," I said. "Nora's in. How about this Mary Bonenberger? I don't remember her."

"She's at the top of my list," Dr. Lee replied. "Her husband is a Baptist minister. They're having a tough time financially. But she's solid as a rock."

We eliminated three others from the list for various reasons. That left Philip Moore, Caldwell Jones, the All-American, and Abdul Shakir. All black.

"OK, then," I said. "I guess the final spot will go to one of these three. I remember Moore and Caldwell. Both young and willing. Who's this Abdul Shakir?"

"He's older. Some experience with fixup. A very religious person—black Muslim, I think. Soft-spoken. You'll like him."

We decided not to let Nora or Mary know they had already been selected but to let them go through the interview process to see how they handled pressure. The interviews with the final people and their spouses were scheduled for seven that night at the Cheshire Inn. John Poelker, the former mayor of St. Louis and an ex-FBI agent, had graciously agreed to act as referee to verify that the selection process had not been rigged in any way.

"This is it," I said, as we retired to our various rooms.

Seven o'clock. The upper room of the Cheshire was beautifully decorated in an Old English motif. A large stone fireplace stood at the far end of the room. Mayor Poelker and I, sitting in leather high-backed chairs, were introduced to the first of the finalists—Caldwell Jones. His financée could not get off work to attend the final interview. Mayor Poelker broke the ice by explaining his role in the Challenge. He then asked the young man some questions to determine his eligibility. When he was satisfied, he turned to me for further questioning. After the young man had been ushered from the room, Mayor Poelker remarked that he seemed to have too much going for him—he was just too All-American. I agreed.

Nora Jean Boles was introduced to us next.

"I have a dream," she began when asked why she wanted to participate in the Challenge. "I want to build a resort. I even have a place for it—975 acres near where I live."

"What if you aren't in the final three?" I asked to test her.

"I won't quit till I have it," she responded.

The mayor and I looked at each other. It was the answer we were looking for.

The mayor questioned further. "Are you working now?"

Nora hung her head. "I'm on unemployment. But to be honest, I do have a side job. I don't report it to the unemployment office. They'd cut off my benefits."

"I see," he responded. The mayor, a kind man with empathy as deep and wide as the Mississippi, looked the other way, so to speak.

"Have you ever read any of my books?" I inquired.

"No, sir. Not because I didn't want to. I just couldn't afford them."

There were some more questions, and then Nora was escorted out. Nora whispered to Dr. Lee out in the hall that she just knew she had blown it.

The next interview was with Mary and Steve Bonenberger—a clean-cut couple obviously behind the financial eight ball. My purpose in interviewing them was to find out if they were goal-oriented—the first clue to finding a go-getter. When asked for specific goals and dreams, they didn't hesitate a moment. They had always wanted to start their own church. This answer and others confirmed that Mary should be one of the final three.

The fourth interview was with Abdul Shakir and his wife. They were older—he was fifty-four, she about the same—but the fire was gone from their eyes. Allah had other plans for these humble servants.

Last came Philip Moore and his wife, Karen. They made a smart couple—both dressed tastefully but not expensively, she in a brown dress, he in a tie and cream-colored sport jacket. They were about the same height—fairly short, five foot six. Her hair was frizzed and longer. He had short-cropped hair. They both wore glasses. Her face was tight, and her black skin radiated. She looked down shyly. But she was not shy. Philip had obviously chosen his companion well.

After some small talk, I began the serious questioning to see if they both understood the kind of sacrifices they would be asked to make.

"Is security important to you?"

Philip answered first. "Yes, it is. I have a family."

"What is security?"

"It means not worrying about money. Karen only brings in $320 a month working part-time. Rent is $160, so we don't have much for anything else. We have to pay a little bit on each bill and then wait till next month. I scrape up a little money by mowing lawns, collecting pop and beer cans or selling roses on a streetcorner. I don't want to do that all my life."

I turned to Karen. "Are you willing to put your security on the line—take some risks—to improve your situation?"

Karen responded without hesitating. "I'm willing. I think both of us are."

I cautioned further. "The only real security is in having lots of opportunity. But risk is the price you pay for opportunity. And risk is scary."

"But it's worth it," Karen shot back. "I believe in myself. I believe in us. We've been together eleven years. Whenever we put our minds to something, we came out on top."

Philip broke in. "There've been setbacks. But I'm not going to let that stop me. If I don't make it today, I will tomorrow. It won't come to me if I don't go after it."

I felt an incredible feeling come over me—a whoosh of confirmation—as I listened to these young people talk. Tears welled up in my eyes. I was so proud of them. Here they sat with nothing, and yet they had everything. I looked at Mayor Poelker. He nodded. We had found our third couple.

"Who taught you to be so determined?"

"My mom." Philip looked at Karen. She nodded her agreement.

"My mom raised eight kids all by herself, working two jobs . . . with no man in the house. She was able to take us from the inner-city ghetto and find us a home in a middle-class area. She didn't have to give us away or anything. If she could make it, I know I can. She said so many times. 'Don't ever let anyone discourage you. If you really want something in your heart, go after it.' "

"Well, we thank you for coming tonight."

"Well, I'm excited," Philip replied. "This is an opportunity of a lifetime. I fit the description perfectly. I'm unemployed. I've got about two dollars to my name. But I do have desire—a heart full of desire—and if that's all you need, I have that in abundance. I've got nowhere to go but up. I've been down. I'm tough. I've lived in the ghetto, where they would rob you blind every time you stepped in the street. But that's behind me now. I'm still young and I want to grow."

I was mesmerized. This marvelous, plain-spoken young man had just delivered the most moving speech I had ever heard in my life. The fear that had paralyzed me only a few hours before began to ease.

I knew that we had found three go-getters.

And I could hardly wait to teach them.

As the five finalists left that evening, they were given a copy of a tape entitled "The Blue Vase—The Story of a Go-Getter."* They were told that it contained a secret that every successful person had mastered—a secret that they themselves would have to master if they wanted to be successful.

Before 10:00 P.M. Caldwell Jones and Abdul Shakir received a phone call informing them that they were not in the final three. They took the bad news without much fuss—something a go-getter would not have done. Mary Bonenberger, Philip Moore and Nora Jean Boles were notified that a final decision would not be reached until the next morning. We wanted to give them another night to think about it. Besides, George, the film director, wanted to capture their reactions on film the next morning as I informed them personally on their own doorsteps.

4. _____

The next morning just after 10:00 A.M., I rang the doorbell of a modest white tract house in a clean, lower–middle-class neighborhood of north St. Louis.

If you would like to listen to "The Blue Vase: The Story of a Go-Getter" go to www.RobertAllen.com.

Mary answered the door and on seeing me she let out a shout. "We did it!"

"How were you feeling last night?" I asked.

Steve joined us and answered for her. "We didn't know what to feel. We just felt that if this was right it would work."

I then gave them two assignments. First, they were to place the following two ads in the next day's classified section of the *St. Louis Post Dispatch*:

In the "Real Estate Wanted" section:

A firm offer to buy your propety will be made in 24 hours after you call Mary. [number]

In the "Investment Property for Sale" section:

How to find real estate bargains in St. Louis. Free 1-hour seminar with valuable handout. Call [number] for info.

Then I gave them twenty dollars and asked them to rent a video machine and the movie *Rocky* and watch it before the seminar, which was scheduled for eight o'clock the next morning at the Daniele Hotel.

My next stop was the home of Nora Jean Boles—a small house at the end of a cul-de-sac in the town of Eureka, Missouri (population five thousand), about thirty miles southwest of St. Louis.

Nora answered the door dressed in cutoffs and a halter top.

"Do you want to be part of the Challenge?" I asked, smiling.

She answered, a bit shy of the cameras. "Yes, I do. Very much. When I got done listening to the Blue Vase tape last night, I said to myself, 'Nora, if you want this thing you're going to have to go after it like the man on the Blue Vase tape. That's the kind of person Mr. Allen is looking for—a go-getter.' So I've been trying to reach you all morning."

"You got the message, all right!" I said.

I proceeded to give her the two assignments—her ads were slightly different—and directions to the hotel the next morning.

She waved good-bye as we left.

An hour later I stood on the front porch of the Moores' older brick duplex on Leduc Street. Philip was excited to hear the news. Karen joined us at the door as her husband spoke.

"I was listening to the tapes and reading the literature up until 4:00 this morning," he said. "I couldn't sleep."

"He's like that," Karen said proudly.

Then I gave them the same assignments I had given the others. Philip's classified ad was to read:

I buy houses cash or terms. Fair. Philip. [number]

When we said our goodbyes, the happy Moores ran back upstairs to their apartment. Screams of excitement coming from the top floor of the building could be heard a block away. Some curious neighbors began to gather in the street as the camera crew dismantled and packed the equipment.

One curious woman approached Dr. Lee, who had been with the entourage that morning.

"What's going on?" she asked him. "Did someone win the lottery?"

"You could say that," he replied, chuckling. "Except this is the kind of lottery where you have to earn the million dollars."

She looked at him, puzzled, and then walked away shaking her head.

4

THE BLUE VASE TEAM: "WE WILL NOT BE DENIED."

1. ———————————————————————————————

"Good morning and welcome," I said.

We sat around the glass dining table in the Presidential Suite of the Daniele Hotel. A bright crystal chandelier sparkled above the sumptuous breakfast before us. It was 8:20 A.M.

"Did any of you sleep last night?" I asked, smiling.

"No!" they all replied in unison.

Two handsome tuxedoed waiters carrying the main breakfast dish—eggs Benedict—had to maneuver gingerly around a confusion of cables, sound booms, cameras and the bright helium arc camera lights that illuminated the scene. I sensed that my guests were intimidated by the presence of the camera crew.

"Don't feel any pressure to perform for the cameras. Their job is just to record what happens. In time, you'll forget they're even here.

Don't feel any pressure from me. My job is just to help you reach your goals—whatever they might be. Try not to be intimidated. Just relax. Let's have a great time."

"That's exactly what I say to a couple when they are about to get married," Steve, the minister, joked.

"And it doesn't do any good, does it?" I added.

Everyone laughed. The ice was broken. As we ate, I reviewed their assignments. All but Nora had been able to find the ads they had placed in that morning's classified section. I explained that the reason for running the ads with the precise wording would become clear later on in the day.

"Why do you think I had you watch the movie *Rocky*," I asked. "It's a rather crazy request."

Karen replied first. "You wanted us to watch someone with great determination. Courage. The will to keep going on."

"Where did he get that will?"

"From within himself," said Mary. "He had the ability to be a great fighter, but he didn't develop it. But when he was challenged to a fight by the heavyweight champion of the world, he rose to the occasion."

"It was the chance of a lifetime for him," Nora added.

"Like us now," said Steve. "It's like each of us is Rocky."

"Yes," I said. "But this is the real world. The opponents we fight are going to fight back. And who knows what the outcome will be. Think we're going to fail?" I was trying to test them.

"No!" They all responded simultaneously with raised voices.

"If you never give up, you never fail," said Steve in his preacher's voice, as if he had sounded this advice before.

I weighed each answer. The Moores were excited. I could tell from the eagerness in their voices. Frankly, I had been concerned that there might exist a racial barrier between us. But I quickly found that there was no barrier at all. Mary was bright. I had no qualms about her. I knew she would be able to pick things up quickly. As for her husband, his answers were too glib, too quick, too pat—as if he understood the answers only intellectually, not emotionally, not deep down. Nora answered the questions in her deliberate manner. I knew that in the next forty-eight hours I'd be stuffing her head with a totally foreign mass of information. I wondered if she could handle it. I continued to probe, seeking to understand each person.

"Do you have any doubts about this?" I asked.

Philip was the first to answer. "Karen and I were talking last night. I said, 'Well, this is it. Do you think we can do it?' And she said, 'Let's put all our heart in it.' We're ready. In fact, I already have a property in mind to buy. It's right in my own neighborhood. You just teach me the steps and I'll buy it."

"You weren't wasting any time," I chuckled.

"I found one, too," Nora said. "In the paper last night. I even went to see it. When I asked the seller his bottom line I thought to myself, 'You don't know it, but I'll own it.' "

We were off to a good start. They were beginning to feed off each other's enthusiasm. Next, I reviewed with them the message of the Blue Vase tape. Philip gave a summary for us.

"It's about a young Vietnam vet," Philip began. "He's a cripple—limps on a bad leg and lost an arm. So nobody wants to hire him."

Philip went on to tell how the young man weaseled his way in to talk to the aging chairman of the board of a big oil outfit. The chairman admired the young man's determination and offered to test him out selling one of the company's toughest products. He did so well that he was offered a permanent job. A few months later, when a management position needed filling, the chairman decided to test the young man's mettle by giving him the supreme test—the test of the Blue Vase—a specially designed obstacle course for go-getters. If he passed the test, the job would be his. The chairman called the young man on a Sunday afternoon and told him he was in urgent need of a particular expensive blue vase he spotted in a store window the day before. Unfortunately, the stores were all closed. The young man offered to get it for him by that evening, not realizing that the situation was rigged. For starters, he was given the wrong address. At each step in the test, the young man had to use his creativity, persistence and determination to overcome ever-increasing obstacles to get the vase. The tape is a dramatic way of showing the benefits of being a go-getter.

When Philip had finished relating the story, I quizzed the group. "What did that teach you?" I asked.

Philip was ready with an answer. "After I listened to that tape, I said to Karen, 'Hey, if Mr. Allen doesn't choose me for the Challenge, I'm not going to take no for an answer.' I wasn't going to be denied. I'd have come to the hotel and begged to sit in the back of the room and listen."

"You know," I said, "if any of the thirty-nine others who were not chosen had asked me to do that, I'd have let them."

"Really?" asked Steve incredulously.

"Absolutely. That would have been evidence that they were go-getters—exactly what I was looking for. But no one asked. They just took rejection and gave up. Just like you said, 'If you never give up, you can't fail.' Isn't that the message of the Blue Vase tape?"

They all nodded their agreement. I surveyed my little group of go-getters. They didn't have much of what the world would call success. But they had that one secret ingredient and that was more than enough. Success cannot be denied a go-getter.

I continued, "To be successful, you need two things: attitude and aptitude. Which of the two is more important?"

"Attitude," they replied in unison.

"Come, now," I badgered them, "do you really believe that a positive, go-getter attitude is more important than knowledge or talent?"

"If you have the right attitude, you can always persist until you get the aptitude," said Steve. "But if you don't have the right attitude, it doesn't matter what your aptitude. How does the saying go? 'It's your attitude that determines your altitude.' "

Another pat comment, I thought. We'd have to see if he felt the same in ninety days.

I continued. "The man in the Blue Vase story had no special talent or education. But he was a go-getter. If an obstacle was placed in his way, he just went over it or around it or under it. To a go-getter, there are no obstacles. Just temporary inconveniences. In the next ninety days, each of you will be tested with some pretty hefty obstacles. You are on the Blue Vase team. If you are a 'blue-vaser,' you will have to accept tough assignments without a lot of instruction. You'll just have to 'blue vase it'—to go out on your own and not come back until the job is done. Do you understand?"

I looked at each one of them seriously. Each one of them nodded back in the same way.

"The seminar I have designed for you in the next forty-eight hours is part aptitude training, but mostly attitude training. You'll learn how to think like a go-getter. You'll also learn twelve wealth secrets. These secrets form the foundation of all wealth. Master them, and you will never have to worry about money again. I think you'll recognize the first secret."

WEALTH SECRET NO. 1. THERE ARE NO MONEY PROBLEMS. THERE ARE ONLY ATTITUDE PROBLEMS. A GO-GETTER, WITH THE PROPER ATTITUDE, CANNOT BE DENIED.

I could tell that they understood.

HOW DO YOU KNOW IF YOU ARE A GO-GETTER?

- You love a challenge.
- Adversity seems to make you stronger rather than weaker.
- When someone tells you no, you don't take it personally. You try another way to get a yes.
- You are goal oriented—you know where you are going.
- You don't look upon obstacles as permanent barriers but as temporary inconveniences.
- You don't make excuses. When given a job, you don't return until it is done.
- You are always thinking of new ways to do things better even if it means breaking with tradition.
- You are willing to put up with criticism since you realize that most criticism comes from negative thinkers.
- You are a positive thinker—you love to find the good in every bad situation.
- Anyone can learn basic go-getting skills as described in the following pages. And with practice, you'll be surprised not only how much easier but also how much more rewarding it is to be a positive, optimistic go-getter than to be a negative, pessimistic loser.

"One more thing," I said. "I want each of you to make me a promise. Within one year from this date, I challenge you to teach three other needy individuals the wealth secrets you will master. And challenge each of them to pass the knowledge on to at least three others."

"I like that," Nora responded. "I know who my three people are right now."

"The purpose of this is twofold," I said. "First of all, on the selfish side, it's a well-known principle that the best way to learn is to teach. Teaching these things to others will expand your understanding greatly."

"Secondly, there is much truth in the ancient Chinese adage: 'Give a man a fish and you feed him for a day. Teach a man to fish and you feed him for a lifetime.' I encourage you to teach others to fish for themselves, to be self-reliant, to be independent instead of dependent, to be masters of their own fate. It's one of the greatest gifts you can give anyone."

Steve, the preacher, made a mental note: "This would be good material for a sermon. There are so many people in my parish who are struggling financially." He forgot for a moment that he and his wife were among them.

"Well," I said in conclusion, "if you're finished with breakfast, let's go down to the seminar room. I can hardly wait to introduce you into a new world."

2.

As soon as the breakfast scene was over, technicians began running about, disconnecting cords and packing up equipment to carry downstairs for the next film shoot. Nora got up from the dining table. Her eyes burned from a combination of the bright helium arc camera lights and too little sleep the night before. She closed her eyes momentarily. It all seemed like a dream; a ray of sunshine illuminating the gray, disappointing background of her life. Someone turned the bright lights off, casting the room in shadow. She joined the shuffle of people heading for the elevators.

Everyone crowded into the elevator excitedly. Nora backed into a corner and leaned against the wall while the elevator descended. She closed her eyes again. She was tired. Very tired. Her mind wandered.

She had been up late the night before excitedly telling her daughters about the Challenge. They were too young to understand completely. To them, it was just another one of Mother's crazy schemes. When Nora had finally crawled into bed it was two in the morning. She set her alarm clock for 5:30, but her mind would simply not shut down, racing from thought to thought. Before she knew it the alarm warned her that it was time to dress.

In the predawn darkness, as she drove along the freeway, she pondered how fast things had changed. Early morning commuters were already clogging the freeway, pushing and shoving their way through another monotonous day at work. Only a few hours before, she herself had driven this road to the unemployment office in South St. Louis with hopes of joining these same commuters to any steady, secure job. Now she was ready to say good-bye to the world of employees forever.

In a few miles she came to a familiar stretch of road. There was barely enough light for her to pick out the real estate sign posted in the trees by the right side of the road. It was a big sign, maybe ten feet across, and in large red letters on a white background were the words:

FOR SALE
975 Acres
Call 555-1234

"That's where I'm going to build my resort," she reminded herself.

Off to the right of the freeway, the wooded hills rolled mysteriously. It would be a marvelous place for a health resort. She imagined the large main building: two residence wings of six floors each on either side of an impressive drive up entrance. In the back would be the swimming pool and spa area. And around the resort, hiking and horseback trails would meander through the rolling hills in all directions.

The sun was just breaking over the tree-covered countryside as she passed through Times Beach, the small Missouri city that had caught the attention of the whole country in 1982 with its dioxin poison pollution scandal and the following year with a devastating flood. For Nora, who had lived in a mobile home in Times Beach during those times of public disaster, it was a time of private disaster. Her divorce became final, and the judge, doubting Nora's ability to support a family, awarded custody of the two youngest girls to her ex-husband. Since the children didn't want to live with their father, Nora defied the court and lived in hiding with the girls until she lost her job at the Chrysler plant. When she finally ran out of money and the bank repossessed her mobile home, she had no choice but to send the children back to live with their father. All that summer, with no place to stay, she slept in the backseat of her car alone, longing for the day when she could afford to get her children back legally.

The elevator bumped to a stop at the bottom floor of the Daniele Hotel, jarring her back to the present. Nora opened her eyes, walking with the others into the exquisitely furnished foyer, past the sunken dining room and down the wainscotted hall to the seminar room. It was a different world.

As Nora was ushered into the room, she noticed the cameras on tripods pointing toward a setting of tables, a blackboard and an easel. She found her seat and took a deep breath, realizing that she was about to start one of the most difficult and frightening experiences of her life. And yet she felt more at peace than at any time she could remember.

She glanced at her fellow team members. The Moores, sitting to Nora's right, appeared a bit out of place in this new environment. Mary Bonenberger sat next to her husband, smiling. For the first time Nora realized that she was the oldest person in the room. Even among the camera crew.

"I've got grown children older than many of them," she thought.

Before she had any more time to worry, someone shouted, "Cameras rolling. Sound. Speed. Action."

WHAT SENSES DO WE LACK THAT WE CANNOT SEE OR HEAR
ANOTHER WORLD ALL AROUND US?—Frank Herbert, *Dune*

5

CLIMBING THE MONEY MOUNTAIN

"Let's get started," I began.

In front of me sat the five Challenge participants. To my extreme left the camera crews worked, trying unsuccessfully to be unobtrusive. The large seminar room, already warm from the bright camera lights, was tastefully appointed with plush carpet, fine Oriental prints on the wall, wood trim and valence lighting. It was a fitting place to be discussing wealth.

"On the desk in front of you is your MasterPlanner. You will carry it with you everywhere you go—like a portable desk and filing system. It will be one of the most important tools in your success. Would you please turn to the first page and read the letter there."

Mary scanned the letter of introduction. "No turning back now," she thought to herself.

If you were to total the assets of the wealthiest 8 percent of the U.S. population, it would be greater than the combined assets of the other 92 percent. What do they know that you don't know? Do you need to be lucky, ruthless, brilliant, talented, well connected, charming, unscrupulous or greedy to be financially successful? No. You just need to understand some basic simple principles and have the courage to act upon them. So let's forge on together like pioneers. We have a lot of unfamiliar territory to cover before nightfall.

When I could see that they were finished reading, I held up a recent copy of *Money* magazine with the banner, "How to Become Financially Independent. Four Ways to Start Now."

"I am quoted in this issue of *Money* magainze," I said. "The bottom line of what I say is simple; real estate is one of the surest roads to financial independence.

"It seems a lot of people in this country would like to be financially independent—to declare freedom from their jobs at last. More than 20 million Americans got up this morning and drove to jobs they cannot stand. Millions more found themselves in unemployment lines wishing for financial freedom. You were among them. I have a message for you. No one has to get stuck in a job they hate. You can choose to make financial self-reliance a reality in your lives.

"Financial freedom is a big goal, isn't it? That's what I like about it! It's big enough to scare most people away. It's just like learning to climb a mountain."

I pointed to my left, at a large picture of a beautiful white-capped mountain.

"What mountain is that?" I asked.

"Everest, isn't it?" Philip answered.

"Not Everest. It's Mount McKinley—the tallest mountain in North America, standing 20,300 feet above sea level. Looks rather forbidding, doesn't it? With this in mind, I would like you to imagine something with me. Imagine receiving a phone call from a very official-sounding gentleman. He says, 'Hello, Philip, Nora, Steve, Mary, Karen, your uncle Harry just passed away and has left you a million dollars in his will.'

" 'A million dollars!' you exclaim.

" 'But there is a catch,' the man continues. 'Since your uncle was a bit eccentric, he attached some rather unusual conditions to your obtaining the inheritance. The money has been deposited in a safety deposit box in Zurich, Switzerland. The key to the safety deposit box has been placed in a metal container and hidden in a secret cairn at the summit of Mount McKinley. Your instructions are simple. You must climb to the top of the mountain, locate the key using a map you will be given, descend again, fly to Switzerland and use the key to open the safety deposit box. You will have twelve months to accomplish this, after which time the million dollars will be given to your worst enemy.'

"You are flabbergasted. A million dollars!!! And all you have to do is climb a mountain. But you've never climbed a mountain before. What's worse, you are deathly afraid of heights. Your eccentric uncle has created a situation where you will have to face your fear and conquer it in order to win. Now, let me ask you a question. How many of you really believe that you would be able to overcome your fear, climb the mountain and retrieve the money within the allotted twelve months?"

All of them quickly and without hesitation raised their hands.

"Are you sure?" I asked. "How would you overcome your fear of heights?"

Nora responded first. "I would be determined to have it."

"I wouldn't want my worst enemy to get it," said Mary, laughing.

"What problems would you face in climbing Mount McKinley?" I asked.

They shot a barrage of answers at me. "The weather. The cold. The wind. The sun. Lack of oxygen. Slipping and falling."

"What things would make your climb easier?" I asked.

"A guide. The right equipment. Determination. A goal. A step-by-step plan."

"Good," I said. "Would you read a book on mountain climbing and then start climbing the very next day?"

All of them responded in unison. "No."

"We would need training, practice," said Karen. "You start out on hills, then small mountains. Until you're ready to tackle big mountains like that."

"Well," I summarzied, "you may not have inherited a bundle from an eccentric uncle, but that doesn't mean you don't have a million dollars waiting for you. You won't have to climb Mount McKinley to get it. But it'll be just as scary. Starting, as you are, with little experience in climbing the money mountain, you will need to make a quantum leap to reach financial independence. In fact, many

Americans think it's impossible to improve their financial situation. They're afraid they'll lose what they already have. Afraid to fail . . . afraid to even try. Perhaps you used to be like this.

"But I've been to the top before. I'll be your guide. Before we tackle the big mountains we'll practice on some small hills. You'll get used to heights. With practice, your fear will diminish. I'll show you where the money is. Believe me, it's a lot less scary when you know where to look. And you won't have to look further then a ten-mile radius of where you live.

"When you've climbed the mountain once, it's much easier the second time. If I lost everything I owned today, I could start over again right here. In a few hours, I'd have found my first property. In a few days, I'd have bought it. In a few weeks, I'd be on to my second and third. What are some major obstacles you'll face in climbing the money mountain?"

"People."

"What do you mean by that, Nora?"

"Their attitudes. They look at you like you're crazy. They haven't been able to do it. Why should you?"

"Have you ever been told that you couldn't do it?"

"Lots of times," she said. "Just this morning I was talking to someone about the Challenge. He looked at me and said, 'You don't have it in you.' And I said, 'You watch me.' "

Steve entered the conversation. "When I hear a story like that it just almost overwhelms me. That someone would be that negative and crass."

"You'd be surprised how many people are like that," I explained. "And what's worse, a lot of them profess to love you. They don't want you to get hurt. To fail. But all too often, by discouraging you from risking, they keep you from realizing your full potential. The only way to grow is to risk. Life is risk. Successful people rarely tell you you can't do it. Only unsuccessful people tell you that. And they're usually wrong. Unless, of course, you believe them. In which case, they're right. It's up to you. What other challenges are you going to face in climbing the money mountain, Karen?"

"Our poor finances," she answered.

Others joined in. "Management of the property. Upkeep. Building a system to keep it. Learning the problem-solving tools."

"OK," I interrupted. "But before you face any of these challenges, you first have to overcome the biggest obstacle of all. What is the greatest stumbling block in reaching the top of the money mountain?"

"Fear," responded Nora without hesitation.

"Fear," I repeated, pausing to let it sink in. "That's a biggie, isn't it? The biggest of all the biggies. Whenever I speak to a large group, I always ask them to write down the major roadblock to their success. Over half of the people in every audience have a problem with fear. It's paralyzing them. They want to act, but they just don't dare. How do we get so much fear in us?"

"Its inbred from the day you are born," Nora responded.

"Who teaches you to be afraid?"

"Your parents. Society."

"How do they do that?"

Mary responded. "They teach you to be careful, to not take risks. Just be secure. Get a job. Have a steady income, and that's what there is to life. To seek security."

"And," I added, "slowly we begin to feel that it's not OK to climb mountains. Better to stay secure in the valley. Everywhere we see the word *security*. What are the words witten over the door of the unemployment office where we found you, Nora?"

"The Missouri Division of Employment Security."

"Did that make you feel secure?"

"No!"

"Having a job doesn't guarantee you security. A few years ago, when Braniff Airlines filed for bankruptcy, I talked to some ex-Braniff employees. Some had twenty or thirty years' seniority. But a few bad management decisions put them on the street. Talk to them about job security. Just last Monday, at an Employment Security Office right here in St. Louis, I talked to a fellow who had worked for ten years on a local automobile assembly line. All those years he thought he was secure. Then, two years ago, he got a pink slip. He's been waiting ever since to be called back. I guess he just can't wait to be secure again.

"When will he learn that what he thinks is security is just the illusion of security? It's a myth. He's building his house on the sand of false assumptions. Ten years ago he made the assumption that the union would guarantee him job security. He bought into that myth—bought it hook, line and sinker. And ended up the sucker.

What if, instead, he had acted on a different assumption—that he wasn't secure—that there was no such thing as job security—that sooner or later he was going to be out on the streets unless he took financial matters into his own hands? What if, as a solution, he had gone out and bought just two pieces of real estate on the side for each of those ten years? He'd be a millionaire today. And then, if he lost his job, he wouldn't blame his boss. Instead, he'd say, 'Thanks, boss, I've been looking for an excuse to retire anyway.'

"There is no security in this life. Only varying degrees of risk. And yet millions unquestioningly sacrifice their lives on the altar of *security*. Like lemmings, they march into the abyss solely because that's what everyone else is doing. It's not that they die, but that they die like sheep. They've been taught by generations of example to love security and to be afraid of anything that isn't secure. What are they afraid of, Philip?"

"Failure," he answered with conviction, as if it were his own fear.

"What's so bad about failure?"

"Its humiliating," responded Mary.

"Did any of you ever take piano lessons?" I asked. "A woman in Atlanta recently told me that her fear of failure began as the result of taking piano lessons. Her teacher made her feel guilty every time she played a wrong note. She didn't like that feeling. Slowly she became a perfectionist, avoiding anything where there was a chance of failure."

Karen added, "I can relate to that. In school, some people are great students. They can come to the class a couple of times, take the test and come out on top. Others study and study and study and still flunk. Now, that's hard on a person."

"Sounds like that happened to you," I said.

"Yes, it did," she said softly. "Can't forget it. Wonderin' if the teacher just didn't like me or maybe I just didn't have what it takes."

"We've all had experiences like that. It's hard to overcome the programming. You might wonder, with only a few days to spend together, why I haven't jumped right into teaching you about real estate. But real estate is the easy part. The hard part is overcoming the fear. Once you overcome the fear, success is just around the corner."

I felt it was time to tell them the cliff story.

"When I was a young boy my father took me fishing in Waterton

Lakes National Park in Alberta, Canada. One day, when I was in my early teens, we hiked for about two miles up a mountain trail to the base of a cliff. 'Bobby,' he said, pointing to the precipice, 'in the basin above that cliff is a set of three lakes called the Lineham Lakes. The only way to get into those lakes is to traverse the cliff along a narrow ledge. I've only been to those lakes one time in my life,' he said. 'Crossing that cliff on that narrow ledge was the most frightening experience of my life.' He told me that in some places the ledge was only two feet wide and there were few handholds. In other spots, the ledge was only a few inches wide, and you had to hang on to an upper ledge with your fingers as your feet dangled over a three-hundred-foot drop. But once you got across that cliff, the fishing was fantastic. Big ones. Three-pound rainbow trout. And lots of them. After seeing the cliff, we walked back down the trail and went fishing at another, safer lake where the fish were smaller and less frequent."

"But I never forgot that day at the cliff. In the back of my mind I made a pledge to go there one day. And that day came in 1982, more than twenty years later. By then, I was a successful investor and author coming back to my roots with my young family. We bought a small summer cabin in the park. One day I bumped into Mr. Goble, a man who had been to Lineham many times. He offered to take me into Lineham.

" 'Will it be dangerous?' I asked.

" 'I'll bring along my two young sons and the dog.' He pointed to a small brown-and-white mutt with a short, pointed tail and said, 'If the dog can make it, you can make it.' I was amazed to learn that the thirteen-year-old dog had traversed the cliff dozens of times.

"Not to be outdone by a couple of kids and a dog, I decided to go.

"The day arrived for the expedition. We started off in the early morning and followed the trail as it switchbacked up the mountain to the point where the trail abruptly stopped and the ledge of the cliff lay before us. The Gobles, father and sons, walked right out onto the cliff as if it had been level ground. The dog trotted along behind without a care. I took one look at the ledge and the three-hundred-foot drop and froze in my tracks. I had expected the ledge to be flat and smooth, almost carved out of rock. Instead it was slightly sloping and covered with loose shale. My knees felt weak. I walked out onto the ledge. My fear of looking foolish to my gracious guides temporarily overcame my fear of the height. But after only a few dozen feet my legs turned to butter, and I dropped to my hands and knees. The fear swelled up inside me in thick knots. My mouth went dry. I couldn't decide whether to continue or to turn back. I was paralyzed (There had been only one other time in my life when I had felt a comparable fear—a memorable evening some eight years earlier when I signed the agreement to buy my first piece of property.) There, paralyzed on the cliff, I remember saying to myself over and over again, 'Please, God, help me face my fear.' I continued to crawl along the ledge, inch by inch. Mr. Goble came back to check on me. With his encouragement I raised myself into a crouch and proceeded to the halfway point along the cliff. The boys and the dog had already gone on ahead.

"At this spot on the cliff a large outcropping of rock obliterated the ledge. Below me, the cliff fell to the boulders far below. I was told that I would have to find a firm handhold on my side of the outcropping and then, swinging my left leg out over the abyss, I was to reach around the jutting rock with my free hand, find a firm handhold and pull myself to the other ledge. He demonstrated what I had to do and waited for me on the other side. I took one look down and seriously considered staying there in that spot on the cliff for the rest of my life. Mr. Goble offered me more encouragement and reached his hand around to guide me. I offered him my left hand, which had no strength in it to even grab for a handhold. He held my hand to the mountain, giving me the strength that I could not muster. Somehow, I swung my leg out over the edge, and he pulled me around. We continued along the ledge until we came to a ravine where we climbed straight up using trees and roots as leverage. Finally we emerged into the basin where the three lakes awaited.

"And what fishing! It was even better than my father had described. Although the three-pounders eluded me, I found a small pond in the stream between two of the lakes where I could see the fish swimming in schools. I caught a fish with almost every cast. In the lower lake, dozens of smaller fish would follow my hook in to the shore, their silver bodies gleaming in the sunlight. I have never had a better day of fishing before or since. Apart from us, there was only one other party of fishermen there on that glorious day.

"All went well for me until about four o'clock that afternoon when it became clear that we would have to go back down the same way we had come up. I asked my guide to leave me there and send a helicopter back for me. He laughed and shook his head. As we started back down, I felt more sure of myself. The father and the boys went on ahead. The dog and I brought up the rear. The dog trotted assuredly along the ledge in front of me, disappearing around a corner. I stopped to take a rest.

"And then I heard a sickening sound.

"The dog yelped. Some loose rocks tumbled over the side. And then I heard a distant thud coming from the base of the cliff."

" 'What was that?' I yelled.

" 'The dog,' someone yelled back.

"I couldn't believe it! The dog had slipped and fallen over the edge. Only seconds before—trotting along the ledge so surefooted, so nimble, so confident—now gone. That didn't do a lot for my confidence. The fear came back, only stronger. My heart pounded. My legs went weak. I crouched and waited. One of the boys came back for me.

"Funny things happen in times like these. From deep inside comes a creative impulse suggesting a solution. I remember reasoning with myself. 'Logically, if you take one step at a time, slowly but surely, you must eventually reach the other side.' The fear eased a notch. I proceeded like this, one step at a time, one shoe in front of the other, not looking down or ahead, past the outcropping of rock, until I looked up and found myself on the other side.

"It was over! I was safe.

"The boys had gone to find the dog at the base of the cliff, and, sure enough, it was dead . . . eyes glazed over, legs stiff as pegs. We walked silently toward the car, the boys carrying the dog between them for a proper family burial.

"It was an unforgettable experience. I had come face to face with my fear. And I had won. I learned four lessons from this experience which are going to be essential to your success.

"First of all, the cliff was a piece of cake to the Gobles, but to me, a beginner, it was terrifying. I can still see them walking along the ledge with no fear whatsoever while I groveled along on my hands and knees choking back the panic. I am going to ask you to do things in the next ninety days which, to me, seem normal and ordinary but which, to you, may seem out of your league.

"For instance, I might say, 'Call fifty sellers a day on the phone.'

And you might wonder, 'Fifty sellers! What do I say? How do I start? What if I look like a fool?' Like a blue-vaser, you'll just have to swallow your terror, put one foot in front of the other, make one call at a time, and continue until you reach the other side. Confidence comes with practice.

"I might say, 'Assume the seller's debt of fifty thousand dollars,' which is nothing to me but might look like a fortune to you. Just let me guide you along the cliff. In the places where your hands are too weak to grab hold, I'll make a handhold for you. Soon enough you will be fearless.

"Secondly, don't look at the immensity of the goal. Don't look down—at the penalty for failure. Just keep your eyes on the next step. I won't let you make any fatal mistakes. That does not mean, however, that you won't make mistakes. You will. It comes with the territory. You'll slip and bruise yourself. Maybe even break a leg, figuratively. But you'll heal, and if you maintain the proper attitude, you'll emerge a stronger, more courageous and less fearful person.

"The third point I wish to make is so important that I am going to call it a wealth secret:

WEALTH SECRET NO. 2. FACE YOUR FEAR. YOU ALWAYS FIND THE BEST FISHING HOLES IN THE PLACES WHERE THE AVERAGE FISHERMAN IS AFRAID TO GO.

"Why was the fishing good at Lineham?" I asked. "Because very few ever dared to fish there. The masses are always afraid. This leaves more for the few who dare. We don't have a shortage of opportunity in America. We have a shortage of courage. The lakes are teeming with fish. But you have to dare to climb the cliffs to get them. Where the risks are great the rewards are greater. Once you understand this concept, you'll never lack for anything again. That is, if you're able to overcome your fear.

"As in all fairy tales, if you want to marry the princess, you have to slay the dragon. The greatest dragon you'll ever face is your own fear. I am going to call on you to face your fear a hundred times in the next ninety days. If you can learn to live with the fear, the world is yours.

"And the fourth point I will also elevate to the level of a wealth secret:

WEALTH SECRET NO. 3. WATCH THE CROWD. GO IN THE OPPOSITE DIRECTION.

"Success does not come by following the crowd. Where there are many fishermen, the lakes get fished out fast. You must not be afraid to go against the grain—to go alone to unclaimed territory.

"Here, also, fear paralyzes. One of our deepest fears is the fear of rejection. Aren't we all soft and fuzzy on the inside? We seek acceptance by our peers. We want to be loved. We crave it. Unfortunately, this is not the route to success. To be successful you must learn to be different.

"Many assume that this means that you'll have no friends. Not so. You'll have even more friends—real friends—who will admire you for your courage.

"You don't believe me? Just think of the people you most admire. What kind of people are they? Do they hide in the anonymity of the crowd, afraid to be unique? Or are they courageous enough to be better than the average?

"Yes. Do they lack for friends?

"No. Be like your heroes. And in so doing, you'll be loved and accepted by those who really count. Any friend who encourages you to be less than you can be is not a real friend by anyone's standard. Give him a wide birth.

"Be different. While the masses seek security, do the contrary. March out into the risk.

"If the masses huddle in a corner, afraid, stand out from them. Face your fear.

"Look around you. See the masses standing in lines, waiting for someone to take care of them. Step out of line and form a new line—with you at the head of it.

"If fear of failure causes the multitudes to cower, let this be your cue. Like all great people before you, be determined to fail your way to success if necessary.

"If the masses yearn to be loved, strive instead to be respected. It is greater to be respected than to be loved. For respect is the foundation of love. There can be no love without it. When you learn to face your fear, you will come to respect yourself. And you will be irresistible.

"It takes courage to step out of the line marked 'security' into the line marked 'risk.' I was amused to learn that last Monday when

Tom was handing out those yellow fliers one young man refused to come to the meeting because he was afraid he would lose his place in line. Can you imagine that? Passing up freedom for a mess of pottage. But not you. You answered the call to step out of those lines of an old world of scarcity and enter into a new world of abundance.

"It's difficult for people to believe that you can choose abundance over scarcity. They think I am crazy when I say that it's just as easy to be wealthy as it is to be poor—if not easier. And why is it hard for them to believe? Because they are confused.

"Let me demonstrate. Look at the dotted picture on the page in front of you. Do you see any patterns?"

All of them shook their heads. They couldn't see anything but a confusion of dots.

"Well," I continued, "there is an image in those dots, distinct and clear. I can see it. Can you see it yet?"

"No."

"Would it be easier for you if I told you that you were looking for a horse?"

"No. It's still just a bunch of dots," replied Steve.

"This is the way the world of money looks to most people. It is

just a mass of confusion. They don't know how to connect the dots to make any sense out of it. Thousands of different experts give totally conflicting advice. Your parents tell you to play it safe; your banker tells you to put your money in CD's; others say the answer is in gold or stocks or tax-exempt bonds or the company pension plan or Social Security. The average American is boggled at best, paralyzed at worst. The confused American scratches his head, dabbles in a thing or two, gets burned and retreats to the sidelines feeling like a fool. As in Mark Twain's story, the cat who steps once on a hot stove never steps on any stoves again—hot or cold. Can you see the horse yet, Steve?"

"No. Still can't see it."

"Isn't that interesting. Even when I tell you what to look for, you still can't see it. Let's see if I can make it clearer for you by connecting a few of the dots."

"I've got it," said Mary.

"Me too," Nora said.

"I still can't see it," Steve protested, his brow creased.

I connected a few more of the dots.

"All right. I've got it," he said.

GOING FROM AN OLD WORLD TO A NEW WORLD

Old World Programming	New World Attitudes
They are responsible for me.	I am responsible for me.
I am dependent.	I am independent.
I am the employee.	I am the boss, regardless of whom I work for.
I am afraid to act.	I act in spite of my fear.
I am afraid. Give me security.	I am afraid. Give me opportunity.
I get what I see—scarcity, lack, bondage.	I get what I see—opportunity, abundance, freedom.
I am a victim.	I am a volunteer.
I am sensitive—take it easy on me.	I am precious—challenge me, let me grow.
I need friends even if it means lowering my standards.	I want to make progress even if it means going alone.
I need your love.	Let me be worthy of your respect and love.

Then I showed them the original picture without the dots connected. I asked them what they saw. Steve spoke without hesitation. "I see a horse and rider," he said.

"And from now on, whenever you see this picture, instead of a confused mass of dots, you'll always see a horse and rider. I changed your perception. I taught you how to make sense of the confusion. When it comes to money, most people are guided by a confusing set of assumptions that don't work. They are stuck in an old world where the prevailing assumption is that the world is flat. I tell them that the world is round. They laugh.

"I want to introduce you to a new world. It's the world of opportunity, abundance and freedom. It exists all around us right now—this instant—though very few ever see it. Their world is governed by flat-world concepts—scarcity, bondage and deprivation. With these as their assumptions, how can they even imagine a new world?

"In the next few days, you'll catch glimpses of this new world. It still won't be clear to you by tomorrow night. But sometime during the next ninety days you'll have a burst of understanding. You'll see that these two worlds exist as surely as you can see the sun. You'll realize that you can choose which world you want to live in. You'll look back at your friends and relatives in the old world and wonder how they can think they're living on a flat planet when you know full well that it is round. 'How can they live like that?' you'll say. 'Did I live like that?' You'll beckon for them to join you in the new world. And they will laugh. I want you to remember the first time that someone laughs at you. And when it happens—and it will—I want you to smile and not take it personally.

"In this new world, you're going to be amazed at how free you feel. And yet you'll be the same person you always were. You'll weigh the same. You'll talk the same. You'll like the same foods. You'll have a lot of the same habits. In fact, the day you make the transition from the old world into the new world you probably won't have any more money in the bank than you do right now. But you will be different. Radically different. Because your perception will be different.

"And I will make you another promise. Once you enter this new world, you will never go back to the old world you left behind. You won't even be tempted. Why would a butterfly go back into its cocoon?

"I drove down Martin Luther King Boulevard here in St. Louis a few days ago. People are literally starving to death in the midst of the gold mine. It's the saddest thing I've ever seen in my life. But just like you, Steve, who couldn't see the horse and rider, they can't see the opportunity. Even when you tell them that it's there. They've been programmed to see the poverty, the lack. But just because they can't see it doesn't mean that it doesn't exist.

"Bit by bit, layer by layer, slowly and carefully, you're going to peel away your own programming. I tell you these stories about the mountain, the cliff, fishing, the new world and the old world so that you and I will have a common reference point to use for discussion in the next ninety days. When you call me, paralyzed with fear at the thought of signing your name to a real estate contract, I'll say, 'Remember the cliff. One foot in front of the other.' When you become discouraged at the immensity of the goal, I will say, 'Practice on the foothills. Get used to the altitude. Then the mountain will not seem so big.' When you despair at the people you meet who can't see the world that you see, I will say, 'Show them by your example. Those who have eyes to see will see. Then teach them how to fish.'

"OK. Let's cover one more major point before we break. Since we'll be living round-world concepts in a flat world, give me three quick ways we can strengthen ourselves so that we won't be overcome by our old world programming."

"Knowledge, education," Steve responded.

"Positive attitude," added his wife, Mary.

"Goals," said Nora.

FIVE-STEP SUCCESS FORMULA

1. Determine what you really want.
2. Set a specific goal to obtain it. To be effective, this goal must include a specific time frame and plan for its accomplishment. The goal should also be written down and studied regularly.
3. Gain knowledge about your goal—listen to tapes, talk to experts, go to seminars to learn about it.
4. Associate with people who share your goals and attitudes while avoiding those who don't.
5. Don't stop until you get it.

"Good. Knowledge. Attitude. Goals. The top three. Let's return to our example of Mount McKinley. What was our goal? To climb the mountain. What was our time frame? Twelve months. What was our reward? One million dollars. The more specific the goal the greater the probability it'll be realized. So let's set a specific goal for ourselves on this challenge. Mary, turn over on the next page in your manual and read for us the goal sheet."

Mary read: "Within the next ninety days I will find or create at least one win/win opportunity which will result in my being able to deposit five thousand dollars cash in the bank."

"That's a very specific goal," I said. "Are you willing to sign your name to that, Mary?"

"Sure."

"Once you sign it, place it where you'll see it often."

"For me, that's in the kitchen on the refrigerator," she said.

We all laughed.

"You might consider taping it above your bed on the ceiling," I said. "So it's the first thing you see in the morning, and it's the last thing you see at night.

"One of the reasons you were chosen for the Challenge is because you are goal-setters. Nora, you had a specific goal, to start a hotel/resort. Steve and Mary wanted their own church. Philip, you wanted your own busines. But none of you had specific enough goals with time deadlines.

"Having a specific, written goal with a date for completion is the key to opening the power of your subconscious mind. As you read your goal, visualize or picture in your mind the achievement of what you desire. Visualize sitting in the closing office when the title company officer hands you a five-thousand-dollar check. Visualize a seller happy with the solution to his problem. Visualize a happy realtor or banker. See a positive, win/win result.

"Why goals? Why visualization? Suppose you had access to the most powerful computer in the world. What kinds of questions would you ask it? How would you use it? Well, you do have access to this computer. It's right on top of your shoulders. The brain is among the most powerful and complex entities in the universe. But how do we use it? We program it to find us minimum-wage jobs. Like a good servant, it does exactly that. What a waste of power! It's like having access to the genius of Albert Einstein and using him, instead, to carry out the garbage. I want you to reprogram your computer to find you maximum-income opportunities. The process is just the same. And thus, the powerful computer of our mind, energized by a specific, visualized task or goal, goes to work to find you exactly what you program it to do—even while you sleep.

"Only a small percentage of the masses set goals. And yet, did you ever meet a successful person who wasn't a goal-setter?

"I rest my case.

"That's enough for now. Let's break for ten minutes. And then I'll show you how to find opportunity and take advantage of it."

THERE IS NO SECURITY ON THIS EARTH. THERE IS ONLY
OPPORTUNITY.—Douglas MacArthur

OPPORTUNITIES ARE USUALLY DISGUISED AS HARD WORK,
SO MOST PEOPLE DON'T RECOGNIZE THEM.—Ann Landers

6

OPPORTUNITY: HOW TO FIND IT, FUND IT AND FARM IT

1.

"So what did you learn in the last hour?" I asked when we'd returned to work.

Philip responded first. "Don't let fear conquer you. You conquer fear."

"Wealth is out there. We just have to go for it," Mary added.

I nodded toward Nora for her response. "It's OK to fear, as long as I don't let the fear rule me."

"Good," I said. "Steve? How about you?"

"I'm still thinking about that picture of the horse and rider," he said, still a bit unnerved. "Why couldn't I see the figures in there? Maybe I'm a single-minded person. If I blast an image on my mind, I really can't see anything else."

I was secretly pleased that Steve was a bit rattled by his experience in self-discovery. He had actually experienced blindness—being unable to see what others around him were seeing. Maybe now he would begin to question the way he saw the world. How can you escape from an old world if you don't question the assumptions that keep you a prisoner there?

"Being single-minded and determined is great," I said, "but you can become fixated on the wrong thing. So be determined to be creative—single-mindedly open to every opportunity."

I went on to explain that the key to making more money is to capitalize on more opportunities. Old-world thinkers miss a lot of opportunities because they start off from the assumption that opportunity is scarce. No wonder they can't "see" it. Creative, new world thinkers keep their minds open a bit longer, deferring judgment, expecting to find opportunity, and are not surprised when they do. I had prepared another demonstration to teach them more about the art of recognizing hidden opportunity.

"Mary, would you come up here for a second?" I requested.

I seated her at a small table. Before her lay a royal blue jeweler's felt pad with two sparkling stones in the center of it.

Using a pair of long silver jeweler's tweezers, I moved one of the shining stones. "This is a half-carat cubic zirconium—nothing more than a piece of glass polished and faceted to look exactly like a diamond. It's worth less than five dollars. The stone beside it is a genuine half-carat diamond worth fifteen hundred dollars."

I took a small, round magnifying glass—jewelers call it a loupe—out of my pocket and placed it on the blue pad next to the tweezers. "Mary, I told you that you were going to learn how to spot opportunities. Here's the first one. Pick the real diamond and you can keep it. Choose wrong and you get nothing ... or I'll pay you a dollar to pass up this opportunity altogether. But before you make up your mind," I added quickly, "I need to make one small adjustment."

I then produced a small box containing forty-nine other cubic zirconiums and dumped the stones onto the blue velvet pad, mixing all of them together. I watched the reactions of those in the room out of the corner of my eye. The Challenge participants gasped. Even members of the film crew, who were supposed to be professionally detached, were shocked, assuming that the diamond was now lost in the glittering confusion.

Mary hesitated. I savored her indecision. This was exactly the reaction I'd hoped for. "How much time do I get?" she asked.

"One minute," I said. "Which will it be? The dollar bill or the chance to find the diamond?"

"I want the diamond."

"You could end up with nothing. How much would I have to pay you to not take the risk? Twenty dollars?"

"Nope. I still want to go for the diamond."

"Fifty?"

"You're getting warmer," she said, softening.

"So you can be bought off, can you?"

Steve joined in the discussion. "It's like Bob Barker and 'The Price Is Right,' Mary. You can either have a thousand dollars or what's behind door number three."

We all laughed.

"Isn't life like that?" I asked. "Don't a lot of people go for the sure thing, working at jobs they hate? They get bought off—some for twenty thousand dollars a year, others for fifty thousand. Just like you, Mary. You couldn't be bought off for twenty, but when I got to fifty, I hit your greed button. Some employees will put up with anything for a price: frustration, boredom, anger, humiliation. Why do they do it? Security! But experience has already taught you that job security is just an illusion. OK, Mary, which is it? Fifty dollars or a chance at the diamond?"

"I guess I'll take my chances."

"OK. Your minute just started."

Mary fumbled for the loupe and tweezers and began poking around in the pile of stones.

"What are you looking for, Mary?"

"The brilliance of a real diamond," she mumbled, determined not to lose her concentration.

I slipped a glance at Steve. He was on the edge of his seat. Fifteen hundred dollars would just about pay the past-due hospital bills for his three-month-old son. Besides, he knew something I didn't: Mary had grown up working in her father's modest jewelry store.

Everybody cheered her on. "Come on, Mary. You can do it. Think positive, Mary."

Philip's eyes never strayed from the shining pile of stones. A week ago he had been collecting aluminum cans for grocery money. A lot can happen in a week.

With two seconds to go, Mary isolated one of the shiny stones at the side with the tweezers and looked up at me hopefully.

I examined the stone she had picked. "Nope. Sorry, Mary. Here, you can keep it." I dropped the stone into her outstretched palm.

Then I asked, "Why did you pass up the fifty dollars? It was a fifty-to-one gamble."

"Yes, but I could have had the diamond. I thought you were encouraging us to take risks."

She had a good point. I had encouraged her to be wary of security and more comfortable with risk. But some risks are unacceptable. Many beginning business people overlook this. Freedom is so important to them that they'll run any risk to obtain it. Like opening up a restaurant without any prior knowledge or experience. Safer to take the family nest egg to Las Vegas and blow it on one spin of the roulette wheel. Without knowledge and a workable plan, you are gambling, with little or no chance of success. Smart investors don't gamble. They make sure the odds are stacked in their favor. Then they play. They might still lose, but the risk is significantly reduced.

How do you reduce the risk of failure? You need a system.

"Mary," I said, "let me show you my system for finding the diamond every time. First, turn all of the stones face down with the points sticking up, so that they all look alike. That way the small differences will stand out like sore thumbs."

I bent over the blue velvet, scanning the seemingly identical stones. In only a few seconds I picked out the diamond. I explained that the real diamond had a flaw that was visible to the naked eye. The fancy jeweler's tools I provided weren't necessary. Quite often, fancy tools—computers and calculators—just get in the way of plain common sense and a simple system. It was now Mary's turn again.

"You try it, Mary."

I dropped the genuine diamond next to three fakes and mixed them up. She arranged the four stones as I showed her and examined them carefully. "This one has a spot in it."

"That's called an inclusion," I said. "It's just a speck of carbon. An imperfection. In other words, it has a problem. The cubic zirconiums are perfect. No imperfections. No problems. That's why they aren't worth as much. Isn't that completely backward from the way the world thinks? Most folks never expect to find any value in a problem. This is such an important point that I refer to it as a wealth secret."

WEALTH SECRET NO. 4. ALL OPPORTUNITIES ARE DISGUISED AS PROBLEMS.

"When it comes to real estate investing," I continued, "most properties look pretty much the same to the untrained eye—little houses all in a row. Just like so many cubic zirconiums. But an expert has learned to spot the little problems that are really opportunities in disguise. Maybe it's an obvious flaw, like peeling paint. Or a little flaw, like grass that's too tall. The average person thinks negatively: 'Yuck. What an eyesore!' But the expert sees every problem as a potential opportunity."

I tested Mary with ten stones. Since she now had a system, picking out the diamond from ten stones was simple. When I challenged her with all fifty stones she readily accepted. Before her minute had elapsed she isolated one stone and said, "It's this one."

She had picked the correct stone.

"Unfortunately," I said, "you don't get to keep this one. But you do get to keep something far more valuable. You see, knowledge plus practice becomes experience. Experience over time equals confidence. If you're confident, you won't be afraid. And if you're not afraid, the world is yours.

"It wasn't luck at all, was it, Mary?"

She shook her head. I walked over to the table, surveying each of them in turn. I could see that they were wondering what diamonds had to do with real estate. I felt like an attorney approaching a skeptical jury. The time had come for me to drive my point home.

"Life hasn't dealt any of you a very good hand. You feel down. Discouraged. Your confidence is at an all-time low. But with knowledge and practice and a few small successes, it won't be long before you'll be back on track. I'm going to teach you a system. A simple but effective way of separating real estate diamonds from zircons. Did any of you drive by any property this morning on the way to the hotel?"

They all nodded.

My goal was to convince them that they had blindly driven by millions of dollars in potential profit that very morning, simply because they didn't know how to tap into it. As I built my case, I related a story.

"An expert was called in to fix a broken factory machine. With the superintendent looking on, the expert assessed the situation, spotted the problem, took out a hammer and tapped the machine twice in the same spot. The machine started right up. He informed the superintendent that his bill would be $250. The superintendent was furious. 'Two hundred and fifty dollars!' he shouted. 'All you did was tap it with your hammer. I want an itemized statement of the charges on my desk by tomorrow morning!'

"The next day when the superintendent arrived for work, he found the following bill on his desk:

> Tapping with a hammer . . $ 1
> Knowing where to tap 249
> Total $250

"If you know where to tap, it's easy," I said. "If you don't, it's one of the most difficult things in the world. The rich get richer because they know where to tap. The poor get poorer because they don't.

"The first step in learning where to tap is to understand the next wealth secret."

WEALTH SECRET NO. 5. UNTIL YOU KNOW VALUE, EVERYTHING IS WORTHLESS.

"Suppose you found a dime in the attic and you spent it without knowing it was a rare coin worth tens of thousands of dollars. Since you weren't an expert, the coin was relatively worthless to you, wasn't it?

"Likewise, all of those bargain properties you drove by this morning, were also worthless to you. However, once you learn the difference between a diamond and a fake, then even the fakes are valuable. Mary, didn't you learn something from every stone? Sure! You learned whether or not it was a diamond. So every time you examined a stone, it was a valuable experience. Until you know value, everything is worthless. But once you know value, everything is valuable.

"Unfortunately, you don't find gold lying in the streets. You have to dig for it. In the same way, valuable opportunities are often camouflaged, hidden, disguised. But, once you learn where to tap, you enter a new world where opportunity is everywhere.

"Every day people drive right on by these opportunities unaware—caught up in their old-world problems. Going to work in the salt mine where salt is plentiful and labor is cheap. They opt for a salt miner's secure salary over a diamond miner's insecurity. Did you know that the word *salary* actually derives from the Latin word 'salarium'? Long ago, when salt was a precious commodity, many Greek and Roman workers used to be paid in salt. They received a salarium—salt money. Thus, our word *salary.*

"America is full of salt miners. That's what they've been programmed to do. 'Daddy was a salt miner. So was my grandaddy and his dad before him. All I know is salt mining. Don't teach me about diamonds.'

"Now, I'm not saying that having a job is bad. Even if you don't love your job, it can be an excellent launching pad from which to gain experience, confidence and stability. But some people were cut out to be diamond miners. Good diamond miners don't settle for salt money. Why settle for a minimum wage when you can have a maximum income? They learn where to tap. And the more they tap, the wealthier they become. Do you need a lot of money, a good job or a good credit rating before you can learn where to tap?"

"No," they all replied.

"But most Americans have this just completely backward. They've been programmed all their lives to believe that 'it takes money to make money.' So they don't even look! Let's not be like the masses. Let's do just the opposite. Let's concentrate on finding opportunity. Is each one of you in the process of finding some opportunity right now?"

They were silent, uncertain of where I was taking them.

"Didn't I give you an assignment yesterday? What did your newspaper ad say, Philip?"

"I buy houses."

"You? Buying houses?" I mocked. "Come on, Philip! Get serious. You don't have any money to buy houses!" I paused to make my point. "But the people who respond to your ad don't know this, do they? What else does your ad say?"

"Easy terms."

"Yeah," I joked. "Going to have to be real easy for you. Why do you want people to call you on that ad?"

"Because I want to buy a house."

"Not just any house. You want to buy the right house, the diamond house. The profitable house. The opportunity house. Like a diamond miner, you will sift through a lot of gravel before you spot a genuine stone. Using my simple system, you'll be able to spot the good ones from the bad ones. If someone calls in response to your ad, you'll ask a series of questions. You'll score each answer. If the total of the scores is high, you'll continue. If not, you'll discard it. It's a cubic zirconium.

"Before I share this system with you, I want to pause a moment. I hear some clicking in the room. Can you? It's the clicking of minds turning off. It's hard to keep your mind open to opportunity when you know that you don't even have a job. Try to keep an open mind. You already have almost everything you need. You are all go-getters. Each one of you was dealt a winning hand. It may not look like much to you. But you will soon see how valuable you really are.

"Mary, what did your ad say?"

"Something about a one-hour seminar about investing in St. Louis property." It was obvious she wondered why I had had her place such an ad.

"First you find an opportunity. Then you find a partner to help you buy it. One way to find a partner is to hold a free seminar about finding real estate bargains. Won't this attract potential partners? So now you see that there is a method in my madness.

"What does a bargain property look like? Let me share an example with you. Just a few months ago Tom Painter started out as a beginning investor like you. He placed his ad in the paper. A seller—let's call him Mr. Motivated—called with a problem. A year earlier Mr. Motivated had sold a house in city A to move to city B. The sales price was $52,000, with the buyer putting $8,000 down and agreeing to a balloon (lump sum) payment of $17,000 in one year. Mr. Motivated bought another home in city B, using the $8,000 as a down payment and agreeing himself to pay an additional $17,000 in one year, relying on the money due at that time from the sale of his home in city A. Unfortunately, when the year was up, the buyer of the house in city A stopped making mortgage payments and moved out of the house. Obviously, Mr. Motivated has a problem. What is it?"

"The seventeen-thousand-dollar note is due," Mary responded.

"He has two homes in separate cities," said Philip.

"And two mortgage payments," I added. "The holder of the seventeen-thousand-dollar note on the house in city B has threatened to foreclose if he doesn't get his money. Mr. Motivated could lose both houses! That's when he sees Tom's ad in the paper. What should Tom do?"

Nora could quickly see a solution. "So he gives you a deal on the first one...."

"Now, don't get too creative yet, Nora," I warned. "Before you come up with solutions, first gather all the facts."

I then proceeded to role-play with them a conversation with the seller. I asked Mr. Motivated three more questions: his mortgage balance ($27,000 with payments of $350 per month), the current value of his property ($60,000) and his bottom line (all he wanted from the property is $17,000). Having gathered this information, I held my hand over the imaginary telephone receiver and thought out loud.

"Hmmmmm," I pondered. "The property is worth $60,000, and the loan balance is only $27,000. If I could only come up with $17,000 to buy this property, I would be paying $44,000 for a $60,000 house (27,000 plus 17,000 = 44,000). Sixty cents on the dollar. Sounds like a bargain! I'd better dig a little further."

Speaking to the group again, I continued, "Do you see the creative mind at work? An uncreative investor would have said, 'I don't have seventeen thousand dollars, so there's no use checking further.' But a creative person always wonders, 'What if ...' 'Would this be a good deal if I had the money? Is there a way to solve this problem without a lot of money?' Let's massage the numbers a bit more. Maybe a solution will present itself. Things look like this, don't they?"

"Mary, how would you get the seventeen thousand dollars?"

She pondered for a moment. "I would borrow it using the house as collateral."

"But, Mary, can you qualify for a loan? When you go down to the bank to apply for the new seventeen-thousand-dollar mortgage, what is the loan officer going to ask you?"

"How is your credit?"

"Exactly," I said. "And other questions like, Where is your down payment? How much do you earn? Can you support the payments on this new loan of seventeen thousand dollars? And when you tell him that you are unemployed, what is the banker going to say?"

Nora interrupted. "He's going to laugh."

"Yes. How humiliating! How discouraging! You found a bargain—a problem with a big opportunity camouflaged inside of it. It

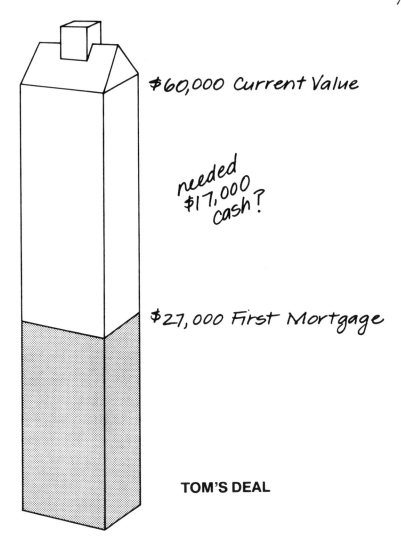

$60,000 Current Value

needed
$17,000
cash?

$27,000 First Mortgage

TOM'S DEAL

was even win/win—didn't have to take advantage of anybody. Too bad. I guess we'll just have to let it go, eh, Philip?"

"Maybe we can find an investor," he wondered. I was glad to see his mind was still searching for solutions.

"That's creative," I said. "If an investor used his credit to borrow seventeen thousand dollars from a bank, how much of his own money would he have to invest in the property?"

"A total of forty-four thousand dollars," Philip guessed.

"Guess again."

"Zilch. Nothing," Steve said.

"Correct. Nothing down. You use creativity instead of cash. With a partner's help, you arrange for a new, second mortgage of $17,000. The cash from the new loan goes to the seller. He is thrilled. The investor buys a property for nothing down. With loans of $44,000 ($27,000 plus $17,000) and a value of $60,000, there's a $16,000 profit in this nice home. Do investors like transactions like that?"

"I think so," Nora said.

"He's used to investments that require lots of cash and yield only ten to twenty percent. Your real estate investment gives him a sixteen-thousand-dollar profit without using any cash. Your partner won't care how broke and unemployed you are as long as you keep bringing him properties like that! Do you think this investor might be willing to split profits with you? He'd be crazy not to. If you know where to tap, you're halfway there."

"But suppose you can't find a partner?" Nora asked.

Philip's mind was abuzz with ideas. "What about asking him to do a second mortgage," he suggested.

The light of understanding also illuminated Mary. "That's it," she said. "Have Mr. Motivated borrow the money himself before you buy his property from him."

I sensed a teaching moment and changed into the role of the seller, pretending that this solution had just been presented to me.

"What?" I asked incredulously "Why would I want to borrow against my own property?"

Steve caught on to the role-play. "Because, Mr. Motivated, this would be a solution to your problem. You borrow the seventeen thousand dollars, and then I'll assume your loans and take the property off your hands."

"Good solution, Steve," I said. "This may solve the seller's problem. But what will we do with an empty bargain house and payments of six hundred dollars a month? That's scary, isn't it?"

"We can rent it out," offered Philip.

"What if the rent doesn't cover the payments?" I asked, playing the devil's advocate.

Mary responded. "We bring in a partner. He pays the negative cash flow for a portion of the profit."

"Look at all of the creative solutions we generated," I exclaimed. "Most people just assume that it can't be done and so they never try.

A creative person is always looking for a creative solution. Question, Nora?"

"But aren't we supposed to make five thousand dollars in ninety days. Where does the cash come from?"

"Maybe you could sell the property," Steve suggested.

"Good," I said. "Suppose you put this property on the market by running an ad like this:

> Excellent rental house.
> Appraisal of $60,000. Will sacrifice for $49,000
> with $5,000 down. Assumable loans.
> Call Philip. 567-8911

Do you think that you might attract some attention?"

Nodding, Mary added, "It's great too for a young couple starting out."

"Win/win," I said. "The buyer would get a super buy. You would end up with five thousand dollars cash for your efforts. Can you begin to see light at the end of the tunnel?"

The creativity in the air was thick enough to cut.

Steve offered another solution. "Maybe you could sell it for nothing down for sixty thousand dollars?"

"Good idea, Steve. You're turning into a raging capitalist—a capitalist without capital. Instead of cash up front, you receive payments of a few hundred dollars a month for the next twenty years. There are several solutions to this problem ... once you begin looking for them.

"Now, let me tell you what Tom actually did. He persuaded the seller to refinance the property. The seller walked away with his money and Tom ended up with the house. Tom then had to figure out how to get his profit out. One day he visited a friend who lived in a mobile home park. He noticed several mobile homes for sale. He reasoned that at least a few of these sellers would like to own their own home but were blocked by large down payment requirements, and strict lending guidelines. Tom put all of these facts together and came up with an ingenious idea. He passed out a flier that said:

> I will trade my equity in my home for your free-and-clear mobile
> home. Call Tom. 555-1234.

His phone rang off the hook. He had guessed right.

"One particularly motivated mobile-home owner agreed to accept

Tom's proposal. Tom traded his house with his $16,000 equity for an $8,000 free-and-clear mobile home, a motorboat worth $4,000 and a note of $4,000 with monthly payments of $100 until the balance was paid in full. They both won. The mobile-home owner moved up to a house. Tom ended up with a free-and-clear mobile home, a boat and $100 a month income."

"But he still doesn't have cash," Steve protested

"How can we solve that problem?" I kept throwing the questions back to the group, forcing them to use and develop their own creativity.

"He could sell the mobile home or boat," Steve answered.

"Yes," I said, "but what he did was simpler. He borrowed five thousand dollars against the mobile home. Mobile home loans are a lot easier to get than house loans. And then he sold the mobile home for little down."

They all nodded.

"Now, let's draw some lessons from this," I said. "First Tom found an opportunity. I call that step one: Find it. Then he used creative financing to buy it. That's step two: Fund it. Then he traded it for a mobile home among other things, which he financed for cash. That's step three: Farm it. It's as simple as one, two, three. Find it. Fund it. Farm it. That's all I'll be teaching you in the next two days."

Karen looked puzzled. "What do you mean by farm it?"

"Just like a farmer, you plant seeds and you harvest crops. An idea is a seed. You plant it by buying the property. You harvest it when you get the money out. How do you get the money out? Whenever you buy a property you have four choices:

1. Keep it and rent it out for positive cash flow
2. Sell it immediately for profit
3. Keep it and refinance it for cash
4. Trade it for something else, which you can either keep, refinance, sell or trade again.

"Tom did all of these things in farming his property. He traded his house for a mobile home, which he refinanced for cash and then sold. He still has the boat and the note.

"He found someone with a problem, and by solving it, he created an opportunity. Most people are programmed to hate problems. Assuming that problems are bad, they run from them, hide from them, divorce them or drink themselves into forgetting them. But a creative person loves problems because he knows every problem contains an opportunity. He is a diamond miner.

"And so are you," I concluded.

"Let's take a ten-minute break."

2.

Mary went to the phone out in the hall to call her baby-sitter. Her head was still swimming with numbers, but she was beginning to grasp the basic concepts. She dialed home.

"Hello, Judy? How are the kids?"

"Just fine, Mrs. Bonenberger."

"Did Kyle take the bottle?"

"He didn't like it at first, but as soon as he could tell that it was your milk, he guzzled it."

Mary breathed a sigh of relief. Kyle was still not weaned from his mother's breast. She had worried that the baby would not take a milk bottle and so, early that morning, she had used a nursing pump to drain some of her milk for Kyle to drink. She was relieved to hear that he was drinking it.

As she stood at the phone she could tell that her breasts were beginning to fill up again. Before the day was out, unless she could empty her breasts, she would be in the kind of agony that only a nursing mother can comprehend. It was just one of the many minor sacrifices that she had made in order to make herself available for the two-day training.

But she was no stranger to sacrifice. Even while pregnant with Kyle, she had contributed her part toward the family budget by making and selling crafts at weekend craft fairs. But the hours were long—sometimes she would stay up till two or three o'clock in the morning sewing—and the dollars were few. She slaved on till Kyle was born in March of 1984.

But when Kyle came, some new feelings began to swell in her. There had been a lot of unspoken pressure from her husband and his family to produce a male that could carry on the name. She somehow expected that the birth of her first son would be the high point in her life and make her happy. But it didn't.

"What's wrong with me?" she asked herself. "I have two wonderful children. A great husband. Why do I cry all the time? Why do I snap at Steve?"

There was a void in her life that beckoned to be filled. Maybe she felt she was wasting away at home—shackled to two toddlers, unable to pursue her dreams, whatever they might be. She was miserable. And guilty. Because a minister's wife isn't supposed to be miserable. She attacked her housework to fight back the guilt. The house had to be immaculate. She ironed everything. Made bread from scratch. No premixed packages for her.

Where did this compulsion come from? Not from her own mother, who had always worked and had employed part-time maids and baby-sitters. Not from Steve. He loved the great home-cooked meals, but peanut butter and jelly would have been just fine for him. Maybe she was trying to live up to her image of the perfect wife and mother, married to the perfect husband. It was a heavy burden, for there is no heavier burden than trying to be someone you're not.

To fight back the guilt and growing bitterness, she threw herself into church work. She taught Sunday school, organized the children's choir, sat on the women's missionary committee. On the outside, she tried to maintain the facade of perfection, the capable woman who could handle everything. But on the inside she was dying—confused and unhappy.

In April, Steve urged her to see an employment counselor. Maybe a job would help her to be happy, to find herself. The counselor just happened to be a psychologist.

"Whose music are you dancing to?" he would ask her. "Why do you think that if you don't spend every second in the home with your children you'll be a terrible mother? Who told you that working mothers don't spend enough time with their children?"

For the first time, she felt she was getting somewhere. But the counselor was expensive—fifty dollars an hour. And that made her feel even guiltier. You can buy a lot of groceries for fifty dollars. So she stopped seeing him.

Instead, she threw herself into trying to find a job. But she wouldn't settle for anything less than a perfect job. One that would allow her to spend as much time as possible with her children. When she told this to prospective employers they would laugh. "You'll have to choose between work and family," they said.

She chose work. She took a job at Hertz, where she lasted less than a week. And so the spring passed by. She rode the roller coaster of her emotions—self versus family. A churning pot of mixed desires. Until the morning in June when she had been selected for the Challenge.

Mary hung up the phone. As she did so, the sparkle of the diamond in her wedding ring caught her eye. She pulled it closer to examine it. "Until you know value, everything is worthless." She repeated the lesson in her mind. And she knew that she would never look at a diamond the same way again.

She walked back into the seminar room. The room was still hot. She joked with the camera crew. They liked her. She could tell.

David Benjamin, the film producer, came over to talk to her. He was fast becoming the father figure to the group. Maybe it was his bald head and red, bushy beard. Even dressed in his jeans, he might have been a monk in disguise.

"How's it going, Mary?"

She sensed that he cared. "I'm getting it, David," she replied. "I'm feeling good." It had been a long time since she'd said that.

3. _____

The little wealth class reconvened. It was 11:15 A.M. I stood in front of them, taking in their enthusiasm. I had hidden my doubts well. But there was still so much material to cover. I was already behind an hour. Maybe more. The two days were slipping away. Could I instill in them the confidence necessary to withstand the rejections of the next ninety days? On the drawing board, the Challenge had seemed noble and possible. But in front of me sat real people with real problems. Serious problems. Maybe I was just adding to them. We had come such a short way. The task before us seemed insurmountable. The cliff looked so steep. The rocks of failure seemed to far below. "One foot in front of the other," I whispered to myself.

"So," I began, "find it. Fund it. Farm it. Three simple steps. But not so easy to execute. Your job is to find what glitters; I'll tell you whether it's gold or not. But how can you tell if it glitters? Let's talk about the five components of value. Look at the chart."

"When all five components of value intersect perfectly, you've found a possible bargain property. But if one or two of them are not

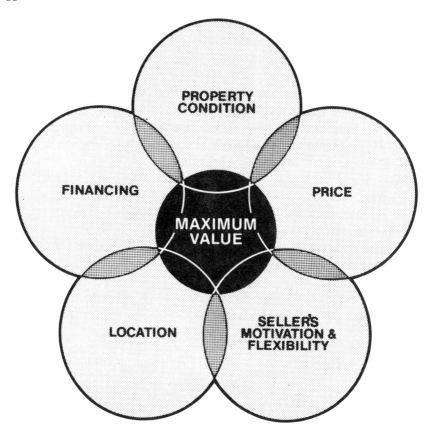

THE FIVE COMPONENTS OF VALUE

in alignment, you must be careful. Suppose you find a highly motivated seller. His property is fairly well located. Financing is good. The price seems right. But the property is completely boarded up, totally gutted. You'll need to spend more to fix it up than to buy it. Should you buy it? Probably not. Let's try another one. Everything about it is perfect except the location is lousy. Is that a good value? Probably not. What about a property that scores well in all areas except financing—the seller wants thirty thousand dollars down tomorrow. No, thank you!

"With a little practice you'll become proficient at understanding these five concentric circles. You'll learn to tell the diamond from the cubic zirconium. For the time being, while you're floundering

PROPERTY SCORING SYSTEM

	POOR	AVERAGE	EXCELLENT
LOCATION	**0 NEVER**	**2 POINTS**	**3 POINTS**
	No pride of ownership. Junk and debris in streets. High crime. No appealing shopping close by. Declining neighborhoods. Abandoned buildings and boarded up properties. Close to major streets, industrial areas, or commercial zones (across the street). Far from employment centers or commuter accessibility.	May be clean older neighborhoods. Close to shopping, churches, schools etc. but not very appealing. Working class tenants, neat established. May be poor location on the upswing with pioneer fixer-uppers. Nicer inner city neighborhoods.	Easy accessibility to all necessary amenities and transportation. Middle class, suburban neighborhoods. Not on busy streets. Cul-de-sacs ideal. Properties nearby very similar in price. Good foliage and landscaping except in brand new subdivisions. Only high class inner-city locations.
PROPERTY CONDITION • Analyze and assign a point value to each factor of a property. • If in doubt about a point value always pick the lower number. • Add up the numbers and total. • The lowest acceptable score is 9, the highest possible is 15. • Greater fools always buy property in the 9, 10, 11 range. • Great investors always buy property in the 12, 13, 14, 15 range.	**1 POINT** **Consider only if price is excellent.** Needs major cosmetic and structural improvements. At least 10% of purchase price will need to be spent immediately to make unit rentable. Improvements do not significantly improve the rent roll because of quality of tenants and location. Improvements not to increase value more than 10% above purchase price. Usually associated with poor locations. Possible to find this property in excellent locations where prices are so high that improvements do not increase value but just make units acceptable to renters. Viewed as making a larger down payment (for improvements) and receiving an averaged priced property.	**2 POINTS** This is the true fixer upper! Cosmetic improvements would be nice but not immediately necessary. Costs not to exceed 5% of the purchase price. Cosmetic improvements immediately affect the value upwards and make the property more desirable, saleable and attractive. Not much structural work if any is necessary — only paint, landscaping, drapes and other inexpensive improvements. This type of property should not be bought if the buyer does not have the time or mental capacity to undertake supervision of improvements. This property can prove to be the most profitable in the short run. The worst house in the best neighborhood.	**3 POINTS** Newer property or older property with recent renovation. No problems, clean inside and out, good landscaping. New components to replace major items. May have been a recent fixer-upper project which is being sold by a don't wanter at an excellent price. No work necessary before renter moves in. Solid property with a hassle factor of zero. Quick closing, quick rent-up, quick cash flow.
PRICE	**1 POINT** 10% or more above the reasonable market price. **Consider only if financing is excellent.**	**2 POINTS** Within + or - 5% of market price.	**3 POINTS** At least 10% or more below market price.
FINANCING	**1 POINT** More than 15% down. Seller needs lots of cash and wants all of his equity. Or property will have heavy negative cash flows for more than two years. Or there will be a large balloon payment due in less than three years from date of purchase. **Consider only if price is excellent.**	**2 POINTS** Financing required from an institution with up to 15% down of buyer's money. Credit checks. Institutional secured loans for part of the down payment (high interest, high monthly payments). Seller carries small amounts. Cash required from buyer. Balloons due in less than 5 years.	**3 POINTS** Less than 5% of buyer cash involved. Seller carries most of the financing at lower than market rates with no balloons in less than 7 years. No negative cash flows projected beyond the first year. Contract sales, no credit checks.
SELLER'S MOTIVATION AND FLEXIBILITY	**1 POINT** Won't budge on price or terms. "Take it or leave it." Doesn't need to sell. Not anxious at all. In the driver's seat.	**2 POINTS** Might consider a small discount in price. Needs cash for new house or property. Needs cash for bills etc. May carry small second or contract but leery of unusual deals.	**3 POINTS** Needs cash for pressing items i.e. behind in payments etc. Or doesn't need cash at all — has tax management, transfer, time problems or divorce, retiree or investor looking for a solution without major need for cash. Flexible in price or terms.
		TOTAL SCORE	

around, I'll look over your shoulder. It won't be long before you're on your own. The next chart shows a more detailed explanation of how to use the concentric-circle scoring system.

"The chart tells you to give a score to each of the five factors of value. Poor is one. Average is two. Excellent is three. Add up the scores from the five factors. If the total comes to twelve or more, you are on the right track. Then, you'll call me, Tom or one of the hot line staff and say, "I've found something that glitters. Is it gold or not?" We'll brainstorm together. We'll come up with three or four solutions. Pick one. And then make an offer. And you'll be on your way to owning your first investment property.

"There are many ways to find bargains. One of the best ways is the classified section of your local newspaper. Isn't the classified section just a collection of people with problems to solve? And what are we?"

"Problem solvers," they replied.

"Here's an actual ad found in the 'Real Estate Wanted' section of a Tulsa, Oklahoma, newspaper:

> Looking for good tenants—last one
> a bummer.
> Must have good references. Fix-up
> needed.
> Will trade your efforts for part of
> the rent.

"Let's role-play," I said. "I'll be the prospective seller. You call me on the phone and find the opportunity in this situation."

SELLER: Hello.
PHILIP: I was wondering if you wanted to sell your property.
SELLER: I suppose, I'm just so tired of this doggone thing!
MARY: Get rid of your headache; let us take it off your hands.
SELLER: Well, I'm not that desperate. I'd want cash.
PHILIP: What's your property worth?

I stepped out of the seller's role for a minute to make a point. "You're in control when you're asking questions," I said. "The more you know the better the solution."

SELLER: My property is worth about sixty-eight thousand dollars.
KAREN: Do you have a mortgage on it?

SELLER: No. It's free and clear.
PHILIP: How much would you be looking to get out of it?
SELLER: Well, I wouldn't need all cash. Might carry some financing. But I would want a substantial down payment.
PHILIP: How much money will make you happy?

"Where did you learn to ask such good questions, Philip?" I asked, stepping out of my role again. "You're doing great."
Philip smiled proudly.

SELLER: I'd need at least ten thousand dollars down.
PHILIP: And you'd carry the rest?
SELLER: Yeah, I suppose. It would be nice to get a check every month instead of a bunch of tenant headaches.

"You make it sound so simple," Nora said.
"We haven't bought the property yet, Nora," I replied. "Keep asking questions. What are you curious about? What do you need to know? Didn't I just teach you five areas in which you need to have answers before you can determine value?"

MARY: How much would it take to fix it up?
SELLER: A couple thousand dollars.
STEVE: Where's it located?
SELLER: Over by the university. Great location.
PHILIP: Let's see, ten thousand cash will make you happy.
SELLER: I can handle that, ya.
STEVE: This is going to sound absolutely crazy, but would you be willing to go down to the bank and borrow some money against your free-and-clear property?
SELLER: Why would I do that?
STEVE: I don't know why. Ha. Ha. [speaking to me] Why would he want to do that?

I could tell they were beginning to bog down. They had started giving solutions without first having answers to the five most important questions.
"Let's see if we can give this property a score," I said, changing the subject. "How would you score the seller's motivation and flexibility?"
"I'd say two points," Nora said.
"OK. Now, location. Seemed to be in an excellent location by the university. We'll score it a three and inspect it later to revise our

score if necessary. How about financing? He says he wants at least ten thousand dollars down, and then he'll carry the financing. That's not so hot. It's just a one or a two. What's next, Philip?"

"Price."

I then explained that the seller had said the property, which was a duplex, was worth sixty-eight thousand dollars, but that they had never asked him what he would take. So they couldn't determine whether the price was above or below market. I told them that the seller would take sixty-five thousand dollars with a large down payment, or less if he was cashed out. With this information we came up with a score of three for financing. And the property condition scored a three. This gave the property a total score of eleven.

"That's a borderline score," I concluded. "This property glitters, but we aren't sure if it's gold yet. If we could improve any of the individual scores by using our creativity, the property might deserve a second look. Maybe this is the time to make a written offer to see how flexible the seller really is."

This is a true story, and the diamond miner actually made four separate offers to test the waters:

$5,000 down and a $65,000 price/$60,000 loan with payments over 25 years at 10 percent interest

$10,000 down and a $60,000 price with a $50,000 loan with payments over 25 years at 9 percent interest

$15,000 down and a $55,000 price with the balance over 25 years at eight percent interest

or $53,500 in cash

The seller looked at all of these offers and countered with fifty-five thousand dollars in cash. "And that's the price they settled on," I said. "Now, the buyer had a problem, didn't he? It was time to put his creativity hat on. He'd found a bargain. Now, what does he need to do?"

"Fund it!" Mary exclaimed.

Karen seemed confused. "But he made the seller a firm offer. What if he can't fund it?"

"Good question. Before tomorrow night, you'll learn how to write an offer that obligates the seller but doesn't obligate you. It is virtually riskless. Now, back to funding this bargain. Let's say the buyer's wife worked as a teller at a bank. She asked her boss how to finance this property. He suggested that she finance it through their bank. But first they'd need a current appraisal. Guess what the appraisal came in at? Eighty thousand dollars!"

Nora could see immediately. "So you gained right there."

"Not yet. We don't own the property yet. But we've got the opportunity! Why was the seller willing to sell for fifty-five thousand dollars, when it was worth eighty thousand dollars, Nora?"

"Maybe he didn't know its value."

"Was he happy with the sixty-eight-thousand-dollar value? Yes. Was he happy with our fifty-five thousand dollars cash offer? Yes. How do we know he was happy?"

"He accepted our offer," she said.

"Is this moral?" I asked. "He's happy with your offer, but you know that it's way under market. Now, Steve, you're a minister. Doesn't this bother you a little bit? Don't you feel like you're taking advantage of this seller? Is this fair?"

"Well, I think it's fair. We paid him what he wanted."

"Let's get to the bottom of this. More than a few people are concerned about this issue. Suppose you walk in a store to buy a suit. You find one you like for $300. You know that the merchant only paid $150 for it. Is that fair? Do I care what the wholesale price is as long as I'm satisfied with the retail price? Nora?"

"No. Because he's a retailer and that's businesss. He's in business to make a profit."

"That's right. That's business. And what is business? Buying products at wholesale and selling them at retail for a profit. You may call yourselves real estate investors, but you are really in business. You have to learn how to buy right in order to sell right. If not, you'll go out of business."

Steve jumped into the discussion. "I'd go deeper than that; business is basically human services."

I agreed. "You serve people best by solving their problems! If you help enough people solve enough of their problems you'll never have a money problem. That's just what business is, solving problems for fun and profit. Nora?"

"But what about excess profits?"

"Hmmmm," I said. "Excess profits. A lot of people attach a bad connotation to the word *profit*. And if profit is bad, excess profit must be horrible! But let's think this through. Suppose you invented a product that solved my problem. You're the only one who has it. Everybody wants it. If I want it, I have to pay your price. You get greedy. You raise your prices. You make tons of money. But your success does not go unnoticed. Other businessmen see your success and come in with similar products at lower prices. Your business loses sales. You're forced to lower your prices in order to keep your doors open. Isn't this what happened to OPEC? They raised the price of oil sky-high. They got greedy. The competition came in, drilled more oil wells. People began to conserve energy. And now there's a glut of oil. Prices tumbled. If you get too greedy, the market will get you. In order to be a good businessman, you have to solve problems at a price that the competition does not undercut. That's the way it works. Whether you like it or not. It keeps prices low, profits in line and businessmen honest."

Nora wasn't entirely sold. She wasn't concerned about macroeconomics. She wanted to get specific. "In the case of this duplex, you wouldn't want someone to leave you in the dark! Say you're the person that owns this property, and you think it's worth sixty-eight thousand dollars and it's really worth eighty thousand. Wouldn't you want someone to tell you that you're selling it way too cheap?"

Mary responded to Nora's question. "But don't they have just as much right to go to an appraiser as you do? And that's just using your knowledge."

Nora fought back. "But you have knowledge and he doesn't! Your knowledge is worth something, but maybe this is too much."

"I like to think of the word *fair*," I said, rejoining the conversation. "How do I know what fair is? Let's ask the seller. When I make him a written offer, I say, in effect: 'Mr. Seller, this isn't your first real estate transaction. You seem to understand the market. I'm offering you a lot of cash but a low price. You've looked it over and have decided to accept it. In doing so, you probably considered the time and difficulty to find another bona fide buyer, the hassle and cost to repair damage caused by the tenant, the negative cash flow you might incur until this work is done, the mental anguish to you and your family in owing a property that you no longer want, the uncertainty of the market, the future of property values. And after all of this, you still accepted my offer. You must have thought it was fair or you wouldn't have done it.' Nora, the seller may not be willing to take the same kinds of risks as you and I. Maybe he would rather take his money and run than stay around for an uncertain profit. It's not a sure thing, you know. There is risk involved. Most of the time, if we're careful, we win. But there are losses. We may have had losses on other properties. The man in the clothing business sometimes has to sell clothes at deep discount because he bought things that would not sell. He takes losses on some things and makes profits on others. In light of this, let me ask the question again, Nora. Will we make an excess profit on this transaction?"

"No. I guess not."

"Stick to your guns, Nora. There are situations that involve excess profits. Like the proverbial widow who naively turns over all of her financial dealings to an unscrupulous smooth talker. This is clearly a case of taking unfair advantage. It's old advice, but sometimes you just have to let your conscience be your guide."

"Isn't that just the Golden Rule?" Nora questioned.

"Exactly. The free-market system is a practical Golden Rule. If a business person doesn't solve your problems in a win/win way, he's out of business. Business people are forced to want to do good unto others or they won't be done good unto. But you can take this a step further. I believe there is power in being totally honest, totally upright, totally win/win. Living the Golden Rule is the most important and practical business principle ever given to man. You'll go farther living this rule than by any other method. It's just common sense that when you concentrate on solving people's problems fairly, your reputation will spread. And a solid reputation is as good as money in the bank.

"Since so few people really believe this, I'm going to call it a wealth secret and add it to our growing list."

WEALTH SECRET NO. 6. HE WHO LIVES THE GOLDEN RULE GETS THE GOLD HERE TOO.

"Now, back to our example. The buyer and his wife were able to borrow sixty-five thousand dollars, using the duplex as collateral. But how much did the seller want? Only fifty-five thousand dollars. What does that mean?"

Steve grasped the situation. "He's going to make a ten-thousand-dollar cash profit."

"How much money will this buyer have to invest to make this ten-thousand-dollar profit?"

"Nothing."

"And besides the cash, he owns a duplex worth eighty-thousand dollars with an existing loan on it of only sixty-five thousand dollars. That's a fifteen-thousand-dollar equity. He could farm that equity by fixing up the property and renting it out for income. Or he could sell or trade it for a profit. If he decided to sell it, he could run the following ad:

> Illness forces sale (I'm sick of this property!)
> Worth $80,000. Sacrifice for $65,000. You just
> assume my loan. Nothing down. Call Bob, 555-1234.

Think he'd get any calls?"

They responded in one voice. "Oh, yes!"

"Would an investor win by buying this duplex for sixty-five thousand dollars on these terms? Sure. But, how would our diamond miner win?"

Mary responded. "He's already won! He's got ten-thousand dollars cash."

"Right. Suppose you were the seller, Philip, and you couldn't sell the duplex. What could you trade it for?"

"A car."

"Put an ad in the paper, 'Will trade fifteen-thousand dollars equity in beautiful duplex for your car.' What kind of car do you want, Philip?"

"A Mercedes."

"Lower your sights just a bit for now," I said, laughing. "We'll go for the Mercedes tomorrow. Today we'll settle for a Ford."

I continued. "Are you beginning to see how you can solve your own money problems by solving the problems of others? It's whole new way of looking at the world. And it works."

"But," Nora interjected, "it's still hard work; I know that."

"But it's worth it! In this example, I've been talking as if there were only one duplex. But in reality there were three duplexes. And out of this one transaction the buyer pulled not ten thousand dollars but *thirty thousand dollars in cash!* And let's not forget the fifteen-thousand dollars equity in each duplex. All told, he earned more money than most folks earn in several years working at jobs they can't stand. Sure, it's hard. But the rewards are incredible! How many transactions like this do you need to find in a year to reach your goals?"

"Just one!"

"Do you think you'll be able to find at least one like this if you spend an entire year looking?"

"Yes."

"Maybe," I cautioned. "And if you find it, what will be the next step?"

"To fund it."

"How can you fund it when you are unemployed?"

"We'll have to find a partner to split the profits with."

"Is that fair?" I asked. "He comes up with all the money. You just find the deal."

"But without me bringing him the deal there would be no profit at all."

"Now you're beginning to see. And that brings us to our next wealth secret."

WEALTH SECRET NO. 7. MONEY IS ATTRACTED TO GREAT IDEAS.

"Money always flows to great opportunities. If you don't have money, your motto should be, 'If I don't have it, somebody does.' Whatever you need, you can always find a partner to fill it. If you don't have cash, somebody does. If you don't have the credit or financial statement, somebody does. You provide the opportunity. Let someone else provide the financial strength. You be the idea person; let someone else be the money person. Nora, which is more important, the financial strength or the opportunity? The idea or the money to fund the idea? The cash or the deal?"

"I'd say the deal."

Steve broke in. "You've got to have both, don't you?"

"Sure. But you'll run out of money before you run out of knowledge to find good deals. If you know where to tap, you'll always be able to find willing partners. A person with just money and no knowledge of where to tap will never do as well as you in the long run. How about that building full of eye doctors across the street from this hotel? They make a good income, pay most of it in taxes, live well, invest in a lot of dubious tax shelters. They're so busy earning a living they don't have the time to find the. . . ." I waited for them to fill in the blank.

"Bargains." They could see where I was going.

"Right! At least you have the time. Let's look at this issue closer, because it's the essence of wealth. What are the financial resources that you have to have to *fund it* . . . to put a deal together?

"Credit."

"Cash."

"A strong financial statement."

"Cash flow from a job or other source of income."

"You're lacking in most of these resources," I said. "But what nonfinancial resources do you have that are extremely important?"

"Time," Philip said. "Got lots of that."

"Knowledge," Nora added.

"Willingness," said Steve.

"You have all of these things and more. So let's add up our non-financial assets:

> "Time.
> "Knowledge.
> "Enthusiasm or willingness.
> "Courage.
> "Faith.
> "Creativity.
> "Desire.
> "Life."

This was an important concept. It was the crux of everything I would be teaching them. How could I drive it home in such a way that they would never forget it?

"Steve," I continued. "All of the world's greatest philosophers since the beginning of time have pondered this issue and have come to the same conclusion: "What you are is more important than what you have. What's inside of you is more important that what's outside of you. Your nonfinancial resources are more important than your financial resources.

"And yet people act as if the opposite were true. Instead of the substance, they yearn for the appearance of wealth—fancy cars, cash in the bank, big houses. But these things are just the by-products of wealth, not wealth itself. The ability to create wealth—the knowledge, skill and courage—are infinitely more valuable than the wealth itself. One is the goose, the other the golden egg. If you were forced to choose between the two, would there be any hesitation which one you would choose?"

"I want both," said the pragmatic Philip, causing the whole group to break up laughing.

"And you will have both, Philip," I assured him. "It's just a matter of time before you 'get over.' But realize now that you're already wealthy. It may sound crazy but it's true. You've already read about my challenge with the *Los Angeles Times* to buy a property in seventy-two hours with only one hundred dollars in my pocket. When that reporter took away my wallet, he bankrupted me! He took away my financial resources—everything the world thinks is wealth—my cash, my credit, my cash flow, my financial statement! But did he leave me with nothing? No! I still had my experience, my knowledge, my desire, my creativity. All of my nonfinancial resources were still intact. And then it dawned on me like a revelation as clear as sunlight:

"*I* was my wealth!

"I may have been bankrupt by the world's standards, but I was still wealthy. And that is our next wealth secret."

WEALTH SECRET NO. 8. YOU ARE YOUR WEALTH. THE MONEY THAT FLOWS TO YOU IS JUST A BY-PRODUCT OF YOUR NON-FINANCIAL RESOURCES.

"Wealth is not having. It's being. Nothing you have is as important as what you are. If you acquire every property in the whole world and destroy yourself in the process, you are truly a pauper.

"About a month ago, after a speech right here in St. Louis, an ex-con came up to tell me his story. He had been one of the top three drug dealers in St. Louis until he was arrested and sentenced to seven years in prison. As he sat in Leavenworth with a lot of time to think, he wondered if there was a way to 'make it straight.' One of the inmates gave him a copy of *Creating Wealth,* my second book. He realized that he'd made a lot of money selling drugs, but he'd actually been destroying himself—his true wealth. He's out of jail now. In a halfway house, trying to get his act together. It's not easy to go from an old world to a new one. But I think he'll make it.

"I tell you these things in order to strengthen your nonfinancial resources—to strengthen your courage, increase your faith, build your desire. The financial resources are cheap. You can get those anywhere. Build your real wealth. That's what's rare.

"I know that this is heavy stuff. But it's the truth.

"Let's break for a few minutes."

It was 12:25 when we reconvened. We were more than a half-hour away from lunch with still so much material to cover.

"How do I find a bargain?" I began. "What kind of a seller would be flexible or crazy enough to sell a property to someone who doesn't even have a job? I call them don't-wanters or highly motivated sellers. What might cause someone to become a don't-wanter?"

They shot a barrage of answers at me.

"Divorce. Death. Can't handle the payments. Bankruptcy. Transfers. They need money for whatever reason. Just don't want to be bothered with it. Management."

"What about inheritance?" I added. "Just yesterday a local investor drove me around to see some of the properties he'd purchased since taking the *Nothing Down* seminar. He picked up eight properties from one seller who had inherited them and couldn't wait to dump them at an unbelievable price.

"On the next chart you'll find a list of twenty reasons why people become highly motivated sellers.

"The chart clearly indicates that the major reason for 'don't-wanteritis' is more a result of personal problems than a result of owning a bad property.

"I know it's hard to believe, but 'don't-wanteritis' is a very real condition. In many cases, there is nothing wrong with the property. Just the seller's attitude toward the property is bad. One of my very first real estate investments involved a three-acre parcel of land. The owner had bought a large parcel of farm ground and subdivided it to sell to 'city slickers' wanting to live in the country. The dimensions of the acreage were—and I'll never forget them—100.5 feet of frontage by 1,326 feet of depth. Sounds ridiculous, doesn't it?

"The seller told me that I could build a house on the front of the lot and then sell the package to a pilot who could use the back of the lot for a landing strip. I fell for it. Boy, did I fall! Three thousand dollars down and monthly payments on the balance. When I came to my sense a few weeks later, I became a don't-wanter. For over a year, I tried to get rid of it. Finally, another investor offered to trade me 2.5 acres of free-and-clear desert ground in California. I knew his ground was good only for holding the world together—but at least I wouldn't have to make monthly payments. I took it. To this day, I still haven't seen my California acreage (I doubt anyone has). But I keep it as a reminder that don't-wanteritis can happen to anyone. The person who took my country acreage eventually sold it and profited. He had more patience than I did. He wasn't a don't-wanter.

TWENTY REASONS WHY PEOPLE BECOME HIGHLY MOTIVATED SELLERS

	Don't-Wanter Conditions	Personal	Process of Management	Property	People
D	Divorce	X			
O	Obsolescence			X	
N	Negative cash flow		X		
T	Transfer	X			
W	Wrong management		X		
A	Arrears in payments		X		
N	Negative location			X	
T	Taxes	X			
E	Estate situation	X			
R	Retirement	X			
C	Competition		X		
O	Out-of-area owners	X			
N	Neurotic fears	X			
D	Debts	X			
I	Ignorance	X			
T	Time (lack of)	X			
I	Investment capital needs	X			
O	Ornery partner(s)				X
N	Need for status symbol	X			
S	Sickness	X			
	Totals	13	4	2	1

I'm going to teach you the subtle and not-so-subtle clues that lead you to the don't-wanters."

Then, I led my small group of diamond miners through a discussion of the many sources of don't-wanters—the newspaper, 'for sale' signs, friends, contacts, word of mouth. I explained how Realtors are an excellent source of flexible sellers. Using the Realtors' *Multiple Listing* book is a quick way to get an overview of the broad real estate market. We talked about various methods of self-promotion—ways to advertise—the use of business cards and fliers. I encouraged them to pick a specific area of town and become an expert in it, to always be on the lookout for properties that weren't being cared for—tall grass, peeling paint, broken windows—obvious clues that the owner doesn't want his property.

TEN CLUES THAT MAY INDICATE AN OWNER DOESN'T WANT HIS PROPERTY AND MIGHT BE A MOTIVATED SELLER

1. Tall grass, weeds
2. Peeling paint
3. Discarded trash
4. Abandoned vehicles on property
5. Broken or boarded-up windows
6. Posted notices from city or country officials, such as condemnation, public health hazard, etc.
7. Fire damage
8. Water or wind damage
9. Any sign of property mismanagement due to tenant abuse, such as several cars parked on lawn
10. Any sign that the property is vacant. Owners become more flexible when their property is empty.

I told them that you buy neighborhoods, not properties. If the neighborhood is bad, forget it. We talked about the county courthouse with its listings of divorces, evictions, bankruptcies, defaulted loans and probate records. I told them how to shortcut the courthouse by using legal newspapers that cost pennies an issue and yet contain thousands of dollars' worth of information. Each of these sources was like a diamond mine.

"Many say that by focusing on don't-wanters we are taking advantage of other people's misfortune. How do you feel about that, Nora?"

"We're problem solvers. We're just helping people solve their problems," she answered.

"It's such a fine line," I said. "That's why win/win is so important. There *are* thieves out there. Try to be different. One of my students in Seattle specializes in foreclosures. She learned of a couple who were about to lose their home. The wife was Asian. Didn't speak much English or understand the customs here. Her husband took a job in Malaysia as a pilot and left her in Seattle. She neglected to make the house payments. My student explained to the woman that she was about to lose her home to foreclosure. Then she called the husband long distance to warn him. He flew home immediately and solved the problem. My student never made a penny! This was a circumstance where helping was more important than making money. For every situation like this, there are three others where legitimate profit can be earned. And you sleep nights, too.

"While we're on the subject of foreclosure, one expert has estimated that about 90 percent of all foreclosed properties go back to the bank. Does the bank want them? No! So banks can become don't-wanters. By dealing directly with banks, you can find excellent prices on foreclosed properties.

"Quick example. One graduate in Dallas located a bank foreclosure worth about sixty-thousand dollars. The bank wanted to dump the property for thirty-five thousand dollars, just to recoup its costs for interest and attorneys' fees. He used a line of credit he had established to get the thirty-five thousand dollars cash to buy the property. Anyone with a sizable equity in a piece of property and good credit can set up a line of credit like this. So he found it and he funded it. How is he going to pay back his line of credit? Philip?"

"He's got to farm it—either sell it, keep it, refinance it or trade it."

"First, he refinanced it. He went to a local savings and loan association and applied for a new first mortgage against the property. He had good credit, the ability to borrow. The property appraised high enough for him to be able to obtain a new fifty-thousand-dollar first mortgage. Where does this fifty-thousand dollars cash go?"

"To him," Steve answered.

"With the fifty-thousand dollars, he repaid his line of credit, the thirty-five thousand dollars, leaving him with fifteen-thousand dollars gross profit. Of course, there were closing costs, loan fees, interest charges on the line of credit, as well as $600 to fix up the property and other miscellaneous expenses. But the net profit was over $10,000. Not bad for a month's work! And he hadn't finished farming it yet. He put an ad in the paper: 'Nice house, $61,000. $2,000 down. No qualifying.' In a matter of weeks he found a buyer to assume the nonqualifying new loan. The balance of the seller's equity—$9,000 ($61,000 less the first mortgage of $50,000 minus the $2,000 down payment leaves $9,000)—was in the form of a second mortgage on the property with monthly payments of $100.

"Let's review. The graduate finds an opportunity. He buys it with a line of credit. He fixes the property up. Refinances it. Pays his costs, repays his line of credit. Ends up with ten thousand dollars in cash as a profit. Then he sells the house for two thousand dollars down. He also gets a note for nine thousand dollars. What can he do with that, Mary?"

"He can keep it and get the monthly payments."

"Or?"

"Can you sell a note?" she wondered out loud.

"Absolutely. Smart investors buy these notes as an investment. they don't pay full face value, though. The seller of a note may get only fifty cents on the dollar. But some people would rather have cash now than a monthly payment for years to come. Suppose our graduate sells his nine-thousand-dollar note for forty-five-hundred dollars cash. Now he has more money to invest in another property.

Let's add up the cash profit from this one transaction."

> $10,000 net profit from the refinancing
> $ 2,000 down payment
> $ 4,500 from the sale of the note
> $16,500 net profit

"Let's be conservative and reduce this by another $1,500. Our total profit, then, is $15,000. Only one percent of the people in the world earn $15,000 or more in a year. Many Americans earn less than $15,000 a year working at jobs they can't stand. And this savvy investor makes $15,000 in one transaction that takes a total of less than ninety days!"

"And I didn't earn five thousand dollars last year at all of my jobs combined," Nora complained.

"Unfortunately," I said, trying to test her, "since you don't have a fat line of credit, you won't be able to take advantage of deals like this, will you?"

"Not so fast," said Steve. "If I don't have it, somebody does."

"Get a partner," Philip suggested.

"How do I get a partner?" I asked.

"Put an ad in the paper," Karen volunteered.

"What do I say?" Nora asked.

"Try this," I answered. " 'St. Louis investor needs partner to split a $15,000 guaranteed profit. Need $35,000 for 90 days or less. You'll kick yourself if you miss this. Call Nora 555-1234.' "

"And then you split it fifty-fifty?" Steve inquired.

"Seventy-five hundred dollars each. Your nonfinancial resources and his financial resources. Win/win. Did everyone win in this transaction? The bank got rid of a property it didn't want. Our bank earned interest on the line of credit. The couple we sold the house to got great terms. The investor who bought the discounted note is happy. Our partner, who provided the financial resources for half of the profit, is ecstatic. And, best of all, we did very well by knowing where to tap. We just need to learn how to find the don't-wanters. How many of them are there?"

"Many. Very many," Nora answered.

"How many do there need to be? For you?"

"A very small percentage," said Nora. "One percent."

"Just one," countered Mary.

"You just need one property in the next ninety days. In your city of two million people there might be several thousand highly motivated sellers. But all you need is one. How many properties will it take to make you a million dollars over the next ten years? Twenty? Maybe thirty? Can you find that many in a lifetime? Absolutely. Some people claim that real estate will cease to be a good investment as soon as everyone learns how to deal in it. I respond that there will always be don't-wanters.

"Now, let me share one more example with you before we break for lunch. The *St. Louis Business Journal* carried a story about Don Singer, the president of a local real estate investment group. The title of the article is "Prospectors Look for Money in Land." Isn't

LOGJAMS: THREE FREQUENTLY ASKED QUESTIONS THAT ARE IMPEDIMENTS TO ACTION

Sometimes people get blocked in their progress because a few simple questions act as logjams cluttering up the flow of their lives. Until these few questions are answered a person can become paralyzed with inaction—"on hold," idling in neutral, waiting for the light to turn green.

Maybe I can turn you loose by sharing with you the answers to the three most common questions:

1. How do I overcome the fear?

The only formula I know of for eliminating fear is desire plus knowlege plus action. When your desire to be free exceeds your reluctance to face your fear, to learn and then to take action, freedom will be yours. And you will deserve it.

2. How do I get started?

Are you waiting for things to be "just right" before you start? So is everybody else. Do you want to end up like everyone else? No. Okay, so get started even if things aren't "just right." Where do you start? Start with education. Get the knowledge you need. How do you know what you need? Go to someone who is already successful at what you eventually want to be doing. Ask them. And then do what they say. Do it now!

3. What about the economy?

Are you worried where the economy is headed? Afraid to sink your money into something and have the winds change and leave you holding the bag? It's good to be asking these questions. Unfortunately, most folks use these questions as excuses for not acting. For instance, I hear two very common "excuse" questions:

Isn't the game over? Everyone is into real estate.

Won't the "new" tax law make real estate a lousy investment?

The answer to both of the questions is to realize that regardless of what happens in the future, there will always be highly motivated sellers—always! Therefore, you can be confident that with persistence you will be able to find the ten or twenty wholesale properties to take you to financial freedom. And every time Congress passes a "new" tax law, the fear and uncertainly just create more highly motivated sellers. A fearless investor finds the best of all situations: more properties to choose from with less competition. Buying in such uncertain environments is riskier, but this risk can be minimized if you buy only below-market properties that produce positive cash flows.

I hope the answers to these common questions have eliminated some of your logjams and thus released you to act.

that what you're doing? You may dig through tons of gravel before you find a little tiny piece of gold.

"The article describes how Don became aware of a million-dollar bankruptcy proceeding that was being held up by one property—a $150,000 vacant office building. The court was worried that recurring vandalism might lower the value of the property. They decided to sell it quickly to someone who could occupy the building to stop the vandalism. Don learned by word of mouth that they were highly motivated to sell. He offered $40,000 with a $2,000 down payment. Although it sounds unbelievable that a $150,000 building would sell for as little as $40,000, the court accepted Don's offer. Why?"

"Because they were don't-wanters," Steve answered.

"He then asked the court to allow him to take possession of the property. By doing this he was able to rent it out and collect the rent . . . *even before he closed on the property.* He rented the building, as is, for $500 per month. He also rented the forty-three parking spaces to adjacent businesses for $15 apiece—another $645 per month. But the best was yet to come. Because the bankruptcy took another fourteen months to complete, Don didn't have to make mortgage payments to the court although he was able to keep all of the rent proceeds—over $16,000 income on an investment of only $2,000. When the bankruptcy was finally resolved, Don sold the building to an adjacent property owner for $85,000 cash. Let's total up Don's profit from this one transaction:

$45,000 profit from the sale of the building
$16,000 cash flow from 14 months of rent
$60,000 profit!

All on a $2,000 investment. How do you fall into deals like that? You've got to be out there falling. Got to be looking, studying, finding, sifting through dozens of cubic zirconiums, tons of gravel until you find something that sparkles, something that glitters.

"This afternoon I'll give you more detail on how to find these bargains. This morning I've tried to keep the details to a minimum. I want you to just understand the principles.

"I really believe that each of you already has what it takes to make it. You're already wealthy. How does it feel to be wealthy, Philip?"

"Wonderful."

"Let's go have lunch, shall we?"

FOR AN IDEA WHICH, AT FIRST, DOES NOT SEEM ABSURD,
THERE IS NO HOPE.—Albert Einstein

"I'LL TRY," SAID LUKE SKYWALKER.
THE WISE YODA REPLIED, "THERE IS NO TRY. THERE IS ONLY
DO OR DO NOT."—*The Empire Strikes Back*

7

FROM THE IVORY TOWER TO THE SCHOOL OF HARD KNOCKS

1.

As we all sat down to a catered lunch, I wasn't about to let them
rest. We continued to forge ahead.

"Now," I said, "while we eat lunch I'd like to return to something
we talked about this morning—business cards. All professionals
have business cards—realtors, title company officers, bankers, lawyers and investors. So should you. This lunchtime is set aside for
you to design your own card."

"What should our cards look like?" Nora asked.

"What does an attorney's card look like? It's simple, clean, professional. 'John Doe, Attorney at Law.' Same with a doctor or an accountant. Professionals don't use flashy names like Megabucks
Industries. That's tacky. Try to be classy."

"What business are we in?" Steve asked.

His wife answered for him. "The investment business."

"As we eat our lunch," I said, "be thinking of a name for your business and how your card will look."

Before we'd finished eating, Steve raised his hand. "I think Mary and I have a name for our company," he said. "How about 'Bonenberger and Associates' in the middle of the card? Then we'll put our name and number in one corner. In the other corner, 'Real estate investments.' "

"I like it."

Philip raised his hand. "Karen and I have our name also. Moore and Moore Investments. Has a sort of ring to it. And we put our name and phone number at the bottom."

"Kind of catchy. OK. Nora. How about you?"

"I like to use my name in the middle of the card—Nora Jean Boles. Then at the bottom it just says 'Real Estate Investments' and my phone number. How's that?"

"You're one step closer to being in business for yourself. How does it feel?"

"More exciting by the minute," Mary said.

With that discussion ended, we finished lunch and took a fifteen-minute break. Mary took time to call home again. Nora sat at the table leafing through the written materials in her MasterPlanner. Philip and Karen stepped out into the hall for a cigarette. The camera and sound crew fiddled with equipment in between bites of sandwiches. I took a moment to huddle with Dr. Lee.

"Where are you?" he asked me. It was his special way of asking me how I was feeling.

"I'm OK. Feeling a bit rushed," I answered. "These lights and cameras are really cramping my style."

"I know," he said. "David and I have been putting out the fires behind the scenes. One of the cameras jammed partway through the second hour, but we got most of the footage."

He sat waiting for me to speak, his silence prodding me to reveal my deeper feelings.

"There's so much material to cover," I said finally. "I don't know how I'm going to get through it." I paused, waiting for him to reassure me. I was tired of being the guru.

"Feeling the pressure, are you?" he asked.

I knew what he was doing. But I responded anyway. "Yeah. It's a lot harder than I thought it was going to be."

Sensing the right moment, he rehearsed with me the principles of the instructional model we had designed together for the two-day challenge.

"People are more important than the material you have to cover," he said. "Go where they are. Let them fill up their own buckets. You just provide the well. They won't remember all of what you teach them. Just whether or not you care. Resist the temptation to push them faster than they can run. That will mean more to them in the long haul."

"That's easier said than done," I sighed.

For months this had been my greatest struggle—the battle between short-term results versus long-lasting progress. After all, my reputation was on the line. I needed short-term results. Five thousand dollars cash in ninety days. Dr. Lee had tried to show me that you can't change people with megadoses of information. People change themselves after minidoses of acceptance from people who care. "Acceptance is harder to give than advice," he'd told me, "but infinitely more valuable."

It was strange advice. Moreover, it was risky advice. And I wasn't sure I was ready to take that kind of risk. Now he said, "What's your main message? To be self-reliant? Yes! To let go of security? Yes! To take a risk? Yes! Why don't you follow your own advice? Take a risk! Yes! Forget the five thousand dollars in ninety days. Forget yourself and your reputation. Teach them what you can. But let them be responsible for their own lives. Allow them the privilege of learning from their own failures. And above all, love them. Accept them. That's your real challenge."

"But if they fail, I fail," I responded.

He pondered for a moment. "Yes," he said, "but you've given them opportunity. Hope. You can't do more than that."

2.

It was time to begin again. The director called, "Lights! Action!"

"Well," I began, "principle time is over. Nitty-gritty time is here."

I explained that they needed to learn how to read the classified ads—to notice the subtle clues that indicate seller flexibility. "It's a numbers game," I said. "Only one in twenty ads is really flexible. You have to keep calling till you strike pay dirt."

I had designed an exercise to test them. "On the next page there are ten sample ads," I said. "Check the one you think is the don't-wanter."

"Just do these ten?" Steve inquired.

"Would a blue-vaser ask that question?" I asked.

"Not on your life," Steve shot back.

"You are opportunity detectives. You don't need my permission to do anything." I wanted him to think like a blue-vaser—not dependent on other people but thinking for himself, acting independently in all things.

"Which ad shows the most flexibility?" I asked.

Mary pointed to number five.

> Moving out of state. Must sell 2 bdrm, 2 bath upstairs flat fully equipped. Asking $49,500. Bring offers. Will take back second. Will consider lease purchase. See to appreciate.

"This has several good clues in it," she said. " 'Bring offers,' 'will take second' and 'consider lease purchase.' "

" 'Bring offers' is the weakest clue," I told her. "It's like 'must sell'—everybody uses it. On the other hand, 'lease option' really means something. Common sense tells us that if he'll sell it or rent it, he might not need cash. This opens the door for a nothing-down offer to buy."

"What about 'moving'? Is that a good clue?" Mary asked.

"What do you think?"

"Yes, especially if he's moving out of state."

I nodded. "The more clues the better. And here's a tip. The larger the ad, the smaller the flexibility. The seller who gives lengthy descriptions of his property using words like 'immaculate' and 'custom built' is hinting that the house is great but the financing is lousy. He's a wanter. You're looking for a don't-wanter who runs smaller ads with blatant financing clues like 'low down,' 'will carry financing,' 'will trade for equity.' Once you find the don't-wanter, then you can check out his property. Do your prospecting on the phone, not in your car. No use looking at a property if you can't finance it. Let your fingers do the walking."

We went on to analyze several more ads until I felt they were catching the subtle nuances—reading between the lines. Then we opened actual newspapers to the "Condos and Townhomes for Sale" section and started circling real ads. This brought out more clues and tips such as:

- If an ad says "nothing down," make sure it doesn't allude to obtaining a new loan using a Veterans Administration program designed only for veterans.
- The best kind of flexibility is in price and terms.
- The ideal situation is when the seller is carrying the financing with low or no down payment and a below-the-market price. These are rare but so are diamonds.
- The best kind of loan is an existing FHA or VA loan. Anyone can assume them—veteran or not, employed or not. In fact, all it takes to assume one of these loans is fifty dollars, a social security number and the ability to fog up a mirror held under your nose.
- Ads run by real estate companies are generally less flexible than for-sale-by-owner ads because of the added commissions. But creative Realtors can earn their keep.
- Think wholesale! Got to have either the price or the terms or both well below market. If not, you're just gambling.
- "Vacant" is a good clue. Someone is making the payments without the benefit of occupancy.
- "Just reduced" means the seller priced his property too high and has now lowered his price to market. You want something that is 10 to 20 percent below market.
- Never buy a property from a seller who is not highly motivated to sell.
- "Financing available" means the buyer will need to obtain a new loan. It's harder to qualify for new bank financing than for seller financing.

Next I shared with them a one-page sheet—a Bargainfinder—that they could use in telephone prospecting to reduce the anxiety of cold calling. As you can see from the sample, the Bargainfinder is organized so that the easier, ice-breaking questions are asked up front in preparation for the tougher questions, which assess the seller's real flexibility.

The purpose of the questions is to gather information needed to score the property. The Bargainfinder has a place for a property score as well as sections for brainstorming creative sources of down payments, generating a positive cash flow and making a profit.

HOW TO READ ADS LIKE AN EXPERT

The key to finding the right property is finding the right seller—someone who is flexible enough to sell at wholesale prices and/or wholesale terms. In reading classified ads, you look for bargains indicated by a combination of the following clues:

1. Seller will carry financing: "will carry," "will finance," "contract," "agreement for sale," "contract of sale."
2. Transfer: "moving out of state," "out-of-state owner."
3. Vacant: "purchased other home," "renter just moved," "unoccupied."
4. Lease/option: "rent to own," "rent to buy," "lease/purchase."
5. Little or nothing down: "little down," "low down," "no down," "no cash," "little cash to loan," "low equity."
6. Priced below market: "under market," "priced to sell," "a steal," "a bargain," "wholesale."
7. Will consider trade: "trade for part of equity," "will consider anything."
8. Assumable loan: "FHA," "VA," "no qualifying," "no credit."
9. Flexible: "open to all offers," "consider all offers," "bring all offers," "creative financing."
10. Desperate: "need a sale," "highly motivated," "don't-wanter," "need to move property quickly," "hurry!"
11. For sale by owner: "FSBO," "no agents," "owner/agent."

Less than 5 percent of real estate classified ads contain the right combination of clues that lead to truly highly motivated sellers. Many Realtors like to use these clues as bait to attract potential buyers even though the clients they represent may not be highly motivated to sell. Thus I often find more flexibility in dealing directly with for-sale-by-owner ads (FSBO).

I took them through a demonstration of the Bargainfinder by pretending to call a seller on the phone and playing both roles.

"Mr. Seller," I began, "I'm calling about your ad in the newspaper. Will you tell me a little bit about it please?"

"What is it you want to know?"

THE BARGAINFINDER™

FIND IT

Name _____ □ owner □ agent   Sq. Ft. _____ Age _____

Address _____   Bedrms _____ Baths _____

City, State, Zip _____   □ Carport □ Garage □ None

Neighborhood _____   □ Brick   □ Frame

Phone _____   Other: _____

LOCATION 2 0 3

Why are you selling? _____

Plans if it does not sell: _____

Any offers? _____ How long on mkt? _____

CONDITION 2 1 3

Value _____

Price _____

(−) _____

(=) _____

Down _____

Balance _____

PRICE 2 1 3

RENT

(←)

Payment

(←)

1/12 taxes

(←)

1/12 Insurance

(←)

Utilities

(=)

positive or negative
CASH FLOW

FINANCING 2 1 3

FARM IT

What do you feel would be the best price and terms
you would accept for a quick sale?

FLEXIBILITY 2 1 3

Loan	Amount	%	Payment	Term	Holder	Assum	Balloon
1st						Y/N	Y/N
2nd						Y/N	Y/N

DOWN

10 Areas of Flexibility	Seller	Short-term
	Buyer	Long-term
	Realtor	Partners
	Property splits	Investors
	Renters	Options

TOTAL SCORE _____

The BOTTOM LINE:
(How can I profit from this property?)

2 1 3

Sell	Trade	Refinance	Keep
Could I sell it for a quick profit?	Can it be fixed up for long term equity profit? Will it enhance long term cash flow?	What benefits could come from financing the property?	Is there enough built-in equity profit to trade for something else of value?

FUND IT

"Tell me the address, some information about the neighborhood and any general information about the property itself."

(The seller responds. This information is not as important as the financing information but tends to put the seller at ease. As the seller responds, just fill in the blanks of the Bargainfinder.)

"How did you determine the price?" (I want to get a feel for value. Is the property priced above or below market? Is there a written, professional appraisal? A Realtor's opinion is not as valid.)

"We've priced the home at sixty-five thousand dollars to sell fast."

"Oh? What should it sell for?"

"About sixty-eight."

"I see." (This is not very flexible. If he had said seventy-five or eighty, we would have gotten excited.) "Why do you need to sell it fast?"

"We're moving to California."

"When?" (The closer the moving date, the more flexible he will be.)

"Two months."

"Have you had any offers?" (This question brings him back to reality. If he hasn't had any offers, his price is generally too high. If he has had several offers, ask what they were. This tells you what he doesn't like. It may also indicate that he's not a don't-wanter.)

"Haven't had any offers."

"How long has it been for sale?" (The longer the better.)

"Six months."

"What is the current financing?"

"It has an assumable FHA mortgage of $50,000 at eleven percent with payments of $525 per month."

"Are the payments current?"

"Yes."

"What are you trying to accomplish?" (That's a nice way of saying, 'What are you going to do with the money?' Most buyers never ask that question and therefore never really understand the seller's problem. How can you solve a problem that you don't understand?)

"Well, we really wanted to cash out. But the market is slower and we need to move soon. I suppose we'd accept a down payment and carry some financing."

Ah. Now you're making progress. The seller understands he has a problem and is willing to be flexible to solve it.

108

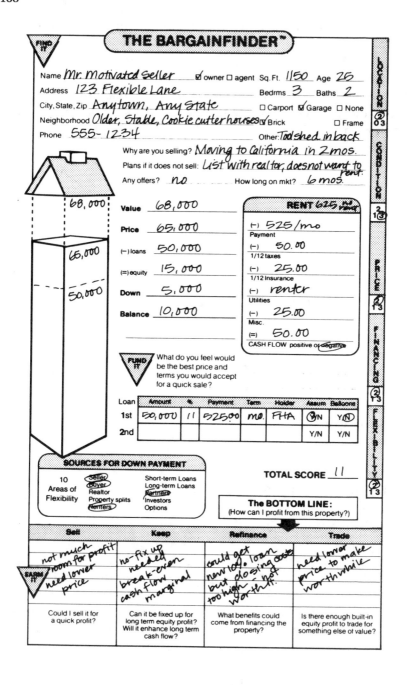

THE BARGAINFINDER™

Name **Mr. Motivated Seller** ☑ owner ☐ agent Sq. Ft. **1150** Age **25**
Address **123 Flexible Lane** Bedrms **3** Baths **2**
City, State, Zip **Anytown, Any State** ☐ Carport ☑ Garage ☐ None
Neighborhood **Older, Stable, Cookie cutter houses** ☑ Brick ☐ Frame
Phone **555-1234** Other: **Tool shed in back**

Why are you selling? **Moving to California in 2 mos.**
Plans if it does not sell: **List with realtor, does not want to rent.**
Any offers? **no** How long on mkt? **6 mos.**

68,000

Value **68,000**
Price **65,000**
(−) loans **50,000**
(=) equity **15,000**
Down **5,000**
Balance **10,000**

65,000
50,000

RENT 625 mo.
(−) **525/mo** Payment
(−) **50.00** 1/12 taxes
(−) **25.00** 1/12 Insurance
(−) **renter** Utilities
(−) **25.00** Misc.
(=) **50.00** CASH FLOW positive or ~~negative~~

FUND IT — What do you feel would be the best price and terms you would accept for a quick sale?

Loan	Amount	%	Payment	Term	Holder	Assum	Balloons
1st	50,000	11	525.00	mo.	FHA	Y/ⓝ	Y/ⓝ
2nd						Y/N	Y/N

SOURCES FOR DOWN PAYMENT
10 Areas of Flexibility: ⓢeller, ⓑuyer, Realtor, Property splits, ⓡenters — Short-term Loans, Long-term Loans, ⓟartners, Investors, Options

TOTAL SCORE 11

The BOTTOM LINE:
(How can I profit from this property?)

Sell	Keep	Refinance	Trade
not much room for profit need lower price	no fix up needed break-even cash flow marginal	could get new 10% loan but closing costs too high - not worth it	need lower price to make worthwhile
Could I sell it for a quick profit?	Can it be fixed up for long term equity profit? Will it enhance long term cash flow?	What benefits could come from financing the property?	Is there enough built-in equity profit to trade for something else of value?

"What would be the lowest price and best terms you feel you could live with in order to sell quickly?" (We're getting to the bottom line.)

"I imagine we'd need at least five thousand dollars down. We'd carry the rest."

"Remember," I concluded, addressing the Challenge team, "the purpose of asking these questions is to generate enough information to score the property. If the property scores well, you're onto the next step—calling the hot line and letting us help you draft up an offer. But the first step is to find a highly motivated seller.

"And finding a highly motivated seller is what we're going to do right after we take a break."

3.

On returning from our break, I had each contestant pick a telephone and get ready to make some real phone calls. Mary and Steve settled on a couch at the far end of the room. Karen and Philip found a table in the center of the room. Nora took up her position at the other end of the long room. I stood next to the Moores' table and barked out the following instructions.

"Each of you has circled ten or fifteen potential don't-wanter ads that I'd like you to call. When you find someone home, take them through the questions on the Bargainfinder. If you determine they aren't flexible, excuse yourself and go on to the next ad. Always be courteous. Never burn your bridges. When you get to the tough questions, be sensitive. A house is the largest investment most people ever make, and they are very touchy about it. Try to understand their problem while getting a property score."

Philip chose his most promising ad, picked up the phone and dialed the number. A man answered,

MAN: Hello.

PHILIP: Yes, sir, my name is Philip Moore. I'm calling in reference to the ad you have in the paper, "home for sale by owner."

MAN: Yes.

PHILIP: Yes, could you tell me a little bit about the home, sir?

MAN: It's three bedrooms. It has a real big yard. It has two patios. One about 25-by-25 brick patio with brick sidewalk. It's got a smaller, probably 8-by-10-feet patio in the back. It's got a

> living room, built-in kitchen with appliances. It has another room you can use as a real small family room or something. It has a utility room, place for a gas or electric washer. It has a gas grill and utility shed outside. It doesn't have a basement.

PHILIP: What's the mortgage balance?

MAN: Oh, there's no loan on it.

PHILIP: No loan? Okay. All right, I know this is a very personal question, but could you tell me, what are you trying to accomplish, or what's your goal with this?

MAN: I want to sell it.

PHILIP (Laughing): OK, so you can be flexible?

MAN: Somewhat.

PHILIP: Somewhat? OK. And the price again is how much?

MAN: Forty-six five.

PHILIP: OK. You're the owner, right?

MAN: Right.

PHILIP: OK. Could you give me the square footage?

MAN: I don't know that.

PHILIP: It has a garage, you said?

MAN: No, it has a utility, a storage shed outside.

PHILIP: Like a carport?

MAN: No, it's not for a car; it's probably about ten feet wide and maybe twenty feet long. It's for storing lawnmowers and stuff like that.

PHILIP: Tell me, is it a brick home or a frame home?

MAN: Frame.

PHILIP: All right, thank you very much, sir. 'Bye, now.

MAN: 'Bye.

Philip hung up the phone, looking puzzled. Somehow, he knew he should have gathered more information. I had been watching over his shoulder and decided to assemble the group to process this call so that we could all learn from Philip's experience. We stood around the table where Philip and Karen were sitting. Philip played back the call on his tape recorder. We all listened.

"I sound very bad on tape," Philip lamented.

"For a first-timer, you sounded great!"

"I didn't get all into it. I didn't find out the value of the home. Um, what kind of terms he was interested in. It happened so fast that. . . ."

"That's what the Bargainfinder is for. You need answers in all five major areas: flexibility, location, financing, price and condition. If you hang up without scoring the property, then you're just wasting your time. But on the whole, you asked some very gutsy questions, like, 'What are you trying to accomplish?' and 'So you can be flexible?' But you didn't dig deep enough. When he said, 'I can be somewhat flexible,' you should have asked, 'What do you mean by "somewhat flexible?" ' You also didn't ask about his main motivation for selling. Is he moving? Did he inherit the place. Was it recently vandalized? Did a tenant move out and leave a mess?"

"So," Philip said, "it wouldn't do any harm to call him back. But he'd know my name."

"You've nothing to hide. Call him back tonight."

"OK."

"Let's hit the phones again," I said. "Everyone this time."

After another thirty minutes of calling I gathered the group together for another teaching session. I wanted to show them what a cubic zirconian looks like. For my demonstration I chose one of Mary's telephone calls. We played it back.

MARY: What is the existing mortgage on the house?
WOMAN: Existing mortgage? Why would you need to know that?
MARY: Well, just to know how much you still owe on it.
WOMAN: Why would you need to know that? I don't understand the question.
MARY: Well, you know ... just to know how much financing you're going to need?
WOMAN: Well, we're not doing the financing. You'd have to come up with your own.
MARY: How much of a down payment are you looking for?
WOMAN: That'd be up to the bank.
MARY: Okay, well, what type of interest is on the mortgage you have right now?
WOMAN: We got our loan six years ago, and it's not assumable.
MARY: Has the property been on the market very long?
WOMAN: No, about a week. Had a lot of people look at it.

It didn't take the group long to realize that this was not a flexible seller and that any further time spent on this call would be a waste.

The Challenge participants blue-vased themselves through several more calls. They were groping, but gradually the rough edges began to get knocked off. As they became more comfortable with the process, they made smoother and smoother transitions between questions. I drove them on, encouraging them, knowing that if they could hurdle the fear of talking with strangers about totally foreign concepts their self-esteem would grow. Steve called me over to process his last call.

"Listen to this," he whispered as he turned on the tape recorder. "I think we have a hot one here."

We both listened to the tape. The seller was moving out of state. The three-bedroom house had a small, unassumable mortgage with a price tag of $122,500. This was the first red flag. The seller told Steve that she had recently listed the property with a realtor and that this reduced her flexibility because of the commissions involved. Another red flag. She wanted $60,000 and would consider carrying the balance of her equity.

I called the group together again to process Steve's call. As we listened, I could see that Philip was catching on quickly. Nora, on the other hand, looked tired, suffering from circuit overload.

I showed them a way to buy the property with nothing down and actually pull five thousand dollars out for themselves at the closing. But I advised against trying it.

"Now, let's stop being creative," I said, "and start acting like businesspeople. Let's get to the bottom line. What kind of mortgage payments would we have if she accepted our crazy offer?"

"Shoo-ee!" exclaimed Steve.

"Two or three thousand a month? Couldn't rent it for enough to even make the payments. We don't even have to run this through our Bargainfinder to begin to realize that this one is a cubic zirconium. Remember, use creative financing only to make a good deal great—not to make a bad deal average. And this one was a bad deal. So we pass on it.

"What you're looking for," I continued, "is a lower-priced property with a low loan balance. Now, let's do a role-play. You be the buyer and I'll be the seller. You can ask me any questions you like but remember to get a score. All you know is that my price is fifty thousand dollars and my loan balance is ten thousand dollars. The ball's in your court."

NORA: What's your terms? Will you carry a mortgage?
SELLER: Yeah, I'll carry some. My equity is forty thousand. If you gave me fifteen thousand down, I'd probably carry the rest ... about twenty five thousand.
MARY: What about the location?

SELLER: It's an okay neighborhood. It's coming back.

KAREN: How firm are you on your price?

SELLER: Well, I might be a little flexible.

PHILIP: What's the condition of the home?

"Philip, don't move on too fast. He's indicated some flexibility. Explore it further."

NORA: Um, would you take forty-five thousand for it?

"Nora, the first person to mention a number loses. Avoid suggesting numbers. Keep giving the ball back to him."

NORA: What's the lowest price you would take?

"Not bad. Maybe a little too strong. Better to say, "What price did you have in mind?
"What do you mean by flexible?"
"Good."

SELLER: What do I mean by flexible? You name it. I need out. How long has it been on the market? Maybe eight months. We're behind on our payments. We don't want to lose it.

KAREN: How much cash do you need?

SELLER: I really need about fifteen thousand dollars, but I guess if I got more I could lower my price . . .

STEVE: If we gave you twenty thousand dollars . . .

"Don't give him solutions yet, Steve."

PHILIP: Would you take out a second mortgage on the property?

"That's a solution. Understand his problem first."

STEVE: How can we settle the issue with you? What do you need from me?

"Good. Give the ball back to him. Let him solve it. The person asking questions is in control."

NORA: What are you trying to accomplish?

SELLER: Well, like I said, we're behind on some payments and we need to. . . ."

STEVE: What would you consider a reasonable offer on your home?

"Listen to him, Steve. Let him talk. Keep silent. What does silence mean? It means, 'Tell me more.' "

SELLER: We got a few payments back. We don't want to lose the house. And if we got twenty thousand or thirty thousand out of it we'd probably be happy.

PHILIP: So if I gave you twenty thousand dollars you'd be satisfied?

SELLER: Well, maybe. If I got it real fast.

PHILIP: I could probably arrange for that. OK. Can we come out and look at the house?

"Good. OK. Let's process this example. Here's a $50,000 house that can be bought for only $30,000 if you can just come up with $20,000 cash. Where do you get the $20,000?"

"Get another mortgage," Philip suggested.

"That's one solution. The new loan would have to pay off the existing loan of $10,000 and the seller's $20,000, plus your problem-solving fee of $5,000 and closing costs of maybe $2,000. That totals $37,000. Would you be excited to buy a $50,000 property for only $37,000 and put $5,000 in your pocket? You bet! OK, group. Back to the phones."

The rest of the afternoon was spent on the phones. Toward five o'clock I let them return to their homes. Nora gathered up her new learning materials. I walked with her through the lobby of the hotel and into the parking garage. We chatted by her car while she fumbled through her purse looking for her keys. She looked overwhelmed—like a wet puppy in a rainstorm. We finally found her keys still in the ignition of her car.

But the door was locked.

We finally called a policeman to break into the car. After she drove off I went back to my suite. I crashed on the bed—tired to the bone. Things had gone worse than I'd expected. Our telephoning should have uncovered at least one possible diamond instead of the cubic zirconiums we had ended up with.

"It's a numbers game," I rationalized to myself. "Our number just hasn't come up yet."

4. _____

At 9:00 that evening, the Challenge team reconvened at the Bonenberger's small home for the final session of the first day. We crowded into the tiny living room. The hot camera lights made it even more uncomfortable. It was so far from the intimate atmosphere I wanted.

I began by reminding them of the next day's schedule. We would meet at 8:00 A.M. at a park near the Daniele Hotel dressed in jogging clothes with a portable tape player.

"I got two great calls on my newspaper ad," Mary said excitedly when I'd finished talking. "But I'm still not sure what to do with them."

She explained that the seller wanted five hundred dollars down with a price four thousand dollars below market. She'd given it a score of twelve. I gave her the assignment of calling the seller and setting up an appointment for us to see the property at 10:30 the next morning.

"Let's break camp for tonight," I said, knowing that they must be weary. "It's been a long day on the mountain. Time to pitch the tents, roll out our sleeping bags, make a fire, rest up for the morning. I'll bet you're a bit sore between the shoulder blades—you're probably not used to carrying heavy backpacks. Your face is sunburned. And those new hiking boots are heavy and awkward. Your ankles are tired and aching."

"And the altitude is getting to my head," Mary added, laughing.

"Yes," I said. "And looking back down toward the valley it doesn't seem like we've come very far. Looking up, we can't even see the peaks hidden in the clouds. Maybe Mount McKinley is too tough. Tell me how you feel. Let it all hang out."

"I'm still nervous," Mary said, this time more seriously.

"That's why we practice on smaller mountains at first. But even that won't be easy. You'll slip and fall—scrape your knees. Maybe break a finger, or suffer frostbite. This is where we separate the sheep from the goats, as Reverend Bonenberger would say. Lots of people have dreams and goals, but they get to the place on the mountain where you are now and they turn back. They were just daydreaming. Not willing to pay the price.

"None of us has ever climbed a mountain like this before. We have a rocky road ahead of us. But let's give it our best shot. And if we fail . . . ?"

I paused for effect.

"You'll never be successful unless you learn to handle failure. I know it sounds crazy, but if it hadn't been for failure, I'd never have become a millionaire. I literally failed into my first million. I graduated in the one-third of my MBA class that made the top two-thirds possible. I felt lucky to have graduated at all. I remember sitting in my business classes in college feeling the same way you probably feel right now—totally confused, even dumb. At the end of my second year, I began recruiting for a job. I sent résumés to the top thirty companies that I wanted to work for. I interviewed. I called. I had my hopes up. Most of my colleagues were landing jobs and bragging about their starting salaries. All I received was rejection letter after rejection letter. In fact, I've brought the rejection letters here tonight so that you can see for yourself."

I pulled out a thin, black leather book measuring 8½ by 11 inches. Bound in the book were dozens of letters. I continued to talk while I thumbed through the book slowly.

"In a few short months I received rejection letters from Gillette, General Foods and Kodak, Quaker Oats, Campbell Soups, Lipton, General Mills, Exxon, Nestlé, RCA, Hershey Foods, Max Factor and General Motors. Recognize any of the names?"

"Things were looking bleak, but I had one ace in the hole. Procter and Gamble—the company at the top of my list and the giants of consumer marketing, makers of Crest, Ivory, Charmin and Tide—invited me to come to their headquarters for interviews with the top brass. My interviews in Cincinnati—on April 11, 1974—were thrilling. I fell in love with the people, the company and the city. After so much rejection, I felt I'd finally found a home. I flew home and waited for the offer to come in the mail.

"On April 15 the letter came. I should have known not to open it. Nothing good ever happens on April 15. This is the day that Lincoln died, the day the *Titanic* sank and the day our taxes are due. Nevertheless, I ignored these ominous warnings and ripped open the envelope to find a letter from Michael R. Walker, the personnel supervisor of Procter and Gamble, informing me that they didn't want me.

"I'll never forget that black day. I couldn't understand it! Had God let me down? Why wasn't He answering my prayers? Opening the doors for me? I had no idea where I was going to turn. The semester ended. The few of us without job offers felt like dregs at the bottom of the barrel. One by one, the last of the responses from my thirty hand-picked companies trickled in. Ford, Hallmark Cards, Macy's and General Electric. All said no. I still had no job.

"Do you know what kept me going during the hard times? It was those rejection letters. They made me mad. I put them in a special file and vowed that I would be a success even if some of America's greatest companies thought differently.

"But I still didn't have a job. I shared my predicament with a successful local real estate developer, who offered me a job selling recreational land. At first I rejected the idea. I felt it was beneath me. 'I have a masters degree in business administration. What will my collegues think?!'

"But necessity got the better of my pride. That summer, as I worked beside this man, I learned lessons I could not have learned any other way. With the confidence gained there, I bought my first investment property, and my second, and then my third . . . and so on. You know the rest of the story.

"A few years ago I bound my file of rejection letters into this leather book. I entitled it *The Many Failures of Robert G. Allen.* While there are millions of my other books in print, there is only one copy of this one. It is one of my most prized possessions. Why? It constantly reminds me that from the ashes of failure grew my greatest success.

"Where would I be right now if my prayers had been answered—if Procter and Gamble had hired me in 1974? Probably still be in Cincinnati making a nice living—saying to the world, Please don't squeeze the Charmin. But because I failed to get that job, I was forced to look in a different direction, to take a road less traveled. And where has it led me? To a life of financial freedom. Today I earn more and work less than even the president of Procter and Gamble, and I wouldn't consider trading places with him for the world.

"You see, sometimes God answers prayers by closing doors, not by opening them. And not till years later do we see the wisdom of our failures—when the fruits of our failures become evident. We have to learn to defer judgment until the final verdict. You must learn to see the good in every setback. If you do, your failures will not be so painful. Failure, in fact, will no longer be failure, only feedback.

"For example, look at this letter dated July 7, 1978, from St. Martin's Press turning down the manuscript of a book I had written entitled *Nothing Down.*

"How could I know, when I received this letter, that *Nothing*

Down was a winner? If I had chosen to accept this failure, *Nothing Down* would never have become the all-time largest-selling financial hardcover book in the history of publishing.

"Therefore, if you refuse to accept failure, you cannot fail. You may fall down a cliff or two. But you must learn to get up, dust yourself off and keep climbing.

"Only those who are willing to fail again and again deserve to make it to the top. You three haven't even begun to fail enough to be worthy of success. You may have to call dozens, maybe hundreds, of sellers before you find your diamond. There will be problems to solve, obstacles to overcome. You'll be rejected and defeated at every turn for weeks on end. But if you persist, you'll make it. And won't it feel great to stand on top of that mountain?!"

Mary could hardly contain herself, "When I buy my first property, I think I'm going to fly away!"

"You'll look back down the mountain and remember all your failures with a smile. They will seem only a small price to pay for what you enjoy. And, then, the greatest and most misunderstood wealth secret of them all will be clear to you."

WEALTH SECRET NO. 9. THERE IS NO FAILURE— ONLY FEEDBACK.

As Philip and Karen walked out of the Bonenberger home into the humid Missouri night, they looked up and down the street. It was a white neighborhood. Neat, white houses lined both sides of the street, their lawns immaculate. A jet passed overhead, reminding them how close they were to the airport.

They got into their car—a brown Chevrolet that they had borrowed from Karen's father.

Karen observed her husband as they drove. He was bubbling with enthusiasm.

"He's picking it up so fast," she thought.

As long as she had known him, he had been a budding entrepreneur. They first met when he was fourteen and she was twelve. He always seemed to have money. Or the knack to find it when necessary. And he had a way with words. In the ninth grade, he was on the student council and debating team. A straight A student. Sort of a square until his friends started razzing him. To placate them he began smoking and hanging out with the wrong crowd. At first, his gang was just involved in mischief—breaking windows, vandalizing, cafeteria fights. Just to be cool. Then they gravitated to more serious things, like stealing hubcaps, tires, carburetors. But stealing scared Philip to death. Couldn't even shoplift a pack of gum without the look of guilt on his face giving him away.

At the age of thirteen, he learned a better way to earn money. He couldn't steal the stuff, but he sure could sell it. His friends would rip things off at the mall—a stereo, some women's clothes, a camera or a television—and he'd buy it all for a hundred dollars and peddle it down at the black housing projects of St. Louis. After a while, he developed a regular clientele. He'd call around and find someone who wanted to buy a hot refrigerator. Then he'd flag down a truck driving through the neighborhood and pay the driver five or ten dollars to deliver it for him. It was good money for a young teenager. Sometimes as much as five hundred dollars a week—enough to buy him a gold tooth, fancy clothes and to give some extra money to his mother.

She, like Karen, never suspected a thing. She thought he was working a part-time job after school.

It wasn't until Philip had been arrested that they learned where the extra money came from. By then, Karen was pregnant with Marcus. She was only fifteen. Philip came to see her.

"I've been busted," he told her.

"Busted? What're you talking about?" She acted surprised but she knew that he'd been flirting with trouble. Her friends at school had warned her. "Philip is a bum. He's gonna leave you. He's goin' around with the wrong crowd." She didn't want to believe them. He was always so considerate when he was with her. But the stories about him always got back to her.

"I'm goin' into the group home," he said. "It's a home for delinquent boys. I'm gonna be gone for three months. I'll call you."

"What for? What'd you do?"

He never told her the whole story.

Even in the group home, his entrepreneurial talents flourished. He'd buy a pack of cigarettes for 95 cents and sell it to the other boys for $1.50 on time—until they got their weekly allowances of money. He became so successful at it that the home employees forbade him to do it.

After his stint in the group home, Karen begged him to go straight. By this time, he was a father feeling the responsibility to provide.

He turned to selling balloons. The principles were still the same—
buy low, sell high. Except this time it was legal. Karen remembered
the first day they sold balloons together. It was the first time he had
ever tried to sell a legitimate product. They rented a helium tank and
inflated dozens of balloons and took the city bus to the arch monument on the banks of the Mississippi. Philip gave Karen pointers on
how to sell and what to say, but it was she who sold her bundle of
balloons even before they made it to the riverfront.

Karen smiled at this memory.

Philip then tried selling other things—roses on streetcorners—
with some success. It wasn't like the old days, but he was bringing
in a sixty- or seventy-dollar-a-day profit.

But none of his family ever appreciated his selling skills. His
brothers ridiculed him. "Get yourself a real job," they chided. "Don't
be a bum selling roses and balloons on the streetcorner." He ignored
them. They could not know how much he enjoyed the thrill of the
sale, the freedom of being on his own with no one to tell him what to
do. When things were going right, it was the most exciting feeling in
the world.

As in the fall of 1982, when the St. Louis Cardinals made it into
the World Series. The series went seven games. On the last night of
the last game Philip gambled and bought two hundred pennants for
fifty cents apiece from a wholesaler. He knew that if the Cards lost,
he wouldn't be able to sell them all. Nobody wants a pennant from a
loser. He positioned himself outside the stadium by the statue of
Stan Musial, his ear glued to the transistor radio. Luck was with
him. St. Louis beat the Milwaukee Brewers by a score of 6–3. The
fans poured out, jubilant. They mobbed him. He sold one pennant
for four dollars. Another fellow wanted ten—eight dollars apiece.
He stuffed the money in his pockets until they bulged. If only the
Cardinals would win the World Series every day of the year, he
would be rich!

"Those were good days," Karen thought to herself as they pulled
up in front of their apartment on Leduc. She had been with him that
night at the stadium.

And she was with him now.

THE SEEDS OF GREAT DISCOVERIES ARE CONSTANTLY
FLOATING AROUND US, BUT THEY ONLY TAKE ROOT
IN MINDS WELL PREPARED TO RECEIVE THEM.—Joseph Henry

8

SWEAT YOUR WAY TO SUCCESS

"Good morning," I said. "You all look so fit in your jogging duds."

They sat on the bleachers beside a football field in Shaw Park in the middle of Clayton, Missouri. The early morning sun bathed the surroundings in a warm mist. The green leaves shimmered. It was going to be a beautiful day.

"Did you all sleep OK?"

"I was exhausted," Mary exclaimed, "but my brain wouldn't quit!"

"Comes with the territory," I replied.

"I still can't believe this is happening!" Nora added.

"Before the end of today, maybe you'll wish it wasn't."

We all laughed.

"This morning let's talk some more about the brain. The brain is the most powerful computer in the world—your personal Einstein. Yesterday we learned how to program this computer by setting specific, desirable goals with realistic deadlines. Today you'll learn how to stretch the grooves in your brain in order to use more of this marvelous tool on your shoulders. What do I mean by 'stretch the grooves'?

"Oliver Wendell Holmes once said, 'Man's mind, stretched to a new idea, never returns to its original dimension.'

"One day, after a long jog, I happened to glance at the soles of my jogging shoes. There, stuck in the grooves or treads on the bottom of my shoes, were dozens of little pebbles. Waxing a bit philosophical that day, I wondered to myself, 'Why are these pebbles stuck in the treads of my shoes?'

"I reasoned that the grooves must have been the perfect width to capture this size of pebble. Other pebbles were either too small or too big. They just bounced off. I took a stick and began prying out the pebbles when the next question popped into my mind.

"If my shoes had bigger grooves, would I catch bigger pebbles?

"Yes, this seemed reasonable. Then, another question came.

"If my brain had bigger grooves, would I catch bigger ideas?

"Every day we are bombarded with dozens of million-dollar ideas. But most of them bounce right off because the grooves in our brain are too small to accept them. This morning we are going to discuss how to stretch these grooves that have become so shriveled by negative thinking.

"How do you stretch your brain to accept bigger and bigger ideas?" I asked.

"You associate with big thinkers," Nora said.

"Right. Most of us, however, are influenced by small thinkers—small-minded people who take pleasure in telling us what we can't do. With constant exposure to small ideas, we gradually begin to think smaller thoughts. Small thoughts lead to small results—a diminished life and a smaller amount of income. Yesterday we learned that money is attracted to ideas. Big money is attracted to big ideas. Small money is attracted to small ideas.

"If you expect to have more than the average person, you have to learn to think bigger thoughts. The best way to do this is to increase your exposure to bigger ideas. To associate with big thinkers. I'd like to give you a set of audio tapes that contain speeches from some of America's finest big thinkers. By listening to these tapes daily you

HOW TO DEVELOP PMA (POSITIVE MENTAL ATTITUDE)

Program your mind with positive thoughts.
Master your body.
Associate with a network of positive people.

Practice your skills to perfection.
Motivate yourself with goals and deadlines.
Always look for the good in every problem.

Pray: Count your blessings and ask for guidance.

Magnify your talents.

Act optimistic (fake it till you make it).

Plan your work, work your plan.
Maintain your perspective: See the big picture.
Appear successful: Dress for success.

Persevere.
Model attributes from other great and successful people.
Aspire to be the best you can be.

will gradually stretch the grooves in your brain and increase your capacity to accept bigger ideas.

"Each tape will expand your mind, excite you and motivate you to act.

"I'm going to encourage you, even challenge you, to listen to one of these messages every day—a minimum of thirty minutes. Listen while exercising, cooking, driving around looking for bargains or working in the yard. I'm not kidding when I say that you can get the equivalent of a college education listening to tapes while you're stuck in traffic.

"Advertisers spend billions every year to influence our behavior with repeated commercial messages. If it works for them, why don't we start changing our behavior by introducing into our habit pattern a regular diet of great ideas on tape. I listen to tapes almost every day and never fail to learn a new thought, strategy or technique. If you make a daily habit of listening to mind-expanding ideas from

GREAT THOUGHTS FROM GREAT
THINKERS ON AUDIO TAPE

Every success-oriented person can benefit from the inspiration and savvy of other successful people by listening to audio tapes. As your self-confidence grows, the negative thinkers in your life will have less influence on you. Some of my favorite brain stretchers are:

Motivational and Inspirational Classics

How to Stay Motivated	Zig Ziglar
The Greatest Salesman in the World	Og Mandino
The Richest Man in Babylon	George S. Clayson
Think and Grow Rich	Napoleon Hill
Acres of Diamonds	Russell Conwell
The Strangest Secret	Earl Nightingale
Seeds of Greatness	Dennis Waitley

Technical and Informational

You Can Do It!	Robert G. Allen
The Power of MasterPlanning	Robert G. Allen
The Challenge	Robert G. Allen
Diamonds in the Rough	Wright Thurston
Personal Power	Anthony Robbins
Total Financial Protection	Jay Mitton
The Bottom Line	Thomas Painter

Would you like to listen to excerpts of some of the above audio recordings? Go to the listening booth at www.RobertAllen.com.

successful people, the small thoughts will be crowded out of your life forever."

"What are some other ways of expanding our thinking, Mary?"

"Read great books."

I turned to Steve. "What books ought to be in your success library?"

"The Good Book, of course," he said.

"A must!"

"Zig Ziglar has a great book," Nora contributed. "*See You at the Top.* I love Zig. He's the greatest."

"I agree. Your success library should include the following classics:

See You at the Top	Zig Ziglar
University of Success	Og Mandino
As a Man Thinketh	James Allen
Magic of Thinking Big	David Schwartz
Psycho-Cybernetics	Dr. Maxwell Maltz."

"*Psycho-Cybernetics* is a classic," Steve interrupted. "It's about a plastic surgeon who watches the transformations that happen in people once they've had plastic surgery."

Mary joined the discussion. "Steve read that book about two years ago when we were at a low point in our ministry. He wrote the principles in the book on a sheet of paper and stuck it next to the bathroom mirror. And I started reading them, too. It really helped us through a tough six months."

"I still recall one principle," Steve added. "I'll be cheerful, and positive things will come my way."

"That reminds me of something I read," said Nora. "If your mind can conceive it, your heart can believe it, you can achieve it."

I agreed. "If you want to be successful, you should have these books in your library and read them often. In addition to these great success books, there are some great how-to books. Can you think of any?"

"I would read your books," Karen said, pointing to me.

"As you might suspect, I highly recommend them." I laughed. "Other classic books for your success library include:

Nothing Down	Robert G. Allen
Creating Wealth	Robert G. Allen
Making Money	Howard Ruff

The last book was my first real estate book. I spotted it in my brother-in-law's bookshelf. He had been successful in real estate investing. Why did I notice it? I'm sure that my subconscious mind, working overtime to help me reach my written financial goals, sent a signal to my conscious mind to notice that particular book. It's a great one.

"I also particularly recommend *How to Write a Nothing Down Offer*. It will be especially practical during the next ninety days because it analyzes fifty real estate case studies with sample documentation using fifty nothing-down techniques.

"As with the tapes, I encourage you to read books from your success library for at least an hour a day. Consider this study time just as vital to your success as the air you breathe.

"As you listen to and read the great thoughts of others, your own computer will begin to want to create great thoughts of its own. You'll begin to awaken this sleeping giant. You'll feel subtle hunches that point you in new directions.

"What is a hunch? A hunch is a thought or a feeling that something is right or wrong.

"How do hunches come? The best way to answer this question is to think about how our minds work. Each of us has a conscious mind and a subconscious mind. Generally speaking, it's the nature of our conscious mind to be literal, rational, logical, serious and negative. The nature of the subconscious mind is to be more positive, creative, playful and visual.

"One is the source of doubt; the other is the source of faith. One tends to have a negative mental attitude; the other a positive mental attitude. However, this is not to say that one is bad and the other is good, that one is right and the other is wrong. Not so. It is the healthy dialogue between these minds that encourages us to make progress tempered with caution. Being more aware of how we think, we can learn to use our brains more effectively.

"Most likely, hunches come from our subconscious mind, which processes information twenty-four hours a day whether we are aware of it or not. It sorts and sifts through these data, ponders and analyzes and then presents to our conscious mind a faint thought or hunch. Most of the time this hunch is not a direct 'do this' or 'don't do that.' It's rarely that strong. It's better described as a leaning toward, a penchant to accept, a gentle nudge in the direction of, a subtle feeling about, or the broadening of one's attitude with regard to a certain proposed action.

"Hunches are subtle hints and are very fragile. When a hunch passes through our conscious mind, it enters a negative environment. If we're not sensitive, we can prematurely kill it off. True, some hunches, after careful evaluation, should be rejected, but often hunches are correct.

"Each day, several good, positive and ultimately profitable hunches pass through our minds unnoticed, because we've never trained ourselves to be sensitive to them. Listening carefully, you might hear a faint whisper: 'Maybe you should go look at the Shaw property' or 'Why don't you try a lease/option technique?' That's your computer working for you.

"Try to create an environment in which hunches can be nurtured. How? Let me illustrate by describing a scene I witnessed on television as Marvelous Marvin Hagler, the middleweight boxing champion, and his challenger Thomas Hearns were being interviewed about their upcoming fight. The champ was asked if he ever thought of losing, and he replied, 'I don't think about losing. I'm feeding the faith and starving the doubt.' This is great advice on how to nurture your hunches. Feed the faith, starve the doubt. (By the way, Hagler knocked out Hearns in the third round.)

"Finally, don't forget the source of many special hunches. I believe that we also receive spiritual hunches—those nudges of inspiration that many call 'the still-small voice.' Learning how to recognize and follow this still-small voice can lead us to levels of success that we could not attain otherwise.

"Thus, by listening to positive thinkers, reading positive books and by learning to follow our hunches, we can actually program ourselves to be more successful.

"And that brings us to the reason I had you come dressed in jogging clothes this morning. One of the best brain-stretching activities is some form of regular exercise. When you sacrifice the time to improve yourself physically—whether you jog, run, walk, swim, bicycle or play tennis—the result is the same. You feel better about yourself. Your physical health improves. Researchers have discovered that poor physical health and high levels of fear seem to go hand in hand. So one way to be less fearful is to get in better physical shape. But for me, the internal advantages are even more important than the obvious physical benefits. Put simply, exercise builds self-esteem. And self-esteem is the fuel that keeps us running after other people give up. The better you feel about yourself, the more willing you will be to accept those big ideas from others and those hunches from your own computer.

"My own favorite exercise is jogging. It's tough. It's hard. I hate it. But when I get back from my jog, all sweaty and sore, I feel great inside. I look at my body and say, 'I conquered you another day. I'm in control here.'

"When I jog I feel better, my legs and stomach look better, my face looks thinner, I sleep better, I eat better. But the major benefit is the inner strength that I develop. It builds my self-esteem.

"Now, to compound the effect, at the same time I jog I also listen to tapes. It's a wonderful way to exercise body, spirit and mind simultaneously. It only takes twenty to thirty minutes a day. But if you can conquer yourself in this one area of your life, success comes easier in every other area. It builds your desire to be a better person and to be less influenced by the world around you.

"To review, then. First, set your goal. Second, stretch your grooves with tapes and books. Third, follow your hunches. And, fourth, stretch your muscles. Develop these habits.

"This is the formula I have followed. When I got started, I was living in a student apartment with five other single guys. Rent was fifty-five dollars a month. I was making two hundred dollars a month at odd jobs while going to school. I set my goal then to have a hundred-thousand-dollar net worth by the time I was thirty. A hundred-thousand-dollar goal was the biggest goal that my unstretched mind grooves could hang onto. Slowly, the grooves in my mind expanded. I read great books. I listened to great tapes. I followed my hunches. My wealth grew—inside and out.

"It wasn't easy for me, and it won't be easy for you to establish new success habits. I've taken you out of your world and placed you temporarily in an unnatural environment—a fancy hotel for a couple of days of high-powered training with camera crews and experts hovering about. But when you leave this unreal environment, you'll return to your own world, where a habit pattern is established. This habit pattern includes friends and family pressures, support systems (or failure systems), demanding children, ringing telephones, job and money problems. If you don't form new success habits, you'll automatically fall back into a pattern of failure.

"But if you daily stretch your brain and the muscles of your body, you'll form new habits that will, in time, lead to the stretching of your pocketbook.

"Well, that's enough talk. Let's plug in a tape from our success collection and go stretch our brains and our muscles. If you haven't done this for a while, take a moment to warm up. You don't want to blow a gasket."

With that, we jogged off, with positive thoughts resounding in our ears.

KNOWING IS NOT ENOUGH; WE MUST APPLY. WILLING IS NOT
ENOUGH; WE MUST DO.—Goethe

TO KNOW AND NOT TO DO IS NOT YET TO KNOW.—Zen saying

EXPERIENCE IS KNOWING A LOT OF THINGS YOU SHOULDN'T DO.
—William S. Knudsen

9

EXPERIENCE IS THE BEST TEACHER

1. _____

Any good teacher knows that the ratio of teaching effectiveness is
one by hearing, ten by seeing and one thousand by doing. Translated, that means the best way to teach is to get the student as close
to the actual experience as possible. That's why I had them do cold
calling on the telephone instead of just teaching them about telephone technique. That's also why I took them jogging—instead of
lecturing them on the benefits of exercise.

And now I wanted them to experience the negotiating process.

After sprucing up from our morning jog, we jammed into the
rented yellow Cadillac and made our way to visit a property owned
by a flexible seller whom Mary had turned up through her phone
prospecting the night before. As we drove to our appointment, I
filled them in on what to expect.

"What happens when we go inside, Bob?" Mary asked.

"You take charge, Mary. It's your don't-wanter. My own preference is to wander around the house alone, but some sellers like to show you through to point out special features. While you inspect the house you try to assess the seller's flexibility in price and terms."

"We already know he's indicated a flexibility in terms," Mary reminded us. "His ad said he wanted five hundred dollars down. And he said on the phone he was willing to carry financing."

"In the jargon, 'terms' is another way to say financing. It includes down payment, interest rate, monthly payment and the length of the loan. As buyers, we want to negotiate the best terms possible. We do this by offering lower interest rates and longer payback periods. This makes for lower payments. You might start the process by saying, 'Your ad indicated some flexibility in financing. What did you have in mind?' Notice I avoid mentioning numbers. If he mentions numbers, you can indicate your position by wincing or saying, 'That's a bit steep, isn't it?' From there you can move on to price. 'How flexible can you be on the price?' If he balks on price, you might say, 'Could you be more flexible on the price if I gave you more down or a fast closing?' You're trying to gauge the seller's flexibility."

"Another way to do this is to talk in terms of the seller's equity. This seller has a price of about forty thousand dollars and loans of twenty-one thousand. Subtract the latter from the former, and that leaves an equity of nineteen thousand. You might test the seller's firmness by saying, 'Let's see, if the price were thirty-eight for a quick closing, the loans are twenty-one, that means your equity is about seventeen, which you have agreed to carry, right?' If he says yes, then you say, 'Suppose, instead of carrying the financing, you were cashed out. Would you take twelve or thirteen thousand cash for your equity?' I first try to establish the fact that the seller is willing to carry financing with a small down. Then I try to see if he will discount his equity for cash. The lower the price, the greater the profit. But all negotiations are different. If this seller seems flexible enough, we'll make him an offer."

"Where will I get an offer form?" Mary asked, concerned.

"You have forms in your MasterPlanner. I'll help you fill it out. Do you have a checkbook with you?"

"Uh, yes."

"Do you have five hundred dollars in your account?"

She shook her head. I could tell she was embarrassed.

"How about one hundred?"

"I don't think so."

"Fifty?" I asked, a bit embarrassed for having asked.

"Maybe twenty," she admitted.

"This is wonderful," I said in an attempt to be positive. "OK. Give him a hundred-dollar check and in the bottom left-hand corner write 'to be cashed at closing.' If he asks about that, I'll come to your rescue with an answer like 'That's the way she always buys property.' But let's see how far you can go on your own."

As we drove through the neighborhood, I pointed out the clues to look for. We spotted several for-sale-by-owner signs. Nora was concerned about the number of houses for sale. I told her that in some cases, this can work to the buyer's advantage because the more competition the more flexible the sellers have to be.

"Here's the house," Philip said as we pulled up across the street from a cookie-cutter suburban home with a For Sale sign on the front lawn. The neighboring houses were well cared for. We quickly cased the house. It had a one-car garage. The lawn was green and mowed, with well-placed flower beds. I pointed out the gutters and cautioned them to look closer for peeling paint and water damage. Before we went to the door, I encouraged them to scour the inside of the house for problems—leaky faucets, water stains on ceilings and floors, rotting floors, especially around the toilets, worn carpets and other wear and tear.

Mary rang the doorbell. The seller, a thin man in perhaps his early forties, came to the door, gave us an information sheet on the home and invited us in.

All of the preliminary clues—the well-manicured lawn and the well-thought-out information sheet—were indications that the seller was well organized and in no hurry to sell.

Steve looked down the information sheet and spotted something. "You have an appraisal at forty-four thousand dollars?" he asked.

"We had a contract to sell this house. Got to the point that a bank set up the paperwork and did the appraisal. But the buyers couldn't qualify."

I raised my eyebrows so that Mary could tell that this was an important piece of information. Steve broke the silence.

"Neat little yard you got back here."

"Nice house," Mary added, obviously impressed with the cleanliness. "I can tell you put a lot of work into it."

"Yeah," the seller replied, "it's also got a new air conditioner and a new roof."

"Then why do you want to leave?" I said, fishing for information.

"We're buying a bigger home."

"Are you anxious to move?"

"Not really. We're ready but not anxious."

Here was another clue. We continued to look through the upper floor. Then we went down in the basement, where the seller showed us the new air-conditioning system. Mary noticed some water problems, and the seller explained that he had removed a tree in the backyard and that ever since, when it rained, the water poured into the basement through a window.

"Do you have that solved now?" I asked.

"Not yet."

"So it will need to be repaired again."

"Yeah."

"Tell me about the offer that didn't go through," I asked.

"It started out at forty-two five, and they wanted us to pay the closing costs, so we raised the price to forty-four. But then they couldn't qualify for the loan."

"Have you already made arrangements for financing the new house you bought?" I continued. "Are you just waiting for a sale on this house before you move into that one?"

"We already put some money down. I need seven thousand dollars down from this home to cover closing costs. Plus my wife wants to buy all new drapes and furniture and everything."

"But didn't your ad say you only needed five hundred dollars down?"

"Well, I figured the buyer could get a new ninety percent loan. It's appraised for forty-four thousand. So you'd be able to borrow at least thirty-nine thousand. You'd only have to put five hundred down. Thirty-nine five is a damn good price. The guy across the street bought his house two years ago for thirty-nine thousand, and he doesn't have central air or a garage."

I returned to his first point by saying, "You know, it's hard to qualify for new loans these days."

The seller agreed. "You almost have to be gold. But if I can't sell it

myself, I'll list it again. And if it doesn't sell, I'll just refinance it myself and rent it out for enough to cover the payments."

"How do you feel about being a landlord?" Mary astutely asked.

"That's my last resort. I've rented stuff before, and it's a big hassle."

Mary changed the subject. "Mind if we look more upstairs?"

The seller went upstairs, leaving Mary and me alone to review
some of the facts we had gathered.

"Did you notice he wasn't very flexible?" I asked.

"He wasn't? I couldn't tell," she said, shaking her head.

"He didn't want to carry any financing. Wanted us to get a new
loan. Said he'd keep it if he couldn't sell it. That doesn't sound very
flexible to me. Did you notice how I kept mentioning the problems
he has—as a way of reminding him that his property is less than
perfect? That has a way of bringing the seller back to reality. It was
real smart of you to mention landlording. That got him thinking. If
you had to score this seller's flexibility thus far, what would you
give him? A one, two or three?"

"He's between a one and a two."

"Good guess. Wants his price and his terms. Closer to a one. But
let's not give up yet. Let's see if he'd take a substantially lower price
for quick cash."

We made our way back upstairs. Philip and Nora were asking
questions about the area, the garage, the hardwood floors. At the
proper moment Mary approached the seller.

"I want to ask you what would your equity be in the house if you
sold for thirty-nine thousand dollars?"

"Let's see...." The seller scratched his head. "At thirty-nine
thousand it would probably be eighteen thousand."

"Okay. If you could get twelve or thirteen thousand cash within,
say, thirty days, would you be willing then ...?"

"Twelve or thirteen what?"

Mary became flustered at not knowing what to say next. She
changed the subject. Then she excused herself and whispered to me,
"He doesn't really understand and neither do I."

I decided to step in. We found the seller in the kitchen, where he
was explaining how it was only eight years old.

"Excuse me, sir," I said. "Getting to the bottom line, if you could
cash out quickly, would you be willing to come off your forty thou-

sand price? You never can tell how long it will take you to find a buyer."

"No. I'll just wait till I can get thirty-nine five."

"Even so," I countered, "sooner or later it'll cost you an extra thousand or two."

"No, I'm not going to drop my price much."

"Well, what price would you come down to?" I asked.

"Not below thirty-nine five. Why should I?"

I knew that I was just arguing now for the sake of arguing. Obviously, the seller wasn't the slightest bit flexible. Normally, I would have politely excused myself and been on my way to the next, perhaps more flexible seller. But for the benefit of my watching Challenge team, I continued, "So you're saying, 'I'm firm on my price, and I've got to have all cash.' Is that what you're trying to say?"

"Yes, but this house is a good deal. Even at thirty-nine thousand. I've checked most of the homes around here. . . ."

"Tell you what," I said finally. "We'll send you an offer in the mail. If you haven't been able to sell, in a few months, our offer might start to look a lot better."

"Sure. Definitely, as a last alternative."

"Thanks," Mary said as we left. "I appreciate your time."

We all got in the car, and as we drove off we processed the experience together.

"OK," I asked them, "was he a don't-wanter? Obviously not. He wouldn't come off either his price or his terms. Take it or leave it. Mary, I thought you told me last night that he was willing to carry financing."

"That's what he told me . . . at least that's what I thought he said." She was learning to be more careful in her analysis.

"We took an hour and a half to inspect this property," I continued, "but it was a valuable experience—good practice. Now you know what a cubic zirconium looks like."

Nora had a brainstorm. "Well, right now he's a zircon, but a couple of months down the road, he could become a diamond."

"Right. Never can tell when the wind will change. Mary should still send him an offer. But can you see that we could have saved a lot of time and gas money by asking better questions over the phone? I try not to inspect a property until I'm certain the seller is a genuine don't-wanter. If a property fits within my very narrow set of parameters, I proceed further. If not, I keep looking. It's that simple. Let's score this one, shall we?

> Seller flexibility? One.
> Location? Two.
> Financing? One.
> Price? Two.
> Condition? Three.
> Total: nine.

"What do you think?"

"Well," Philip observed, "he was selling below the appraised value. Couldn't we have profited from it?"

"Not unless we could buy it at least twenty percent below market. The seller claims it's worth $44,000, but what if it's only worth $42,-000? Then it's only ten percent below market. We need to get the price to $35,000 or lower—twenty percent to thirty percent off."

"I'm still not sure of what to ask," said Mary.

"Just remember the five questions of value—flexibility, location, financing, price and condition. With practice, you'll become as confident as you were yesterday morning picking a diamond out of fifty pieces of glass."

The next experience I had designed for them was to take them to a title company and walk them through a simulated closing on a house. Within a matter of weeks each of them would be required to sit at a closing table, white-knuckled and nervous.

It was time for a dry run.

2.

In the center of downtown Clayton, on a corner across from the park where we had jogged that morning, is a brown, two-story brick building with white trim. Emblazoned on the front in big black letters are the words "Ticor Title Company." The Challenge team arrived just after lunch and was greeted by Nancy, a senior closing officer for the firm. She ushered us into a quiet conference room in the back on the main floor. We sat around the conference table.

"Nancy," I explained, "is an expert in closing property. She makes sure all of the details come together smoothly."

She took my cue. "This is a closing room," she began. "As soon as you have a signed contract between you and a seller, you bring it, and any other pertinent information, to me. We'll sit down here and create an escrow account for this transaction. We call this 'opening escrow.' That's just a fancy term for starting a file of all of the necessary documents to close the transaction—the sales contract, the earnest money and your loan commitment letter if a new loan is required."

"Nancy, if I could interrupt for a second," I said, "we haven't yet discussed the details of an earnest-money agreement. Earnest money is your deposit to hold the property. If we back out, the seller keeps our money, in some cases, as damages. Nancy will hold this deposit until the closing. If there is any dispute between you and the seller about the earnest money, she'll keep it until things are resolved."

"Correct," Nancy said. "Now, let me tell you about title insurance. Ticor is in the insurance business. We insure titles. The policy that we issue guarantees that there aren't any defects in the title to the property you are buying. For instance, suppose an heir, who was thought to be dead, turns up ten years later claiming an interest in the property that you now own. Since we insured your title, it's our problem to work things out with the heir. Or suppose Mary and John Doe own a piece of property as husband and wife. If John deeded his interest to another party without Mary's consent, this would become a cloud on the title of the property. And you wouldn't want to buy that property until that situation had been resolved. So we search the entire chain of deed. We report any clouds, liens or judgments against the property on what we call a title commitment. And if there's anything on the title commitment report that you or the lenders don't like, we work toward solving these things before closing."

"Just as everyone needs life and health insurance," I added, "every buyer needs property insurance. Nancy guarantees us that the property we are buying actually belongs to the seller."

Nora joined in. "That reminds me. Someone once sold me some property he didn't own. When I went to the title company to search the title, I learned that of the ten lots he was selling, he didn't actually own them all. He's still got $295 of my money."

"I'll help you avoid that mistake in the future," Nancy said.

"What kind of costs might be expected at a closing?" I asked.

"To handle the paperwork, the closing costs run anywhere between thirty-five and one hundred dollars. The next cost would be for the title insurance. The premium for title insurance is based on the selling price of the property. It's not like car insurance, where you have annual premiums. For instance, on a hundred-thousand-dollar house, the approximate premium would be a one-time six-hundred dollar charge. Even after you sell the property, you are still insured for the period of time that you owned the property."

"In some states, the buyer pays for the title insurance," I said. "In other states, it is customary for the seller to pay this. In still other states, only attorneys are allowed to handle closings and check title. Nancy, how is this handled in Missouri?"

"The seller pays it."

"Good. Now, there are other miscellaneous closing costs associated with buying property. This might include fees paid to banks to make loans, appraisal fees, insurance and tax impounds, miscellaneous transfer costs."

"Correct," Nancy said. "You'll find that the largest costs in any real estate purchase are generally the loan closing costs on new financing—points and lender's fees."

"To clarify," I said. "A 'point' is an up-front fee charged by the bank for the privilege of borrowing their money. One point equals one percent of the face amount of the loan. There are usually one to four points involved with any new long-term loan. So on a fifty-thousand-dollar loan one point would be one percent of fifty thousand, or five hundred dollars; two points would be a thousand dollars; three points, fifteen hundred dollars, and so on. Most of the time the buyer pays these points—except on some government-backed loans. But remember, everything is negotiable. There are always creative ways to come up with closing costs without having to pay them out of your own pocket."

"Now," Nancy continued, "let's cover two very important documents. The note and the trust deed. Here I have a standard St. Louis County note." She held up a piece of legal-sized paper for us to see. "When filled out, it shows the amount of the loan that is being made to you, the interest rate, the amount of the monthly principal, interest and payments, and when the payments are due. This note in turn is secured in the state of Missouri by a deed of trust. A deed of trust actually secures the amount of money that the lender's lending you on this note with the property that you're buying. In other words, if

THE RESULTS OF INITIATIVE

Some years ago, three brothers left the farm to work in the city. They were all hired by the same company at the same pay. Three years later, Jim was being paid $500 a month, Frank was receiving $1,000, but George was now making $1,500.

Their father decided to visit the employer and find out the basis for the unequal pay. The employer listened to the confused father and said, "I will let the boys explain for themselves."

Jim was summoned to the supervisor's office and told, "Jim, I understand that Far East Importers has just brought in a large transport plane loaded with Japanese import goods. Will you please go over to the airport and get a cargo inventory?"

Three minutes later, Jim returned to the office. "The cargo was one thousand bolts of Japanese silk," Jim reported. "I got the information over the telephone from a member of the crew."

When Jim left, Frank, the $1,000-a-month brother, was called. "Frank," said the supervisor, "I wish you'd go out to the airport and get an inventory of the cargo plane which was just brought in by Far East Importers."

An hour later, Frank was back in the office with a list showing that the plane carried 1,000 bolts of Japanese silk, 500 transistor radios, and 1,000 hand-painted bamboo trays.

George, the $1,500-a-month brother, was given identical instructions.

Working hours were over when he finally returned. "The transport plane carried one thousand bolts of Japanese silk," he began. "It was on sale at sixty dollars a bolt, so I took a two-day option on the whole lot. I have wired a designer in New York offering the silk at seventy-five dollars a bolt. I expect to have the order tomorrow. I also found five hundred transistor radios, which I sold over the telephone at a profit of $2.30 each. There were a thousand bamboo trays, but they were of poor quality, so I didn't try to do anything with them."

When George left the office, the employer smiled. "You probably noticed," he said, "that Jim doesn't do what he's told, Frank does only what he's told, but George does without being told."

The future is full of promise for one who shows initiative.

—Anonymous

you don't pay that note, the trustee for the bank will foreclose on the property."

"To say it in fewer legal terms," I added, "A note is an I.O.U.—'I promise to pay you this much.' The seller says, 'I believe you but just to be sure I want you to sign this other piece of paper called a trust deed, or mortgage.' It says, 'If you don't keep your word, you'll have to give the property back.' There are other ramifications, but this is the general picture. Speaking of foreclosure, there were people who this very day, about an hour ago, lost their property."

"Yes," Nancy said, "it happens almost every day, at noon, on the steps of the courthouse."

"Why?" Steve wondered.

"They didn't live up to their agreement with the lender," I answered. "They didn't make their monthly payments—due to divorce, neglect, bankruptcy, unemployment, all kinds of reasons. Dealing in foreclosures is tricky, so I'd be careful.

"Let's review, then, what we've learned," I continued. "We learned that a title company officer, such as Nancy, can help us walk through the myriad details that accompany the purchase and sale of a piece of real estate. I'm sure that most of these details, such as trust deed, settlement costs, and title insurance, went right over your heads. It's all rather confusing at first. But so was baking a cake your first time or learning how to drive a car or preaching your first sermon. It always looks so much worse to the beginner. After your first property, you'll wonder what you were so afraid of. Nancy is an expert at this. Let her be your guide. That's what she gets paid for. Nancy becomes a vital part of your network. It is as if this were your own office and Nancy were on your staff. And you don't have to pay her until she performs. She even tries to make it easy for you to use her."

"Absolutely," Nancy agreed. "We try to make it as convenient for the customer as possible. This is our main office here in Clayton; we also have a city office downtown and offices in West County, South County, North County, Charles County and Jefferson County."

"All successful people rely on a network of experts to call on when necessary" I said. "You have already begun to establish your own success network. You have me, you have Nancy, and you will be adding bankers, accountants, real estate people. This will become your own mastermind group. And having such a mastermind group is essential to all success. It is a wealth secret."

WEALTH SECRET NO. 10. A NETWORK SAVES LEG-WORK.

"That's it for now."

HOW TO FIND THE RIGHT EXPERTS

If you plan to be successful you will need a group of experts to guide you.

Attorney
Accountant
Property Management
Mentor
Realtor
Banker

The key attributes are knowledge and creativity. You are looking for creative blue-vasers, just like yourself, who will persist until they find solutions even to the most difficult problems. These are rare talents, and when you find a particularly creative expert, add his name to your growing network. The following tips will guide you in finding creative local experts to guide you.

1. Word of mouth: by far the most effective method. Ask successful local investors which experts they have found effective. One creative professional can usually recommend other experts to round out your network.
2. Attendance at creative financing seminars: Those experts who frequent seminars are usually interested in self-improvement and enhancing their creativity. Ask for their cards.
3. An investor/expert: Someone who not only provides client services but also invests for his own portfolio is going to be more understanding of your needs and desires. You can find such individuals at local investment club meetings. For names and addresses of the presidents of investment clubs in many major American cities call my toll-free number, 1-800-345-3648.

TO DO GREAT AND IMPORTANT TASKS
TWO THINGS ARE NECESSARY:
A PLAN AND NOT QUITE ENOUGH TIME.—*Quote* magazine

10

THE BIG PICTURE

1. _____

The final session was scheduled in the seminar room at the Daniele Hotel. There were still several vital pieces of the puzzle to be put in place.

"Are your buckets getting full?" I asked.

"I feel like you've got a bucket and I've got a thimble," Karen said. "And my thimble overflowed a long time ago. I'm lost."

"I know how you feel. Just the other day David and I got lost trying to find Nora's house. Took the wrong freeway. We didn't panic. Just pulled out a map, figured out where we were, selected a new route and finally arrived at our destination. That's what a road map does—gives you perspective, the big picture. And if you don't have that, it's easy to get lost.

"Let me illustrate.

"Just before speaking at a conference in Acapulco a few years ago, I had a brainstorm. I ran downstairs to the hotel variety store and bought three copies of an inexpensive local puzzle—a picture of the Hyatt Hotel located on Acapulco Bay. I disassembled one of the puzzles and later dumped the jumble of pieces in front of a couple in the front row at the conference, challenging them to see how fast they could put it back together. I gave the same challenge to another couple, except this time as I dumped the mixed-up pieces in front of them I also gave them a completed puzzle to use for reference. Can you guess which couple finished first?"

"The one that had a clear picture of where they were going," Mary responded.

"The other couple didn't stand a chance. How can you expect to make it without a clear idea of where you are going? Up to this point in our training I have not shared with you a detailed road map— only three vague guidelines: Find it. Fund it. Farm it.

"Now I'm going to furnish each of you a Master Checklist. This will be your road map. If you ever feel confused, not knowing where you are, you can pull out your Master Checklist and check your progress.

MASTER CHECKLIST FOR WEALTH

STEP ONE: FIND IT: FINDING OR CREATING AN OPPORTUNITY

A. Find a Don't-Wanter Situation in a Target Property
—scan ads daily
—own ad
—cards, bumper stickers
—fliers
—Realtors, cold call
—creative Realtors
—other professionals

—investment clubs
—foreclosure sales
—call banks selling
  repossessed property
—mailings to expired listings,
  foreclosures, out-of-state
  owners, divorces, evictions

B. Give a Preliminary Score to the Property (see chart, p. 81)

C. If It Scores Twelve or More, Do Final Score
—neighborhood analysis
—market study
—property inspection form
—estimate of repairs
—verify underlying financing

—appraisal if necessary
—determine market rent
—verify utilities
—if uneasy, check police, city
  planner, other experts

payments, impounds,   —brainstorm with seller
assumability, fees,
balloons, increases

D. Make Offer/Counteroffer
—subject to approval of partner within seven days
—subject to financing, etc., if necessary
—extend closing as far as possible
—get right to show, clean up and/or rent before closing
—give note for earnest money if you don't have money
—get signed offer

STEP TWO: FUND IT: FINDING THE RESOURCES TO FINANCE THE OPPORTUNITY

A. Determine What Resources Will Be Needed to Solve Problem

—long-term financing   —time
—short-term financing   —knowledge
—cash down payments   —courage
—cash for fixup, misc.   —connections
—credit   —creativity
—strong financial statement —talent, skills

B. Locate Long- or Short-Term Financing if Necessary
—call banks, s & l's, and/or finance companies
—choose the best rate and most flexibility
—have at least one backup bank
—get all necessary papers from both institutions
—fill out papers
—start appraisal process

C. Locate Partner if Necessary
—prepare partner evaluation of property
—have constant feelers out for potential partners

- seller   • renter
- investment clubs   • cold calling
- investment seminars   • Realtors
- ad in paper   • friends
- fliers   • relatives

—prepare partnership agreement
—have partner sign necessary documents
—have partner deposit funds into escrow

STEP THREE: FINISH IT: FOLLOW THROUGH ON THE DETAILS

A. Open an Escrow: Name of Company/Closing Date
—get estimate of closing costs
—get preliminary title report
—work closely with title company, Realtor or attorney to get all necessary paperwork ready for closing
—deposit necessary cash, financial statements, etc.
—check with city on zoning, etc., if necessary
—schedule a closing date

B. Prepare Property For Sale if Necessary
—general cleanup
—estimates for fixup
—get partner $ for fixup
—start fixup as needed
—ads in paper
—prepare flier
—distribute flier
—list with Realtor if needed
—run ad for investor seminar
—find a buyer

C. Prepare Property to Rent if Necessary
—general cleanup
—get estimates for fixup
—put ads in paper
—check with rental agencies
—find renter
—inspect property w/renter
—check renter out
—sign rental agreement
—collect rent, deposit
—move renter in

D. Close on the Property

E. Set up Files on Property

F. Open Bank Account for Property if Kept

G. Make Regular Inspections

"Thus far in our training we've spent a lot of time on the first step—find it. It's time to go deeper. As opportunity fishermen, you need to place many lines in the water, each hook with a different kind of bait on it—thus maximizing the possibility of attracting a hungry fish. I suggest that you have a minimum of five lines in the water every single day. You will need to sift through at least five different sources of don't-wanters. Such as running your own ad in the paper or using a creative Realtor.

"As soon as you get a nibble on one of your lines, what do you do?"

"Smile," Steve offered.

"Smile and ask questions. Got to score the property. Last night Mary located a property she thought had a glitter to it. But when she checked further, she found it was a cubic zirconium. But if it had scored well, she would have gone to the next step—writing an offer."

Mary looked puzzled. "And that's where I get lost."

Nora and Steve were also unsure of what to do next. I explained that this situation was particularly tough because the seller really wasn't flexible. Things get a lot easier when you're dealing with a person who is motivated to act. I singled out Philip to drive my point home.

"Philip, it's not easy to sell flowers to someone who doesn't want them. Don't waste your time with him. Similarly, it's not easy to buy property from someone who doesn't really want to sell."

I told them of an airline pilot mentioned in one of their success sampler tapes. Every two weeks he'd have to fly to Dallas to mow the lawns of his investment property. It didn't take him long to become a don't-wanter. I asked them if they would like to know what I would have done if Mary's seller had been flexible.

They all nodded in agreement.

"Let's assume that the seller agreed to accept our offer of $39,500—ten percent below market—with only $500 down. How would we pay him his equity?"

"In monthly payments?"

"Right. We'd assume his loan of $21,000 and on the balance—$18,000 after our $500 down payment—we'd negotiate to pay the seller so much a month. Let's say the bank payments are $200 a month, and the seller will take $200 a month for his equity. Our total monthly payments would be $400."

"But," Steve said, "I don't have four hundred a month to spare."

Philip raised his hand. "And where would I get the five hundred down to buy the property in the first place?"

"You tell me," I shot back, wanting to make him think for himself.

"First I tie the property up with a postdated check for five hundred dollars and a closing in thirty days. Tell me when I'm wrong now."

"You're all right so far," I responded.

"OK," Philip continued, feeling more confident, "then you either sell it or rent it. Probably rent it cause I need a quick five hundred to give the seller for the down payment."

"Not bad for a beginner! You put an ad in the paper and rent it out. When the renter moves in, you charge him the first month's rent and the last month's rent plus a security deposit. That could be as much as fifteen hundred dollars, depending on your market. And with this money you buy the property. The tenant actually buys the property for you. And you'd have several hundred dollars left over for closing costs, repairs or a cushion for future repairs."

I paused a moment to let it sink in. That seemed to solve Philip's problem, but Steve still wanted to know where to get the four hundred dollar monthly mortgage payment. I waited until he came up with the answer himself.

"The tenant pays the four hundred dollars."

"Good. Suppose it's worth $44,000 today, and you increase its value to $48,000 with minor fixup. That means you have an equity of $9,000. The property is now ready to farm—to sell, keep, refinance or trade. Which is the quickest method to yield $5,000 cash?"

"Sell it?" answered Steve hesitantly. "Let somebody dicker with me just enough so I could get five thousand out."

"But it's rented. Who would want to buy it?" I asked, trying to test him.

"An investor," someone guessed.

"Good. An investor who needs a tax shelter. And you can afford to find such an investor because the tenant is making your monthly payments. I can see the lights coming on for Mary."

"Slowly but surely," she said.

I then took them through an analysis of what we would do if Mary's seller had wanted to be cashed out at a low price. This concerned the Challenge team because they couldn't imagine where they could get their hands on a lot of cash. The first step is to get a discount of at least 20 to 30 percent off the market price (not to be confused with asking price). Thus, a $44,000 house should sell for $35,000 or less (80 percent of $44,000). We'd assume the existing $21,000 loan and agree to pay $14,000 cash for the seller's equity by bringing in a partner. Once the property is fixed up, it is sold at its increased value of $48,000. The new buyer refinances the house, and the new loan pays off the existing $21,000 loan, returns your partner's $14,000 down payment and leaves a gross profit of $13,000. As-

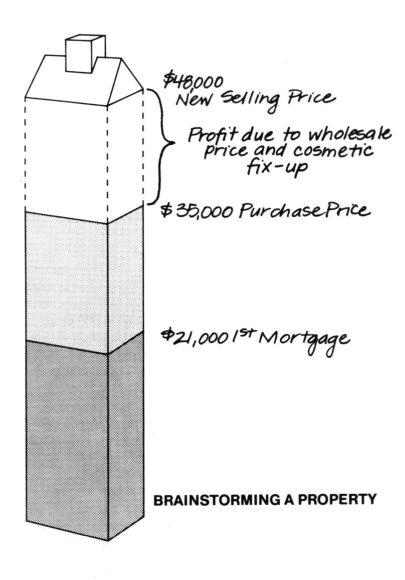

$48,000
New Selling Price

Profit due to wholesale
price and cosmetic
fix-up

$35,000 Purchase Price

$21,000 1st Mortgage

BRAINSTORMING A PROPERTY

suming $3,000 expenses for fixup and financing, you are left with a net profit of $10,000 to split with your partner. Five thousand dollars to him. Five thousand dollars to you. The partner gets a $5,000 return on a short-term $14,000 investment. That's over 30 percent.

Nora raised her hand. "I'm just beginning to realize that flexibility, terms and price are very important."

"It's all part of learning where to tap. For the time being, concentrate on finding motivated sellers. I'll walk you through the negotiation process until you are comfortable with it. It's quite like playing tennis," I said, turning to Steve, who I knew was a tennis buff. "You can't expect to play well the first time you pick up a racket. With practice, you develop a sense of timing, anticipation. Your opponent rushes the net, and you learn to decide in a split second whether to pass him, lob it over him or hit it straight at him. The same holds true with the techniques of negotiating. The seller asks point-blank for an offer. You decide in a split second to change the subject—to lob it over him till later when the pressure's off. The seller asks you how much down payment you have. You pass the ball right by him. You say, 'How much do you need?'

"Sometimes you shoot straight. 'Mr. Seller, let's not play games. I'm an investor. I like to buy properties at bargain prices with small down payments. I can pay cash if the deal is right. If you can win this way, I'll make you an offer. If not, here's my card.' An honest, straightforward approach works wonders with the right seller.

"In any case, always be cordial. You never can tell when a fish might be attracted to your bait. Don't scare them away."

Mary raised her hand. "Speaking of bait, how often should I run an ad in the paper? We didn't get an overwhelming response out of the ad we ran a few days ago."

"All you need is a half-dozen calls a week if they produce a few good leads. And if you can buy just one wholesale property in a year, it will more then recoup the cost of an ad run once a week on Sunday."

"Yeah, that's true," Mary said.

"Suppose no one calls?" I asked. "Change the words. Throw out a different bait. Maybe the fish out there don't like cheese. Try worms. If they don't like worms, try lures. No bites on lures? Try flies. Until you find what the fish are eating that day. But keep trying. In other words, if you snooze, you lose. Most people don't even try. Or they waste time looking for the wrong kind of bargains. They expend

THE FOUR CARDINAL RULES OF NEGOTIATING

1. *Never make an offer until you understand the seller's problem. The first stages of negotiation are for information gathering. Avoid the temptation to jump to solutions. Without proper diagnosis you might be like the doctor who prescribes medicine for the wrong disease.*

2. *Always conduct your negotiation in the context of a win/win philosophy. "This is how you will win, Mr. Seller. This is how I will win. At that price, I can't win. At those terms, you can't win. I don't want you to lose. But I don't want to lose either, etc." This lets the seller know that you are interested in being fair. Being a win/win negotiator may cost you dollars in the short run but will make you more money in the long run.*

3. *In the more advanced stages of negotiation, where solutions to the seller's problem are being discussed, never be the first person to mention a number. Always let the other party make the first move. By avoiding the temptation to mention numbers, you may get the seller to propose a price and terms that could be significantly better than what you had in mind. This one tip alone will save (make) you thousands of dollars over a lifetime of negotiation.*

4. *When forced to mention a number, always start lower than you expect to end up. Why? Because you just might get it and save yourself thousands of dollars. Also, by mentioning a lower number, you leave room for give and take; i.e., the 'let's split the difference' tactic. The other party will be more willing to be flexible if he can see that you are also willing to be flexible.*

enormous amounts of energy pinching pennies—clipping coupons. How much can they save in a year pinching pennies? A hundred dollars? Two hundred? Just one real estate bargain will net more money than a lifetime of pinching pennies. Sometimes there are better ways of making ends meet.

"Be patient. If you didn't feel just a bit confused at this point, it'd be a miracle. Ponder this: You've all heard the story of the movie star who was discovered on a stool at the corner drugstore. Did the movie director give this new starlet a script and put her in a movie the very next day? Of course not! But that's what we did with you. We pulled you out of the corner unemployment line, without training or experience, and put you in front of real cameras to sink or swim. Someday people will watch a video of this and say, 'If they can do it, so can I!'

"Let's break for ten minutes."

2. _____

"If we find a property that looks good, scores well, what is our next step?" I asked as we returned to work.

"We make an offer on it," Steve said.

"So let's write up an offer on the house we saw this morning," I said, holding up a document with tiny print.

"This is a universal earnest-money form. It's designed to be used anywhere in the country, although you will probably be using forms from your own state. Looks real complicated, but it isn't. And yet you'd be surprised how many beginning investors are afraid of this simple piece of paper."

I then took them through the process of filling out the offer, line by line. For a summary of some of the fine points see pages 152–53.

When our discussion was completed, Karen still looked a bit worried. "What happens," she said, "if we agree to buy a property and pay a lot of cash but can't find a partner in time. Do we lose all of our earnest money?"

"That's one of the reasons you offer as little earnest money as possible. And to protect you further, you always include a clause in the conditions section that makes the sale subject to the inspection and approval of your partner. That way, if you can't find a partner, you don't lose your earnest money. How's that for having your cake and eating it too?"

On that note, we took another much-needed break.

3. _____

"Any questions," I asked, hoping to clear up any lingering doubts or fears before the end of the day. It was three o'clock in the afternoon, and time was running out.

Philip raised his hand. "How can I persuade a partner to give me,

Earnest Money Receipt and Offer to Purchase

"This is a legally-binding contract; if not understood, seek competent advice."

- Always sign your offers with your name followed by the words and/or assigns. This makes it easier to deal with partners.

- The legal description is the legal mumbo jumbo for the exact way the property is described on the county courthouse record. It usually tells the lot number, subdivision number and the dimensions of the property. You will rarely have an exact legal description when you write an offer. So just write "to be provided at closing" in the space provided. Your title company officer will research this information for you.

- This includes all items presently attached to the premises including plumbing fixtures, roller shades, curtain rods, etc. Specific exceptions should be noted. As a general rule you will always write 'no exceptions' and let the seller tell you otherwise.

- Personal property is anything that's not attached such as washers, dryers, refrigerators, etc. Always write your offer to include such items. The seller might just be willing to part with them. Remember to give in easily on the little unimportant things like personal property in order to prepare the climate for the seller to give in on the large important items like price and terms. We are business people. We can do without the washer and dryer but we absolutely have to have either our price or terms or both.

- Earnest money deposit. Try to keep this figure low as possible. But high enough to not insult the seller. Start at $100 and move up as needed.

1. **Date and Place of Offer:** _____ 19____ , _____ (city)

2. **Principals:** The undersigned Buyer _____ agrees to buy and Seller agrees to sell, according to the indicated terms and conditions, the property described as follows:

3. **Property:** located at _____ (street address) _____ (city)

with the following legal description: _____

including any of the following items if at present attached to the premises: plumbing, heating, and cooling equipment, including stoker and oil tanks, fixtures, roller shades, curtain rods and fixtures, draperies, venetian blinds, window and door screens, towel racks, linoleum and other attached floor coverings, screen doors, storm windows, attached TV antenna, mailboxes, all trees and shrubs, and any other fixtures, EXCEPT _____ years

The following personal property shall also be included as part of the purchase: _____
At the close of the transaction, the Seller, at his expense, shall provide the Buyer with a Bill Of Sale containing a detailed inventory of the _____

4. **Earnest Money Deposit:** Agent (or Seller) acknowledges receipt from Buyer of _____ dollars
$_____ in the form of ( ) **cash**; ( ) personal check; ( ) cashier's check; ( ) promissory note at _____ % interest
or other _____
as earnest money deposit to secure and apply on this purchase. Upon acceptance of this agreement in writing and delivery of same to Buyer, in the listing Realtor's trust account or _____ closing.

5. **Purchase Price:** The total purchase price of the property shall be _____

6. **Payment:** Purchase price is to be paid by Buyer as follows: Aforedescribed earnest money deposit. _____
Additional payment due upon acceptance of this offer _____
Additio_____
Balance _____

- There are several ways of paying earnest money. Cash or cashier's check: I don't recommend this method. A check is fine if you have money in your account. Using a promissory note is another alternative. The title company or real estate company generally holds the earnest money in escrow.

- Always start lower than what you are willing to settle for. It leaves room for negotiation.

• Title can be vested by *Warrantee Deed* or *Trust Deed.* Most states use Trust Deeds today. Have your title company officer explain the ramifications of both. Just write 'to be designated at closing'.

• The fine print explains that the seller pays for the cost of title search. In some states it is customary for the buyer to pay for the title search and title insurance. This is negotiable anywhere in the country regardless of what is customary.

• This line is very important. Write *'no exceptions'* in this blank.

• Generally, a long closing benefits the buyer. Try for thirty to sixty days on a normal closing. When new bank financing is involved, sixty to ninety days.

• In this area we designate the condition which we expect to be met in order for us to buy the property including such as but not limited to: —subject to inspection and approval of partners —subject to financing —subject to fixing obvious laws

• The quicker you have the right of possession, the sooner you can begin to reap the financial benefits.

(This is not intended to be an exhaustive study of the subject of earnest money offers. An excellent book on the subject is *'How to Write a Nothing Down Offer'.* For more information call 1-800-345-3648.)

7. **Title:** Seller agrees to furnish good and marketable title to the Buyer of a good and marketable title ... Deed or ...

8. **Special Representations:** Seller warrants and represents to Buyer (1) that the subject property is connected to ( ) public sewer system; ( ) private water system, ( ) city water system, and that the following special improvements are included in the sale: ( ), lawn sprinkling; (2) that the Seller knows of no material structural defects; (3) that all electrical wiring, heating, cooling, and plumbing systems are free lighting; (4) that the Seller has no notice from any government agency of any violation or knowledge of probable violation notice or knowledge of planned or commenced public improvements which may result in special assessments or otherwise directly and mi knowledge of any liens to be assessed against the property, EXCEPT _____

9. **Escrow Instructions:** This sale shall be closed on or before _____ 19___ by _____ or such other closing agent as mutually agreed upon by Buyer and Seller. Buyer and Seller will, immediately on demand, deposit with closing agent all instruments and monies required to complete the purchase in accordance with the provisions of this agreement, Contract of Sale or Instrument of Conveyance to be made in the name of _____

10. **Closing Costs and Pro-Ration:** Seller agrees to pay for title insurance policy, preliminary title report (if requested), termite inspection as set forth below, real estate commission, cost of preparing and recording any corrective instruments, and one-half of the escrow fees. Buyer agrees to be met in order for us to ... of conveyance, all costs or expenses in securing new financing or assuming existing financing, and one-half of the escrow fees. Taxes for the current y... rent rental or lease agreements prior to closing. liens, shall be pro-rated as of closing. Renters' security deposits shall ...

11. **Termite Inspection:** Seller agrees, at his expense, to provide written ... property is free of termite infestation. In the event termite are found, the Seller shall have the property treated at his expense and provide accepta... actual repairs are required by reason of termite damage as established by acceptable certification. Seller agrees to make necessary repairs or t... he right to accept the property "as is" with a credit of $500 to the Buyer at closing, or the Buyer may terminate this agreement with the earnest mo... er does not agree to pay all costs of treatment and repair.

12. **Conditions of Sale:** The following conditions shall also apply, and ... , prevail and control:

13. **Liability and Maintenance:** Seller shall maintain subject property, including landscaping, in good condition until the date of transfer of title or possession by Buyer, whichever occurs first. All risk of loss and destruction of property, and all expenses of insurance, shall be borne by the Seller until the date of possession. If the improvements on the property are destroyed or materially damaged prior to closing, then the Buyer shall have the right to declare this agreement null and void, and the earnest money deposit and all other sums paid by Buyer toward the purchase price shall be returned to the Buyer forthwith.

14. **Possession:** The Buyer shall be entitled to possession of property upon closing or _____ 19____.

15. **Default:** In the event the Buyer fails to complete the purchase as herein provided, the earnest money deposit shall be retained by the Seller as the total and entire liquidated damages. In the event the Seller fails to perform any condition of the sale as herein provided, then the Buyer, may, at his option, treat the contract as terminated, and all payments made by the Buyer hereunder shall be returned to the Buyer forthwith, provided the Buyer may, at his option, treat this agreement as being in full force and effect with the right to action for specific performance and damages. In the event that either Buyer, Seller, or Agent shall institute suit to enforce any rights hereunder, the prevailing party shall be entitled to court costs and a reasonable attorney's fee.

a total stranger, ten thousand dollars cash for a real estate investment?"

I decided to return to an analogy from Philip's frame of reference. He had told me at the break of an experience selling roses when he had gone from failure to success. I wanted to illustrate that he had the answers to most of his own questions.

"Remember the afternoon when you were having a tough time selling roses? You decided to try a new strategy on the very next couple to come along. You ran up to the man and said something. What was it?"

"Say, 'I love you' with a rose."

"What a line! What was the price of a rose before you changed your strategy."

"A dollar."

"A dollar! And you couldn't give them away. After you changed your strategy, what did you charge?"

"Two-fifty."

"And was the man glad to pay it?"

"He told me he'd have paid four dollars if I'd asked it."

"Where did that idea come from? From you. You didn't need a fancy expert. When you have a problem to solve, your creative juices start to flow, and soon the answer is presented to you. All creative people will tell you that their creativity increases dramatically the closer they get to the deadline when the solution is required. So what does this have to do with finding partners and convincing them to lend you money? Let's use our own creativity to come up with some solutions to that problem, right now."

We took a few minutes to brainstorm several ways of finding potential partners. I just asked questions, and they filled in the blanks with their own answers. This was part of my strategy of building their self-esteem by allowing them the experience of using their brains—of seeing that they could independently use their own common sense to solve most of their problems.

We came up with six top sources of potential partners:

1. friends and family
2. investment clubs
3. referrals and word of mouth
4. newspaper ads; i.e., "Earn 37% return on prime St. Louis real estate. Call Nora 555-1234"

5. fliers placed in high-potential areas—i.e., near doctors' offices; they have little time and lots of tax problems
6. investment seminars

"Concerning this last point," I said, "Steve and Mary have already had several calls on their ad for an investment seminar. You can organize a seminar in the near future where you take sixty to ninety minutes to teach people the same wealth secrets that I have taught you. Then share with them the details of the properties that you have found. They may become interested enough to help fund some of your deals. And that is an excellent way to build your investor network.

"For instance, on our sample property, you'd call one of your prospective partners and say, 'Are you free for lunch? I'd like to show you my latest bargain. It's a single-family home located in a good area; it's worth $44,000. We can acquire it for $31,000. It has a low-interest-rate assumable loan of $21,000. It will take $10,000 to cash the seller out. I expect to refinance it and have your money back to you within ninety days. Then we'll sell it. I can't guarantee anything, of course, but I do expect to net between $5,000 and $10,000.' If he seems interested, you make an appointment to show him. "The most important thing to know about dealing with partners," I summarized, "is that it doesn't matter how weak you are as long as the bargains you find are strong. If you find enough good deals, they'll soon come to realize that they need you just as much as you need them.

"You have to let your partner begin to appreciate the contribution you are making to the partnership. He may begin to believe, mistakenly, that his money is much more important than your bargain-finding ability.

"You see, Mr. Investor," I said, playing the role of the bargain finder, "there are two kinds of resources. There are nonfinancial resources and financial resources. Your contribution to the partnership is financial: your cash, credit, cash flow, equity or financial statement. These are important. My contribution is nonfinancial: time, knowledge, courage, skill, ability. Both are necessary. That is why we split profits equally.

"Now I know that this sounds very simplistic," I said, returning to teaching. "Yes, there are many t's to cross and i's to dot until you reach your first five-thousand-dollar goal. But in time, you'll build yourself a network—a creative realtor, an understanding title company officer, an adventuresome banker, a cooperative attorney, a few willing investors. Your reputation for fairness and professionalism will precede you. And in a few short months you'll look back and be amazed at how far you have come. Your dreams will begin to be realized. Philip, you'll become a businessman. Steve and Mary will start their own church."

"And," Nora added. "I'll have my resort. And you'll all be able to stay free."

She laughed, and we all laughed with her.

"Any final questions?" I asked. "Are you feeling a little bit better this afternoon than you did yesterday?"

"Yes, a lot better," someone responded.

"This is the first time," Mary said.

"Remember what it was like yesterday?" I asked.

"Oh, yes, confusions," Steve said.

"Total chaos," Nora added.

Mary sat back and closed her eyes. "I remember that feeling. It hasn't been that long ago."

"It's not easy to climb mountains. The weather is not always clear and crisp. Often the fog rolls in, the wind blows, it's cold. You get confused. But every once in a while the fog clears away, the clouds part and you catch a glimpse of the peaks up above you. You are exhilarated to see your goal. You can always radio me from wherever you are on the mountain. I'll give you encouragement. I know that you can make it.

"Now, let's break till this evening. Supper in my suite at 7:00 P.M. I want to introduce you to some special people."

IT AINT'T BRAGGING IF YOU REALLY DONE IT.—Dizzy Dean

11

"IF THEY CAN DO IT, YOU CAN DO IT"

"I've got a surprise for you," I said, handing each of them a small box. "Your business cards have come back from the printer. It's official. You're in business!"

Everyone clapped.

I looked at each excited face. We all sat on the sectional couch in the royal-blue and white presidential suite of the Daniele Hotel. Only yesterday morning we had begun our journey with a sumptuous breakfast in this very room. Where had the time gone?

When the excitement subsided, I continued, "Let me introduce you to some special people." I gestured toward three strangers who were sitting with us on the couch. "Each has a unique story to tell. Mickey Ann Parker from Portland, Oregon. Jeff Rickerson, a fellow Missourian from across the state. And Bruce Fanning of Colorado Springs, Colorado.

"Their stories contain a common thread. Just like Thomas Edison, who failed thousands of times before he was successful in perfecting the light bulb, each of these three continued to fail until they were successful.

"Mickey Ann, tell us a little bit about yourself."

Mickey Ann was a modestly dressed woman with graying hair and a pleasant smile sitting next to Mary. She wrung her hands slightly as if she was nervous.

"Well, about fifteen years ago I was living in the Seattle area where Boeing had its headquarters. It was a bad time for Boeing, and they were laying off people right and left. One day, someone offered to sell me their house. 'Just take over my payments,' they said. It seemed like a good deal. I'd just come out of a bad marriage that had resulted in a bankruptcy. So I bought it and rented it out. Since that one went well, I picked up another one for my retirement. And then one for each of my four kids. Pretty soon I had five houses. I was very lucky then. I ended up picking up twenty-one houses this way. And then my luck ran out. I made the mistake of marrying again." She laughed nervously. "It was the worst mistake of my entire life! Sometimes we don't use our heads, you know?

"Anyhow, I wheeled and dealed and ended up in four and a half years with ninety-seven rental units, and forty acres of Indian timberland on the coast—over a million dollars' worth in all. Oh, I thought I was big stuff! I was feeling very good with my future all laid out. And then, the marriage didn't work out. In fact, it was a disaster.

"My attorney, handling the divorce, cheated me out of every single piece of property. I didn't get one penny out of any of it. I got him disbarred, but I didn't get any of the property back. And so I ended right back where I started."

She began to ramble, unsure exactly of what she should say. I could tell that the cameras were bothering her. It was time to gently nudge her into sharing the story I had brought her to St. Louis to tell us.

"Mickey Ann," I interrupted, "how did you come in contact with me?"

"I wrote you a letter after I went to one of your free seminars," she said.

"Why did you write me that letter?"

"Because I was so mad! I wanted to go to your seminar, but I couldn't afford the $495. And I was so discouraged—depressed. I'd been out of steady work for over three years."

"Let me share part of Mickey's letter with you," I said to the group. She writes:

> Let me tell you what it's like to be unwanted and rejected—almost daily—for over three years. You acquire a feeling of worthlessness that produces a depression that won't go away. You feel that if the world can't see that you have some value—something to offer— there is not much use to go on. You don't know if you'll be able to pay the rent, much less put food on your table. You begin to sell off your belongings to make ends meet (for almost a year I had to sleep on the floor because I had to sell my bed). When something breaks, you cannot afford to get it fixed or replaced. It doesn't make any difference how badly you need a doctor, you couldn't pay him anyhow. You lose hope. So, I would like you to consider this kind of hopelessness when you make claims that someone from the unemployment lines can make good. You know not of what you speak! You are successful and have absolutely no idea what people in my situation (and there are many of us: intelligent, capable, educated) are like. For us, life is hopeless and we only cuss the fact that we wake up alive every morning.

So I immediately wrote back. Basically, what did I tell you, Mickey Ann?"

"You told me that if I had done it once I could do it again—just get out there and do it. And I wrote back and told you that you just didn't understand what it's like to be poor! I tried to explain all the feelings that were inside of me—what it's like. . . ." She broke down. "I'll cry if I do. . . ."

The whole room was caught up in emotion. The Challenge team knew exactly how she was feeling.

"It's all right," I said.

She took a moment to regain her composure.

"No one can understand what it's like. You can't go looking for properties because you don't have the gas. Even if you did, you don't dare leave the house because the phone might ring with someone offering you a job. You eat oatmeal every meal for maybe two or three months until you run out. Then, when eggs go on sale, you eat hard-boiled eggs—one egg a meal for two or three months at a time. It's that kind of existence. When I wrote you, I saw no glimmer of hope out there. I was really ready to do it in."

"Do it in?"

"I didn't see any reason to live anymore. My kids were turned against me because I was such a failure. Nobody had any use for me. I didn't have any use for myself! I felt like such a failure!" She paused again to get a grip on her emotions. "But when I got your letter, I thought, 'If he really thinks I can do this—if he has faith in me—I can't let him down. I've at least got to try.'

"So I went out immediately and found a deal. I knew what to do. I'd done it before. I'd just gotten depressed. It wasn't the best deal in the world. But it was a start. It isn't even in my name—it's a lease option. I used my hang glider for a down payment. That was a real sacrifice—to risk losing my hang glider!"

"Mickey Ann had lost hope," I commented after the laughter had subsided. "I just helped her find it again. In her next letter to me she said:

> Before I got your letter, I was so low that I was thinking seriously of taking my own life. But now, I have renewed hope. I still don't know how I'll pay this month's rent, nor can I buy groceries, but at least I can see a light at the end of the tunnel. Before, there was just the tunnel—with no end to it—just day after day of the same misery. I still don't have as much courage as you would like for me to have . . . but give me time. It's a long way back.

Mickey Ann has come a long way back. Tying up the first property gave her renewed confidence. Then she got another property. And then another. Now she's even starting a new business."

"Several years ago," Mickey Ann explained, taking my cue, "I had a necklace that was just too short. I wondered if there was such a thing as a necklace extender—a short piece of chain with fasteners on each end. When I couldn't find anything like that on the market, I formed a company to make them. I brought in some partners to finance it. We just started and we already have orders."

"She came up with an idea," I interrupted. "Find it. She brought in several partners: Fund it. And now she's marketing the idea: Farm it. If it's a great idea, money will flow to it. If it isn't, it will die. But at least she's trying. And if you find, fund and farm just one great idea, you'll be set for life. Mickey Ann, thank you for sharing your story.

"Now," I said, "let's move on to our next guest, Jeff Rickerson." I introduced a young man in his late twenties, slender and red-haired, wearing glasses.

"Just about a year ago," he began, "I was fortunate enough to graduate from college right into a banking job. You know, one of those high-security type of jobs with a big title to it? It sounded really neat. They told me they'd pay me seven thousand dollars a year. That was big money to me then."

Everyone laughed.

"Whoa," countered Nora. "That is big money! More money than I ever made in a year."

"Then," Jeff continued, "one Friday evening, just before I got off work, the president called me into his office and said, 'You know, it's really been nice knowing you, but we just don't need you anymore.' Five minutes' notice and I was out of a job. Actually, I was relieved to have them let me go. I needed a reason to get out on my own. I'd taken the *Nothing Down* seminar in college and bought a property or two, so I was familiar with the techniques.

"That weekend, I started putting a plan together that would net me more cash than I would've made in an entire year working for the bank. I didn't have enough gas to waste driving around looking for the deal, so I dressed up in my three-piece suit and went around knocking on doors. It was tough—walking around in 103-degree temperatures."

"You walked . . . ?" I asked incredulously.

"I walked up and down the streets and asked folks if they'd be interested in selling or if they knew of someone who was having problems and might need to sell."

"But you didn't have a job."

"I'd learned in the seminar that if I didn't have it, I could always get it."

"So," I inquired, "instead of looking on being fired as a problem, you looked on it as being . . . ?"

"An opportunity."

"The Lord answers prayers in strange ways," I said. "How long did it take you to find a property?"

"About two weeks. I had to hurry. Bills were piling up on my desk. I'd stacked them according to which ones I had to pay first, and I was running out of room."

"How'd you find it?"

"I found a house about three miles from my own home. The grass was several feet high. I could see it was furnished, like somebody was living there, but nobody was home. There was a sticker on the front door from the city health department saying the house was to be condemned. So I went to the library and, using a cross-reference guide, got the name of the owner, his place of employment and the phone number. I called but the number was disconnected."

"This is just like the Blue Vase story," I interrupted.

"Then I called his place of employment. They said he'd been dismissed, and they thought he lived out of state. So I went to the post office and paid the postmaster a dollar for the forwarding address. I typed up a nice letter to the owner explaining how he could sell his house by mail. He wrote me back and sent me a key."

"The house was a total disaster inside—mud had poured into the basement during a heavy rain, and mold was growing on the walls. I'd never seen anything like it before in my life. But I knew there was an opportunity there. I called the owner back and he said, 'Just take it off my hands. I don't want it anymore.'"

"Was the seller behind on his payments?" I asked.

"That was the unbelievable part. He was current on his mortgage payments and his taxes. He just gave me his house for the mortgage balance! It cost me about $2.75—a buck to get his address and another $1.75 to send the contract by certified mail."

"First you found it and tied it up. How did you fund it?"

"I knew a fellow in the Jefferson City area who was a handyman. I offered to split the profit with him. I'd do all of the paperwork if he would let me borrow his financial statement and his fixup expertise. He agreed. Everything fell together."

"Tell us a few details of the fixup," I asked.

"First, I contacted the bank that held the mortgage and persuaded them to forgo the payments while we fixed it up. Then I called the insurance company, and they ended up giving us a check for the damage in the basement. We used that money plus my partner's contacts to get the job done. Fortunately, things looked a lot worse than they really were. We hired some kids to clean up the yard. All told, it took about three months. During this period of time, I found someone to buy it."

"And what was your net profit?"

"We each made about ten thousand dollars."

"And that's way over your seven thousand," Nora added.

Jeff nodded. "And I immediately moved my checking account to another bank!"

This last comment brought the house down.

"And, ever since," Jeff continued, "I've been putting deals together. It's extremely exciting."

"I want that excitement," said Steve.

"I have twenty-three written goals," Jeff continued, "each with a specific time frame. I've already accomplished three or four of them. I'll probably reach another six or seven in this year alone. Some will take me another ten years to accomplish. You've got to have goals, and real estate is the perfect vehicle to take you to those goals."

"Thanks, Jeff," I said, changing the subject. "Now, let me introduce you to our last guest this evening, Bruce Fanning."

Bruce was a genial fellow with long dark hair and a beard—almost hippielike—not at all the stereotype of a successful businessman. He sat at the end of the couch next to Steve.

"I met Bruce last year in Colorado Springs. Bruce, why don't you share your story with us?"

"Well, I was working for a radio station till September 15, '82. I thought I had a great job, but as radio goes, a new manager came along and canned the whole staff. And we were out on the street. I began looking for another job, but I was disillusioned with radio—I got it in the end, you know? No security. A couple of days later, I was in a used bookstore and picked up a copy of *Nothing Down* for a couple of bucks. I was down to my last hundred bucks or so."

"Did you have any real estate experience?" I asked.

"No. I didn't even know what a title company was. But anyway, I got involved in real estate and bought my first property. And as of this past Monday, I closed on my nineteenth property."

"And all of this in less than eighteen months," I commented. "How could you go from no experience, no knowledge, and with just a book to guide you, be so successful in such a short time?"

"I had the desire to do it. I didn't want to go to work every day, punch the clock and sit in the little engineering room and solder wires, and think that I was going somewhere. I wanted to really get ahead. I like to work for myself. I've always been good at fixing things. Real estate was just perfect. I had all the time in the world. I was unemployed."

"How did you find your first property?

"I ran an ad in the newspaper that said, 'I want to buy my first income property. I have no down payment.' A couple of weeks later a

Realtor called with an idea. He'd read *Nothing Down*. So he put me into a duplex down near the army base."

"Did it have a cash flow?"

"Yes, I live on the cash flow from my properties. For a while, at first, I did odd jobs on the side—fixup, hauling trash, doing work for apartment owners."

"Did it bother you to have to take odd jobs?"

"Yeah. It was a step down from what I'd been doing. But it only lasted a couple of months. I just kept telling myself, 'Hey, this hauling trash and flushing toilets and stuff is a good way to meet property owners.' In fact, that's how I bought a couple of my properties."

"So," I said, speaking to the group, "what was he doing there? He was networking, wasn't he? Want to ask him any questions?"

"Yeah," Philip said. "Bruce, how did you fund your first one?"

"The seller carried back a note for the entire purchase price. He had it free and clear. We moved him to Albuquerque in return for the down payment."

"What do you mean?" I asked.

"I found a friend who had a credit card. We rented a truck and packed a lunch, and we loaded his furniture. And we drove him to Albuquerque."

"Can you believe that?" I laughed. "Why was he willing to be so flexible?"

"He was an older man—early seventies. His property was near the army base, and he was just fed up with the GIs—hassling them for rent, and phone calls from the police at midnight about loud parties. He didn't want to be the tough guy."

"What did it feel like, when you bought that first property?"

"Oh, it was a rush!"

Everyone, especially Phil, who knew drug users' jargon, smiled as Bruce told his story. By his down-to-earth manner, Bruce was quickly becoming the favorite of the group.

"We signed the papers at the Realtor's office," Bruce continued, "and went outside. I remember it was a chilly night, but, boy, was I warm. Ha! Ran over there and looked at it. I couldn't believe it. I kept saying to myself, 'I own this'."

"Bruce," Steve asked, "how long after you read the book did it take to get that first property?"

"Forty-five days. I have a friend, Kevin, who's a plumbing contractor who's gotten into this with me now. He's a great help picking up used plumbing fixtures, and fixing things that go wrong. We're doing about one a month now."

"What's the best one you've ever bought?" I asked.

"The best one I ever bought was a three-unit building that had had a fire in the rear unit."

"Problem means opportunity," I said.

"Right. The people had moved out. The owner wasn't making the payments at the bank. And he knew he was going to be in trouble. We bought it for the loan balance of $35,000 and borrowed money on a second mortgage to do all the repair work. We just put the final paint job on the outside last week. It appraised for $88,000 and we've only got $42,000 into it. So that's a $40,000 profit. Now we're going to sell it."

"When Bruce was an employee," I said to the group, "looking for security, he never made that kind of money. Now he's the employer—the boss—he's in control. No one can fire him. That's the difference between being an employee and an employer. I was jogging through the streets of Seattle a few months ago. It was lunchtime, and the streets were thronged with employees. People turned to stare at me as if to ask, 'Who is this crazy jogging fool?' I didn't let it bother me. I stared back at them as if to say, 'I'm not in a race with you. I'm in a race with me.'

"It's amazing how many people in the old world—the losers' world—will try to hold you back, ridicule you. But in the new world—the winners' world—you'll notice there's a helping system. Winners like to help other winners. Big thinkers like to help other big thinkers. You become part of the winners' network. A helping network. You don't find that kind of help down in the bottom echelon."

"It's dog eat dog," said Philip, as if he knew.

"When you get to the top, it's 'dog help dog.' Do you find that to be true, Bruce?"

"Yes. That's one of my daily declarations. Each day I read this: 'You're obliged to help other people in any way you can because it's going to come back to you. Your success is assured if you help enough people get what they want.' "

"Well, folks," I said, changing the subject, "this morning we talked about how it's important to establish habits of success. I like another quote, which says, 'Routine brings perfection within the grasp of mediocrity.' "

"Routine brings results," Philip translated.

"Good, Philip. Let's call that our wealth secret number eleven."

WEALTH SECRET NO. 11. ROUTINE BRINGS RE-SULTS. AN AVERAGE PERSON WITH A MODEST ROUTINE OF DAILY SELF-IMPROVEMENT WILL OUT-PERFORM A DISORGANIZED GENIUS NINETY-NINE TIMES OUT OF A HUNDRED.

"Now, let's design a daily success routine," I continued. "Just as in vitamins, each of us has adult daily minimal requirements for success. What are some of them?"

"Exercise," said Mary.

"Very important. At least thirty minutes a day. While you exercise you can perform another daily requirement—listening to tapes from your success collection. What else?"

"Prayer," Steve suggested.

"I like that one," Nora said.

"Family communication," Karen volunteered. "If you get so busy that you don't communicate, it might ruin everything."

I agreed. "I've been taught all my life that no success can compensate for failure in the home and that the most important work we'll ever do is within the walls of our own homes."

Bruce Fanning offered a suggestion. "What about goal review? I do this every day and it helps a lot."

"Thanks, Bruce. Ten to fifteen minutes a day. I also recommend that you write an affirmation—a positive program for yourself and study it daily. Bruce, weren't you reading from your affirmation a few minutes ago?"

"Yes. I read it every day. I've brought a copy of it for each of you."

He passed out a sheet of paper with his affirmation printed on it.

"I took this in bits and pieces from various people," he explained. "It starts like this:

" 'The most powerful force you have is what you say to yourself and believe. Pursue your goals free of any feeling of ill will toward anyone. Assure yourself every day that you're a warm, friendly, well liked, loved person. Your success is assured. It does not require you to take advantage of any other person. Rather, it obliges you to help others any way you can. See yourself as a success. Be free of limitations. Always be will-do and can-do. Eagerly seek to improve every phase of your life. Stop putting things off and wasting time.

You have the ability to reach creative solutions to your problems. You have a constant flow of new and good ideas. You have guts.' "

Everyone laughed at the last sentence.

"Thanks, Bruce. Now, in addition to goal review, spend fifteen minutes before bed reviewing your day and organizing the next day's activities. This will give your subconscious mind all night to process the information. You'll wake up more organized and ready to hit the ground running. Especially watch for hunches the next morning. Nora, what else should we add to our routine?"

"Study?"

"I recommend thirty minutes a day from both aptitude and attitude books in your success library. You reap what you sow. If you expect to reap a big harvest tomorrow, you have to be planting the right seeds today. That brings us to find it, fund it and farm it. Each day you should spend time on each of these areas. At first you will concentrate on getting your lines in the water—five hours a day of finding those opportunities. You should spend a minimum of two hours a day in the 'fund it' are—calling banks, finding out the terms and conditions for getting loans, finding out the terms and conditions for getting loans, propecting for partners. Finally, spend at least two hours a day learning how to farm it—studying the market, checking rental values, setting up contacts with realtors, sending out fliers."

In summary, then, adult daily minimal requirements are:

_goal review and visualization:	fifteen minutes
_organization and overview:	fifteen minutes
_exercise:	a half-hour
_read attitude books:	a half-hour
_read aptitude books:	a half-hour
_listen to tapes:	at least a half-hour
_find it:	five hours a day
_fund it:	two hours a day
_farm it:	two hours a day

"That adds up to almost twelve hours a day," Steve said. "That's more than a full-time job!"

I agreed. "Someone once joked that an entrepreneur is a person who will work sixteen hours a day for himself just so he doesn't have to work eight hours a day for someone else. Besides, I only want half of your twenty-four-hour day. The rest of the time is yours to do with as you please."

Everyone laughed.

"These are just guidelines, of course. Organize your day in a system that works for you. I'm not going to tell you to get up at six, brush your teeth at six-oh-four, jog at six fifteen, read till seven-twelve, etc. I don't care when you get up. I don't care when you go to bed. I'm not responsible for you. You are responsible for you.

"If you were average people with jobs, you would not be able to maintain such a rigid schedule. You would have to cut back on your hours and stretch out your expectations of results. But you would still have to establish a daily routine to fit your life-style. None of us would consider sitting down with a banker unshaven, unshowered or ungroomed. We take fastidious care of the exterior, outward, physical aspects of our lives, spending upward of two hours a day on our appearance. But how much time do we spend on our interior grooming? Which is more important to long-term success?

SUCCESS GUIDELINES FOR
THE AVERAGE WORKING PERSON

Adult daily minimal requirements:

__goal review and visualization:	five minutes
__organization and overview:	ten minutes
__exercise:	fifteen to thirty minutes
__read attitude books:	fifteen to thirty minutes
__read aptitude books:	fifteen to thirty minutes
__listen to tapes:	fifteen to thirty minutes
__investments:	thirty minutes
__family, friend time:	as needed

Weekly minimal requirements:

__take one local expert to lunch to build your network

__make at least one written offer to buy a property

Monthly minimal requirements:

__read one attitude book

__read one aptitude book

__attend your local investment club meeting to build your network

Yearly minimal requirements:

__buy at least one property

"Now, for the last few minutes of tonight's session, let me explain to each of you how the MasterPlanner works."

This led to a discussion of the importance of using a planning tool that simplifies the task of organization. For this purpose, the MasterPlanner was specifically engineered, containing sections on goal-setting, calendar planning, activity checklists, networking, references, meetings and finances.

"Your MasterPlanner becomes your portable office," I concluded. "It contains information that will help you to find, fund and farm your first property. All of the paperwork is there—blank offer forms, handouts, fliers, form letters, Bargainfinders, Financefinders, rental checklists, lease agreements, master checklists, etc. The MasterPlanner is as important to your success as listening to tapes or reading books." (For more information call 1-801-852-8700 .)

THE SECRETS OF BEING ORGANIZED

Do you ever feel like your life is out of control? Like you're drowning in details? Like you're never going to get your life together? It doesn't have to be that way. You can take some simple steps now to get on top of things and stay there.

In my opinion, the major reason why successful people always seem so "together" is they set specific written goals with realistic deadlines. This sends a message to their subconscious mind to automatically sort through the confusing detail of life and only notice that which advances them toward their objectives. Since they know what they want and when they want it, they don't have to agonize over ever decision. This one habit simplifies their life and makes them seem so much more organized. I highly recommend it.

But just having goals is not enough. You've got to use your brain effectively. You've got to get your mind uncluttered.

Did you know that your conscious mind cannot effectively juggle more than five to ten thoughts at a time? If you don't want to feel overwhelmed, write down all the things you have to do. You'll be surprised how much less confusing it is once you get the list down on paper. Most people call this a "to-do" list. But, don't stop there.

You must prioritize your activities or you'll fall into the trap of confusing activity with progress. Being busy often gives one the illusion that things are getting done. What usually happens is that the easy, enjoyable tasks get done while the difficult, unenjoyable and often important tasks get transferred from list to list. But when you prioritize and work first on your top priorities you move from the level of "getting things done" to a new level called "getting the right things done." And that is a quantum leap. Only then can you afford the luxury of working on less important matters.

And last, remember that whatever gets measured improves.

Get in the habit of reviewing your progress on a regular basis. How can you see if progress is being made unless you track it? Take time to look back and see how far you have come. Perhaps you should even record your insights and experiences in a daily journal for review on a regular basis.

This simple approach won't work immediate miracles but with a few weeks of practice you will notice that you are becoming more serene, calm and organized in a world that thrives on confusion and chaos.

"Now, as our final task tonight let me review for you the wealth secrets we have learned thus far:

Wealth Secret no. 1:   You rarely have a money problem. You have an attitude problem. The go-getter with the right attitude cannot be denied.

Wealth Secret no. 2:   Face your fear. You always find the best fishing holes in the places where the average fisherman is afraid to go.

Wealth Secret no. 3:   Watch the crowd. Go in the opposite direction.

Wealth Secret no. 4:   Until you know value, everything is worthless. As soon as you know value, everything is valuable.

Wealth Secret no. 5:   Almost all opportunities are disguised as problems.

Wealth Secret no. 6:   He who lives the Golden Rule gets the gold here too.

Wealth Secret no. 7:   Money is attracted to great ideas.

Wealth Secret no. 8:   You are your wealth. The money that flows

	to you is just a by-product of your nonfinancial resources.
Wealth Secret no. 9:	There is no failure. Only feedback.
Wealth Secret no. 10:	A network saves legwork.
Wealth Secret no. 11:	Routine brings results. A disorganized genius is no match for the average person with a daily routine."

Mary raised her hand. "You said you were going to teach us *twelve* wealth secrets. When do we learn number twelve?"

"It's a secret," I said. "It may take you the next ninety days to learn it. It may take ninety years. When I think you are ready for it, I'll let you know.

"At this point," I said, changing the subject, "our cup runneth over. Let's retire for the night."

"Overload," said Steve wearily.

"Tomorrow morning is our last time together," I added. "My plane leaves at noon. Let's meet at the arch monument in downtown St. Louis at 8:00 A.M. There's a museum underground at the base of the arch that I'd like you to see. We're going to try to discover the spirit of St. Louis."

12

CROSSING THE FRONTIER

No one visiting St. Louis can miss the arch.

It is a giant, silvery rainbow cutting through the skyline of the city, its feet planted firmly in a ninety-one-acre park. Rising 630 feet in the air and spanning the same distance at the base, the arch is the largest monument in the United States. For instance, the arch towers seventy-five feet higher than the Washington Monument. Two Statues of Liberty, one stacked on top of the other, would fit snugly under it.

Very few Americans—very few Missourians, for that matter— know what the arch signifies. Put simply, it signifies a spirit that should burn in every American heart. It signifies the spirit of St. Louis.

But what is the spirit of St. Louis?

It must be important, or Charles Lindbergh, setting out on his history-making nonstop transatlantic solo flight more than fifty years ago, would not have christened his single-engine plane *The Spirit of St. Louis.*

The spirit of St. Louis. We were about to discover what it meant.

We gathered at the base of the monument at 8:00 A.M. and walked down the tunnel leading to the large underground exhibit hall, where tourists were already queuing up for an elevator ride to the very top of the arch and a spectacular view of the city. This was the exciting part of the arch monument. Off to our left was a museum. Only a few straggling tourists wandered in and out. I led my tiny group to the entrance to the museum, where a display of Christopher Columbus lore and maps of the New World greeted us.

"This is the Museum of Western Expansionism," I said. "It's a different kind of museum—few exhibits, paintings or artifacts—just quotes decorating the walls, which recede in concentric circles. These quotes will be your only clue to the meaning of the arch that rises way above us."

"It's like a treasure hunt," Dr. Blaine Lee, who was part of the entourage, observed.

The group dispersed throughout the museum to read the many quotes. Nora stopped in front of a clear Plexiglas panel displaying a quote in white lettering and began to read aloud.

"When, in the course of human events, it becomes necessary for one people to dissolve the political bands which have connected them with another. . . ."

Dr. Lee interrupted her. "Are you ready to make your own Declaration of Independence, Nora? Has it become necessary to dissolve the bands which have connected you to people who don't agree with you?"

"Yes," she replied. "There are things I want in my life, that I need to do with my life."

I stepped in. "Nora, a few days ago you didn't want independence. You really wanted dependence—a job, to be dependent on someone else. But now you've left the old world of dependence behind and crossed into a new world of independence."

Philip, who overheard the conversation, whispered to himself, ". . . where all men are created equal."

After a few minutes, I reassembled the group in the central foyer of the museum near a large, white statue of a man looking proudly toward an imaginary horizon. "This entire monument with the arch, the park and the museum is called the Jefferson National Expansion Memorial. The arch is called the Gateway Arch. Does anyone know why?"

"From this place, they went westward," Steve answered.

"Who did?"

"The pioneers, explorers, trappers, entrepreneurs, preachers, teachers . . . ."

"Why St. Louis?"

"Because it was the furthest point—the only point—of civilization west of the Mississippi."

"Who owned the land west of the Mississippi?"

"The French," Steve answered correctly.

I went on to explain that the city of St. Louis was established in 1764 by the French, who named it after King Louis IX, the patron saint of France. By the early 1800s Napoleon had given up his dream of establishing an empire in the New World. He needed money to prepare for war with England and to further his European conquests. Napoleon became a don't-wanter. In 1803 he offered to sell France's entire North American properties to the United States. This patrimony, known as the Louisiana Purchase, was an 800,000-square mile tract extending from the Mississippi River west to the Rockies and from the Gulf of Mexico to the Canadian border. Thomas Jefferson, who was president, jumped on the idea. In one stroke he could almost double the size of the country and open up fertile lands for colonization. The purchase price was about 15 million dollars—a bargain at three cents an acre! There was even some creative financing—the United States agreed to assume some French debts. With the new territory open for settlement, St. Louis became the gateway to the west. Here, pioneers would gather and outfit themselves for the journey into the wilderness.

"This is a statue of Thomas Jefferson," I continued, pointing to the large statue in the central foyer. "From this spot, on May 14, 1804, Jefferson sent his private secretary, Meriwether Lewis, and William Clark to explore the new territory. The Lewis and Clark Expedition mapped the way for millions of pioneers who would cross the frontier to a new life.

"What is a frontier?" I asked. "Isn't it just the line between an old and a new world? In a sense, you are like those pioneers, leaving behind an old world to discover a new one. Someone once asked Sir

Isaac Newton how he discovered the law of gravity. He replied, 'If I have been able to see farther, it is by standing on the shoulders of giants.' We too are standing on the shoulders of giants—those early pioneers who blazed the way, who sacrificed and died out there in the wilderness in order that we could be free."

Philip listened intently. He whispered reverently in the silence of the museum, "I've never seen the arch in this perspective before."

"What do you mean?" I asked.

"I used to come down here a lot as a kid. But I never knew what it meant."

GREAT MEN AND WOMEN WHO WERE NOT AFRAID TO FAIL

Pick any field of life, name the most successful person from that field, and you will find a person who was not afraid to fail.

Politics: Doesn't Abraham Lincoln come to your mind as being one of the most respected presidents this country ever had? He failed in eight straight elections before he finally won the big one.

Business: Did you know that two of the most respected names in business, Walt Disney and Henry Ford, both had to declare personal bankruptcy before they could rise on to higher levels of success?

Sports: Babe Ruth may have held the record for home runs, but he held the record for the most strikeouts as well.

Writing: The international best-seller *Jonathan Livingston Seagull*, by Richard Bach, was rejected by dozens of publishers before it finally found a home.

Acting: Search the life of any major star from Clint Eastwood to Lily Tomlin, and you'll find at some point they had to pump gas, drive a taxi or wait tables until their break came.

Public speaking: Perhaps America's greatest public speaker, Zig Ziglar gave three thousand free speeches before he ever got paid for one.

Music, Art, Education: The story is the same. The most successful ones endured countless failures and rejections on their way to the top. But they were dauntless (incapable of being intimidated or discouraged). Like them, if we refuse to be daunted (drained of courage, subdued, intimidated), we join the ranks of the great. Fight on. It's worth it. You're worth it.

We moved from the center of the museum into one of the aisles between the concentric walls. We were all silent, soaking up the spirit of the place. Philip stopped in front of a placard displaying an ad from an old newspaper and read,

> February 13, 1798
>
> To enterprising young men
>
> The subscriber wishes to encourage 100 men to ascend over the River Missouri to be employed for one, two, or three years. For particulars, inquire Major Andrew Henry ... who will ascend with and command the party. . . .

Dr. Lee joined us and asked, "Would anyone answer an ad like that?"

"There are a few crazy people," replied Mary.

"Didn't you answer an ad like that, Mary? 'Financial independence can be yours!' " Dr. Lee laughed heartily.

Mary then read from the quotes on the wall.

> 1822. William Ashley, St. Louis trader, places advertisement in the *St. Louis Gazette* asking for 100 enterprising young men to join him in a trapping and trading venture into the Mississippi West.
>
> 1823. Iroquois Indians attack trader William Ashley and his party, the Missouri is closed to white traders and trappers.
>
> 1825. William Ashley, Missouri trader—opens new overland route into Western Wyoming personally piloting a bull boat down the unexplored Green River to establish a Post at Henry's Fort. Indian hostilities had rendered the previous permanent trading post system impractical so he created a more flexible rendezvous system which brought the traders to the trappers

in an annual exchange of furs and
pelts for the supplies required for
the next trapping season.

"Isn't this like the Blue Vase story?" Dr. Lee asked. "Ashley had a
dream and nothing was going to stop him—not the Indians, not the
wilderness, not the weather. Not anything. He was a blue-vaser. Just
like you."

"Look at this," I called to the group, pointing to a quote by Daniel
Webster. Webster had opposed the acquisition of the Louisiana
Purchase.

What do we want with all this vast worthless area, the region of
savages and wild beasts of desert, shifting sands and whirl-winds of
dust, of cactus and prairie dogs? I shall never vote one cent from the
public treasury to place the Pacific Coast one inch nearer Boston
than it is now.

Dr. Lee joined in. "Here was a respected man; people listened
when he talked. He didn't see any value in the Louisiana Purchase."

It was my turn. "A lot of negative thinkers to try to talk you out of
crossing the frontier. People you respect will tell you that you're
crazy. No one likes to be rejected. But if you want to be a pioneer—
to take the risks and reap the rewards of freedom—you'll have to
learn how to deal with rejection. You may have to call fifty or more
sellers before you find someone who is flexible. But suppose, after
fifty calls, you finally uncover a bargain property that nets you five
thousand dollars. Was it the last call that made you the five thousand dollars? No. Each call was valuable—fifty calls makes five
thousand dollars. That's a hundred dollars a call! Each rejection is
not a failure! It's a triumph! It's not something to dread. It's something to look forward to. Who cares what people say, as long as
there is gold at the end of the rainbow? So when someone rejects
you from now on, what will you say?"

"Thank you!" everyone replied.

"Right! A hundred here, a hundred there. Rejection after rejection.
It all adds up."

We moved down the aisle and stopped in front of another quote.

Barrett Travis Message from the Alamo

. . . under siege by a thousand or more of the Mexicans under Santa
Anna, I shall never surrender or retreat.

"Nora," commented Dr. Lee, "the next time you come to this museum and see this quote, you'll say, 'Oh, Barrett Travis, I know just exactly how you felt. I've got a thousand people on my tail telling me I'm crazy. But I'm just like you. I'll never surrender. I'll never retreat.' "

"These people are your people," I added. "Your heroes. Back in their day, people thought they were crazy, too. This museum is a monument to them—to their pioneer spirit. The spirit that made this country great. But lately, this spirit has fallen on hard times. We need to revive it. We have new frontiers to cross. What are they?"

"Outer space," Philip answered.

"Inner space," Mary added. "The frontiers within us."

"And nothing but fear will stop us," I said.

The group split up, and each individual went on alone. From time to time someone would point out a quote that had special meaning. A few minutes later we stopped and congregated in front of a quote dated Thursday, July 4, 1805, written by Meriwether Lewis:

> . . . have concluded not to dispatch a canoe with a part of men to St. Louis as we had intended early in the Spring. All appear perfectly to have made up their minds to succeed in the expedition or perish in the attempt. We all believe that we are now about to enter on the most perilous and difficult part of our voyage. Yet, I see no one repining; all appear ready to meet those difficulties which await us, with resolution and becoming fortitude.

Dr. Lee spoke to Philip, who had obviously been moved by the last quote. "Philip, before today you didn't know what the arch meant. Now it has new meaning. Has this place changed?"

"To me, yes."

"No," countered the psychologist, "the place hasn't changed. You're the one who has been changed. You're looking at it now with new eyes. That's all."

"The veil has been lifted," Nora said.

I interrupted to ask Philip to read another quote for the group.

"This is from Charlie Goodnight Cowboy," Philip read.

> All my years on the trails are the happiest I've lived. Most of the time they were solitary adventures in the great lands of fresh and new, and a Spring morning, and we were free and full of the zest of dare.

Steve found another quote.

Think of it, young men. You who are rubbing along from year to year with no great hopes for the future. Lay aside your paper collars and kid gloves. Work a little. Possess your soul with patience and hold on to your way with a firm purpose. Do this, and there is a beautiful home for you out there. Prosperity, freedom, independence, manhood in its highest sense, peace of mind, and all the comforts and luxuries of life are waiting you.

As we walked through the outside aisle I called the group together one last time. "Above us, a giant silver arch rises to the sky. Do you have a better understanding of what it means now?"

"It is a monument to us," someone said.

"It is a monument to our fathers," replied another.

"It is a message from our fathers that says, 'I did it, and you can do it too,' " said Nora.

"From now on, whenever you see that arch, you'll know it's not just for decoration. It's a monument to those who died so that we might dream. It's a silver rainbow. It's the promise of better days to come. It's the gateway to whatever you want in your life. It marks the frontier to unexplored treasures inside you. It's the symbol of freedom and independence. It represents the spirit of St. Louis."

Steve, the minister, spoke, not wanting to pass up the opportunity. "It's a bridge that reminds us of where we've been. Links us to our past. Makes a launching pad that sends us into the next dimension."

I nodded, pondering his words. Then I spoke.

"In the central terminal of the St. Louis airport hangs an old silver plane. On its side, in black letters, are the words *The Spirit of St. Louis*. Now you can appreciate why Lindbergh picked that particular name for his plane. He was crossing a new frontier. Something that no one had ever done before. Like Lindbergh, you are doing something that no one has ever attempted before. You'll stumble onto worlds that you never expected to discover. You're going to change."

Then, singling Mary out, I said, "You were telling me this morning that you thought you were already starting to change. You're going to discover a whole new person, Mary, that you never thought was in there before. And it's unexplored territory."

Karen agreed. "My father told Philip yesterday, 'Hey, you're not the same person you were Monday. I can see it! I feel it! You've changed!' "

"Before I even opened my mouth," added Philip.

"When we came down here this morning, I said this was going to be like a treasure hunt. Can you tell me what treasures you found?"

"I found my own free spirit," Nora said, breaking down with emotion.

We all waited nervously, yet patiently, even lovingly, until she regained her composure.

"I cry when I'm happy," Nora said finally. "I cry when I'm sad. You've got your everyday pains, and you've got all of your problems. You get so wrapped up in your problems, you can't see the opportunities. And you wonder if you've even got it in you."

Philip comforted her. "You got it, Nora. We all got it. Bob didn't give us anything that we didn't have in ourselves."

"Like the song says," Dr. Lee added: " 'Oz never did give nothin' to the Tinman that he didn't already have.' "

I picked up the thread. "The same with the Scarecrow and the Lion. They went with Dorothy to the Wizard of Oz hoping he would give them either a brain or a heart or a backbone of courage. And on the way, they discovered that they already had those things. I'm not a wizard. I have no magic wand. My answers are simple common sense. I teach you that wealth is not outside you. It is inside you. When you come to know that, you won't need me any longer. You'll be free."

And thus we ended our tour of the museum. We walked back out into the sunlight. Directly above us the arch swept skyward, its surfaces shimmering in the sun. Mayor Poelker was there to meet us, and we chatted as we strolled down the quiet paths of the park that surrounds the monument. The camera crews were setting up their cameras for a final shoot on a grassy knoll on the east side of the arch overlooking the Mississippi. We assembled there on the lawn.

"Earlier today," I said, "Philip asked me to autograph a book for Karen's father. Above my signature I wrote, 'You are your wealth. The money is just a by-product.' I'm happy to have been able to share some of my wealth with you these past few hours. You and I are pioneers. You may think that I came here to change you but you have changed me. I've been reminded again that there are many frontiers for us to cross, many mountains for us to climb."

I pointed to the top of the magnificent arch where the sun's reflection dazzled the eye. "See that sparkle up there? It glitters like a diamond."

"It's the most beautiful glitter I've ever seen," Nora said.

As the group dispersed and the camera crew dismantled its equipment, Mary stood to the side and surveyed the scene, lost in thought.

She felt like Cinderella when the clock struck twelve. The illusion evaporated. The ball was over. The carriage turned into a pumpkin. She found herself in the old world again. She was tired, exhausted—her brain grooves overstretched by too much hope and too many positive thoughts and too many big ideas.

Steve broke into her trance.

"Let's go home, honey. I've got a sermon to preach tomorrow."

She nodded. Together they walked to their car.

On their way home, Philip and Karen stopped at a McDonald's and over a Big Mac and fries set down their game plan for the next ninety days.

"I'm scared," said Karen.

"I'm more than scared. I'm petrified," Philip said. "Do you think your Dad will let us borrow his car for a few weeks?"

"Yeah. I think so."

"I won't be able to help you around the house as much as I used to."

"I'm ready to tough it out," she said.

That's the same thing she had said the night she gave birth to their son, Philip remembered. At the time, Philip was still in the youth detention home with eight other boys. Karen called to tell him that she was going to the hospital alone. He couldn't stand not to be with her. Philip went to the group foreman, Stan Williams, an ex–St. Louis Cardinals football player.

"Take me down to the hospital," Philip demanded.

"It's too late."

"You either take me to the hospital or I'll break out of here and steal your car."

And so on that night, July 13, 1977, Stan Williams and all eight juvenile delinquent boys piled into the group van, drove to the hospital and worried together in the waiting room until Philip learned that he had become the father of a six-pound, thirteen-ounce baby boy. The proud parents named him Marcus.

Philip had just turned seventeen. Up until that night he had been just another young boy in trouble, laughing when people warned him that at the rate he was going he wouldn't live to be twenty. But when he saw that baby boy, his own son lying there in a bassinet in the hospital nursery, something snapped.

Stan Williams, sensing a teaching moment, spoke to Philip. "You're not a kid anymore. You've got a kid of your own. You gotta stop doin' all the crazy, stupid stuff that you're doin'. Look at your own father. Do you want your kid to look at you like that?"

These words sunk in. His own father had left home when Philip was four years old—too young to understand. Then, when Philip was fourteen, his father had been murdered. Philip didn't want his son to remember him like that. He wanted his son to have the kind of father he never had. And that would mean he would have to change.

And now, eight years later, Philip was ready to make another quantum change. He looked at his young wife and smiled.

"I'm ready to tough it out, too," Philip said.

Nora drove her kids home and got ready for work at the Elks club. She didn't look forward to spending her evening in a bar after such an uplifting day.

"Hiya, Nora," called out one of the boys at the bar as she walked in the door. "How's your day?"

She put on her bartender's apron and flashed a smile.

"Actually, I had a beautiful day today. I been down to the arch this morning with my girls."

"Yeah?"

"I was one of three people chosen for a challenge. I'm going to make myself where I don't have to work here anymore."

This piqued their curiosity.

"Gimme a Miller Lite, would'ya, Nora? So what about this challenge?"

She removed a glass from the shelf behind her and pulled on the beer tap, and while the glass was filling with the clear, amber liquid topped with white foam, she told him some of the details of her last forty-eight hours.

"Cm'on, Nora. That only happens in the movies."

"That's what you think. I got dreams. I don't want to work here for the rest of my life for no four dollars an hour," she laughed.

They all laughed—more at her than with her. She could tell that they didn't understand. They were in another world. As the evening wore on she listened to their problems and watched them drown them, laugh, and waste their lives away.

At one-thirty in the morning she kicked the last drunk out, locked up the lodge and drove home depressed.

The arch seemed a million miles away.

NEVER GIVE UP AND GOOD LUCK WILL FIND YOU.
—Falcore the Luck Dragon in *The Never Ending Story.*

13

WHAT ARE THEY BITING ON?

1. _____

Reading the Sunday paper is a ritual to most Americans—a time to relax, kick back and rest from a busy week of work. For Philip, however, the Sunday paper had meant something else: disappointment. For over a year now, he had dug through the large section of Sunday classifieds without finding a single job opportunity.

But in the past seventy-two hours the Sunday paper had taken on a whole new meaning for Philip. Instead of disappointment, it meant new hope, a ticket from the world of dependence to the world of freedom. A few days earlier he had wanted a secure salary. Today, he wanted only the opportunity to turn a profit. A few days earlier he'd wanted to be a loyal employee. Today, he was the employer—the owner and president of Moore and Moore Investments. In a few hours, he had gone from laborer to boss, from dependent to independent, from socialist to capitalist.

It felt good.

The *Sunday St. Louis Globe-Democrat* landed on Philip's door-step at exactly 6:17 P.M. on Saturday evening, June 9. Within seconds of the thud, Philip pounced on it like a lion on fresh meat. He avoided the job classifieds, vowing never to look there again, and tore immediately into the real estate ads. He first went to the "real estate wanted" section to look for his own ad.

"One line in the water," he mused smiling as he read it silently.

Then he spent the next hour systematically searching the ads for clues to highly motivated sellers. When he was finished, he shared the results with Karen. The classified section was covered with red circles—perhaps thirty or forty. They decided to go to bed early and to take Sunday off to relax and set some goals for themselves.

But on Sunday, Philip couldn't relax. He made some calls before noon. Then he had a brainstorm. He rushed to a spare bedroom and surveyed the musty stacks of yellowing, old newspapers that reached almost to the ceiling. A few hours earlier, the entire roomful was worth at most fifteen or twenty dollars at a nearby recycling center. But now Philip saw them with new eyes. They looked like piles of gold ore waiting for the smelter. His heart raced.

He plowed through the stacks and retrieved the Sunday real es-tate classifieds for the four previous weeks. He reasoned that even though most of the ads would be dated, a few might pan out. If not, he would have lost nothing but a few hours—and time was the one thing he had plenty of.

He systematically compared the current weeks' ads with previous weeks'—June 3, May 28 and May 21. There were different ads. It amazed him. And then he spotted a small ad in the bottom left-hand corner of page 12D of the June 3 paper:

> 4 units on Leduc
> Four unit building to be liquidated
> in divorce settlement. A bid should
> be submitted in writing to 4008
> Olive Street, Suite 206, St. Louis,
> Missouri no later than June 15.

"Leduc! Hey, that's *my* street!" he shouted.

The ad contained some great clues, too. "Liquidated," "divorce." It sounded too good to be true.

He made a call. No answer.

"This is a good one. I can feel it," he thought. He resolved to call the number first thing Monday morning.

At about eight o'clock on that Monday morning, June 11, the phone rang. Philip rushed to the phone, thinking that perhaps someone might be calling on his classified ad.

It was David, the film producer, calling to make arrangements to do some filming in Philip's apartment. About every four days, the film crew would follow Philip's progress and record his activities. David asked Philip to call immediately if something started cooking.

"Actually, I got something cookin' right now," Philip said. "On a home right across the street from me!"

"Really?" David seemed surprised. He'd expected results but not this quickly.

Philip read him the ad.

"I wonder if it's a foreclosure," David said. He was no stranger to the real estate game, having bought, fixed up and profited from several properties himself.

"I don't know," Philip said. "I've been calling the number and nobody answers. I'll keep calling."

David thought for a second. He had a hunch it might be a property sold through a city-sponsored low-interest program, then repossessed by the city when the buyer defaulted. If so, it could be a hot lead. He told Philip to keep him posted. If things started popping, David wanted to have the cameras there to capture the action.

That concerned Philip. He didn't want cameras to blow his deal.

"We can stay out in the background," David reassured him. "By the way, you ought to talk to the tenants. They're a great source of information about the building. You know, problems with plumbing, water damage or electrical malfunctions."

"Yeah, I've already been over there today."

"Oh, good. You're ahead of me."

"Yeah. They're only paying $165 a month. They didn't even know the building was for sale. I didn't go inside myself. It doesn't need any major work outside. It's all brick."

"Oh, it sounds like a good one."

"Bruce Fanning, the guy from Colorado, thought so too. He called me last night, and I told him about it. My network is starting to help."

"Be sure to call Bob Allen."

Philip hung up the phone, feeling more encouraged by the second.

Wouldn't it be great if he could be the first of the Challenge team to buy a property? He hurried to call the number again. This time someone answered. It was a law firm. The receptionist informed him that the attorney handling the situation, a Miss Anne Marie Clark, was not in. He left his name and number and hung up, feeling very frustrated. He forced himself to continue his newspaper calls. It wasn't long before he got another nibble.

"Yes, hi. My name is Philip Moore. I'm calling in reference to the apartment you have for sale. Could you tell me about it?"

"It's a four-family. All two-bedrooms. Rents total $925 per month. Three of them are $225, and one is $250."

"OK. What's the value?"

"Well, I'm asking sixty-one nine."

"Has it been appraised at that value?"

"Well, I bought it two and a half years ago and paid sixty-eight thousand. The only thing that's changed since then is that I've put in a new furnace and got sick."

"Oh, I'm sorry to hear that."

"And I'm selling it for what I owe."

"OK, are you willing to carry terms?"

"Well, if I owe sixty-one, how could I carry terms? That's got to be paid off. Do you follow?"

"Yes, I do now," Philip lied. "Who's carrying the note?"

The seller explained that there were two mortgages—a first mortgage of fifty-three thousand dollars and a second mortgage of eight thousand dollars.

Philip still didn't quite understand. "OK, so what you want to do is really look for cash and get the heck out of there, huh?"

"You don't have to have cash. You can, you know, finance the same way I did." The seller was trying to tell Philip that it was a nothing-down deal.

"Tell me a little bit about how you finance it because I'm new at this."

"I paid sixty-eight thousand dollars for it two and a half years ago. Put a first and second mortgage on it through a bank. And then, last year, I came down with cancer. I got through with radiation therapy and came down with shingles, which I'm still recovering from. It's just too much for me to handle. I decided I'd make somebody a good deal, get out for what I owe, and be done with it."

"What are your payments?"

"Well, what I'm paying wouldn't be the same as what you'd be paying."

"Yeah, I know, I know," Philip said, not knowing at all.

"And what I'm paying is $687 on the first and $80 on the second. Why don't you just drive by and take a look at it?"

"I'll do that."

"From the outside. Now, don't bother the tenants."

"Oh, no, I wouldn't dare do that."

Philip ended the call and made a note to drive by the property. The seller seemed to be a classic don't-wanter. Unfortunately, in the paper shuffle of the ensuing telephone calls and the excitement of chasing down other leads, he never followed up on this call. (Too bad, it was a good one!) Before noon, he placed another call on the Leduc property.

The receptionist put his call through immediately. Miss Clark answered, and all of a sudden he felt unsure of himself, even rattled. "I'd like to know how much is the value of the home on Leduc," he said finally.

"It was appraised, I believe, at twenty-three thousand dollars."

Twenty-three? That couldn't be right, he thought. The duplex he lived in was worth twenty thousand dollars, according to his landlord. A fourplex had to be worth forty or more. "What are you asking for it?"

"We're simply taking bids."

"Okay. Fine." Philip stalled. He glanced down the Bargainfinder and chose another question at random. "What are the taxes and insurance per year?"

"I don't have any of that information. I'm not a real estate agent. I'm an attorney who was appointed by the court to sell the property. We're just taking bids."

"So, is it like a repossession?"

"No. It's not a repossession." She explained that the court had ordered the property sold in a divorce decree. She had set the date of June 15—this coming Friday—to be the last day for submitting bids. She gave him the number of a man who would give Philip a tour of the property. He might have more information.

"OK. Thank you very much, Miss Clark. I'll take a look at the property and then get back to you."

"Fine," she said. "Are you representing a real estate company?"

"No, ma'am. I'm representing myself."

It felt so good to say that. Yes, he was representing himself—for the first time. Before, when he let other people represent him—his employer or the government—all he ever got was poverty and a feeling of powerlessness. But now that he had taken charge of his life, he felt a sense of power.

"Which ad did you see, sir?" Miss Clark asked.

"The one in the *Post Dispatch*, ma'am. Have you had any offers on the property?"

"One."

Philip made a mental note that he had some competition. "Okay. Thank you very much, ma'am. And I'll be getting back to you."

His adrenaline was pumping now. He couldn't wait to talk to someone about this glitter he had just uncovered. He picked up the phone to call the hot line number, his fingers shaking with excitement.

He was on a roll. And it was only his first day.

2.

While Philip was running hard, chasing down opportunities without regard to structure, form or organization, Nora was taking a more methodical approach. She awoke Sunday morning with a determination to play this one by the book. "One foot in front of the other," she reminded herself. This is unfamiliar territory. Best move slowly. Can't afford a mistake.

She started off her day with a forty-five-minute jog/walk while listening to a tape by Zig Ziglar. His message was simple but powerful: 'You can have everything you want in life if you'll just help enough other people get what they want.' Returning from her jog exhilarated, she picked up the thick Sunday morning paper on the doorstep and went in to shower and prepare for the day.

After breakfast she sat at the table in her office—one of the bedrooms in her small home—stared at the Sunday paper lying in front of her and took a deep breath as if facing an unpleasant task.

"Got to get my lines in the water," she whispered to herself.

She carefully went through the newspaper looking for the ad she had run. There it was. It was about to expire. She made a mental note that she would have to call and renew it tomorrow. Then she began circling ads in the classifieds. She knew she was looking for flexibility, but all of the ads seemed the same. She had trouble discerning any clues. She set a quota of five calls, picked the ads she felt most promising and dug in.

She dialed a number. A woman named Gertrude answered the phone and described a four-bedroom home with a two–car garage that her son and daughter-in-law were selling. They were moving to a larger home.

So far, so good. Nora thought to herself. "Could you tell me how much you're asking for it?" she continued.

"Fifty-four thousand five hundred dollars."

"Could you tell me what you owe on it?"

"There's no loan on it."

"How was the price of the house determined?"

"It was appraised for fifty-eight thousand dollars."

Nora made a mental note that the asking price was almost ten percent below the appraised price. "Could you tell me where the house is located?"

It was in Afton, Missouri, a suburb of St. Louis, the woman said.

"Well, my name is Nora Boles and I'm new at this," Nora continued. "I'm an investor. And I would like to know exactly what you want to accomplish—what you would like out of it?" She felt foolish, not understanding exactly why she had to go through all of this.

"The house belongs to my son and my daughter-in-law. They're firm on their price. They want $54,500."

"How much would they like down?"

"Oh, I would say at least four thousand or five thousand dollars down."

Not knowing what she should ask next, Nora returned to familiar territory, "What's the neighborhood like?"

After the woman had completed her answer, Nora excused herself and hung up. She sat back in her chair, not knowing what the five-minute call had accomplished. She shrugged and dialed another number. A woman answered.

"Hello, my name is Nora Boles, and I'm calling in regard to your house. How much are you asking?"

"We're asking forty, but it's negotiable."

Nora noticed that last word. This is what she wanted to hear. "Okay. What's the existing mortgage?"

"About nine thousand."

"How much cash do you have to have down?"

"We're asking like five hundred."

"Five hundred down?" Nora asked incredulously. Was this the flexibility she was looking for? She glanced at her Bargainfinder form. "Would you consider carrying any financing on it?"

"No, we can't do that."

"No?" Nora was surprised by the answer. They only wanted five hundred down but weren't willing to carry financing. How could that be? She didn't know what to ask next. She got the name of the seller and the location of the property and again excused herself. "I'll get back with you after I talk to my partner."

She hung up the phone, confused. Why did she feel such a tightening in her stomach when she started to get near the critical questions? It was uncomfortable, even frightening to her. She reminded herself that she had faced much tougher situations. Still, no rationalizing could cause the fear to subside. She continued to call all morning with little success, and the next morning the ritual was the same, with one exception. As it was Monday, she called the newspaper and renewed her ad. It would cost $3.50 for another week—a lot for her—but it was money she was willing to risk.

A day or so later, after a particularly discouraging morning on the phone, Nora called Tom on the hotline phone to have him school her on what she was doing wrong. They played roles; he the motivated seller, she the investor. She stumbled through the dialogue. He corrected her.

"OK, Nora. Are you ready?"

"I guess so."

"Get a Bargainfinder. Here we go. Ring-ring-ring. Hello." Tom played his role to perfection.

Nora asked the first question. "I'm calling in regard to the ad you had in the paper. Are you the owner or the agent for the property?"

"I'm the owner."

"OK." Nora paused to fumble through her Bargainfinder for a question—any question—to fill the awkward silence.

"Could you tell me how many bedrooms and baths?"

"It's got three bedrooms, one bath."

Another painful pause. "Could you tell me how—how many stories?"

"Just one."

"OK, could you tell me the square footage?"

"Oh, around fifteen hundred square feet."

Tom left his role to instruct her. "Listen, Nora. I think you ought to maybe move down into the financial stuff a lot sooner, you know?"

"Oh, OK." It took her a moment to shift gears. "Has it been appraised?"

"Yeah. It was appraised for fifty-five thousand dollars."

"Where do I write that, Tom? Is there a place on the Bargainfinder for it?"

He instructed her where to look. Then they ploughed through a few more questions. Tom tried not to push her too fast. He could see that she had a lot of ground to cover. And the failure of the past few days seemed to have sapped her self-confidence. Tom wondered why she had such trouble addressing the sensitive questions. Maybe her many financial ups and downs had taken their toll. Maybe the embarrassment and humiliation of having so many strangers—bankers, lawyers, bill collectors—zero in on the disarray of her own personal finances made her uncomfortable about prying into other peoples'.

Each day, Nora waded back into the same frustrating battle. At times, it seemed as if she was winning. But an enemy waited for her—an enemy I took great pains to warn her about the first day of training. Its name is Fear—and it was gaining the upper hand in Nora's life.

Finally, she called me. "Sometimes I just get so scared I can't see straight," she admitted, her voice shaking with pent-up emotion. "I feel that fear and that dread, and I just can't think what to do. I'm not a quitter, but sometimes that phone seems like my worst enemy. When that happens I just have to get up and go outside for an hour or two until things get back to normal."

After one particularly frustrating morning, Nora escaped the heat and frustration collecting in her tiny office and walked out into her backyard. It just wasn't working. She wrestled with the problem. "Why does it have to be so hard?" She stared across her back lawn through the row of tall trees standing guard like old friends at the back boundary of her property. The familiar scent of wild things growing calmed her. Slowly the superficial feeling of futility was washed away by the steady undercurrents of resolve that flowed in her at the deepest levels. The fog began to clear. She could see that talking directly to sellers on the phone was never going to be her strong suit, no matter how hard she worked at it.

"What would a blue-vaser do?" she wondered aloud.

Then she had her answer. An hour later her battered car rolled to a stop in front of the Franklin County courthouse in Union, Missouri. Nora was about to put another line in the water.

"Hi, my name's Nora Boles," she said to the woman at the counter in the clerk's office. "Can you show me how to find a list of people who own property in this county but live out of state?"

The woman at the counter was fiftyish, gray-haired and cheerful and seemed eager to help. She walked Nora through the process, showing her how to dig the information from huge leatherbound volumes that lined an entire wall. "If you need any help," she said, "I'll be right here."

Nora eagerly thumbed through the heavy, timeworn pages. "This is more like it," she thought to herself. It was a lot easier then dragging information out of a total stranger on the phone. Besides, she had someone right there to help her.

What made Nora think of visiting the county courthouse? Jeff Rickerson, the investor from Missouri, had mentioned this idea to the group on the evening of the second day of training. "That's a good idea. Write it down," I told them that night. "Out-of-state owners are likely to be more flexible in selling because of management hassles." Nora dutifully wrote the idea down, unaware that her subconscious was quietly filing it away for a rainy day. That day had come sooner than expected. Her computer was feeding her hunches.

And like seeds of winter wheat beneath the frozen ground, her budding confidence was beginning to send tender shoots toward the surface.

3. _____

"Hi, girls! Are you ready to pass out some fliers for me?"

"Yeah," responded the girls in unison watching the cameras out of the corners of their eyes.

Mary Bonenberger surveyed the small group of girls gathered in front of her. The day before she had prepared a flier to hand out to houses in her neighborhood. Then she had gone to a print shop to get several hundred copies. It took her only a few calls to line up some girls from her church to help her distribute the fliers. The cameras were there to capture the scene. In a way, Mary resented the presence of the cameras. They slowed her down. And she had work to do!

"Tell you what, girls," she said. "Split up the fliers fifty-fifty. Some of you take one side of the street, the rest take the other. And just pass out as many as you can. Roll them up and stick them in doors. But, whatever you do, don't put them in mailboxes. That's illegal."

The girls divided up the fliers, and Mary watched them run off, full of excitement. "Got to get more lines in the water," she fretted.

4.

Philip came stomping up the stairs and flopped onto the chair in his tiny office. Karen was in the kitchen preparing meals in advance. She didn't have to go to work for another hour. When she heard Philip come up the stairs, she wandered in from the kitchen.

"Hi," she said sheepishly. She could tell by his mood that things were not going well. "What have you been doing this morning?"

"I'm getting a runaround on that fourplex property. Nobody knows what's going on! So I can't get the information I need. It's like pulling teeth. So I went over to the city offices and asked about their foreclosed properties. But that's a lot of red tape, too." Philip started to gain some of his enthusiasm back. Just sharing this information with his wife seemed to lift at least half of the burden off of his shoulders. "It's nice," he thought to himself, "to have someone to face the world with."

Karen still stood silently, leaning on the doorjamb. He glanced up at her and motioned her to come inside. He pulled out some papers from his briefcase that described some of three hundred properties the city was trying to unload. There was a property in Lafayette Square for only seventy-five hundred dollars. And another on Cobrillan that had some potential.

"So I just have to go and check out which ones are feasible for fixup. Like this on Cobrillan Street. It's a one-story brick residence, and it looked very nice in the picture. And there's a tenant in it."

"So it's got to be OK, if someone's living in it," Karen observed.

"With a positive cash flow," Phil added. "Some of these properties are all cash. Some require ten percent down. The list of the properties for sale comes out in Sunday's paper. It's a complicated bid process to get them," he explained. "But you can deal with certain brokers who know the ropes. For example, this property in Siston is just fifty-five hundred as is, and with existing taxes of forty-nine dollars. That's not bad." Philip stood up and pointed to the map of the city that he had attached to his bulletin board. As he talked, he pointed to the various areas in the city.

"Right now, I'm concentrating my efforts in University City, Wellston, Central West End and also in Hyde Park, where they're doing a lot of redevelopment. In these areas we can get federal loans to fix up properties. And the houses are very cheap. Also, properties down in the city close to the river front could triple in value in the next three to five years. So I cross-reference the address of the city properties with this map. Here's one in University City. And here's one on Crest. . . ."

5. _____

Mary sat down with her husband to fill him in on what she had been learning about using the county courthouse to find leads for don't-wanters. "I met an investor today who hires a full-time employee to work in the courthouse and check through the county records every day."

"Every single day?" Steve exclaimed. "What does he do with the information?"

"Well, he's looking for people who're facing foreclosure. He immediately sends them a letter, which says, 'I buy properties. I can save you from having to go through foreclosure.' I guess it works or he wouldn't do it."

"I see," Steve said. "So that's how you get the fresh stuff."

"Well, not really. Because the same information has already been published in the *St. Louis Countian*—the legal paper that anyone can buy for thirty-five cents. But if you can catch it before it gets published, then you're ahead of the pack. You see what I'm saying?"

"Yes."

"Like if you can get a banker to tell you about all of his delinquent loans *before* he files the notice of default, then you've got a gold mine. Well, I've found a banker who has agreed to share this information with me. He's got so many delinquent loans right now, he's got to get rid of them—dump them right away."

"You know," Steve said, "I'm feeling there's a system that we're not a part of yet."

"I know. It's all learning the ropes. This may all be fruitless. You never can tell whether you're wasting your time or making progress. It's just important to build a network, get a little exposure, get to know some bankers, make some initial contacts. In the future, who knows, some of this legwork might come in handy...."

6. _____

It was time for Nora and me to have a chat. I dialed her number, and we exchanged greetings.

"Have you decided on a daily routine?" I asked her.

"Yes. I get up at 7:00. Then, from 8:00 to 8:30 I've been jogging around the subdivision listening to tapes. I make my calls from noon till about 4:00. And then I take a break till 7:00, when I call for another hour or so."

"Are you doing your reading on a regular basis?"

"Yes, a chapter a night."

"Are you getting the hang of using the telephone?"

"Yes and no. I still get nervous."

"What five lines do you have in the water?"

"I have one ad in the *Globe* and one in the *Tri-County* in this area—the ad Bruce Fanning told us about: 'I want to buy my first income property. I have no money down.' I'm reading and calling on ads every day. That's two lines. I have an appointment with a Realtor this afternoon at two. That's the third line. When the paper boy comes tomorrow, I'm going to ask him about inserting a flier in the paper. And then I'm doing a mailing to out-of-state-owners. I'm keeping busy."

"Good."

"By the way, I've got a good lead on a duplex. A woman I used to know is having financial problems. I'll get more information and call you or Tom about it."

"You're great! Saying your prayers?"

"Yes, every day."

"Been discouraged at all?"

"Doubt but not discouraged. I was sittin' here thinkin', 'Nora, you must be crazy! You're doing all this and your own life is so messed up.' The old devil has a way of getting to you at times."

I BUY PROPERTY!!

I buy real estate in any condition.
If you or someone you know is thinking about selling a house or other real estate property, call me before you list with a real estate agent. I just might be able to save you a commission and the anxiety of waiting for the right buyer to come along.

Call Mary 555-1234

**FLIERS THAT ATTRACT
HIGHLY MOTIVATED SELLERS**

"What about your bills? Are your creditors bugging you?"

"Well, I'm back a few payments. I'm goin' to see the loan officer today and see if he won't give me some time. I think he will."

"What do your friends think of the new Nora?"

"I stay away from some of them. Because they can drag me down. One friend came by last night, and I told her before she even started: 'I don't want to hear any negativeness. You make your life and let me make mine.'"

"Good for you!" I laughed.

"She can't see what I see."

"Do you see it?" I asked.

"Oh, yes. I've always seen it. I just never had my chance or knew how to get there. And I've got it now. I'm going to make it. I know that."

7.

I called Mary on Tuesday, June 12, to find out how she was doing.

"Hi, Mary. It's Bob. I thought I'd let you get settled in before I called."

"Well," Mary said, laughing, "I guess I'm settled in. I think I'm thoroughly confused, is what I am."

"Oh?"

"Well, I started calling Sunday afternoon. I got so excited when the paper came out, I called for two or three hours. But I was still fuzzy on how to tell if a property is a good deal or not. Then I called all yesterday morning and about two hours yesterday afternoon. I called one of the consultants on the hot line, and he told me that I need to ask more financial questions. Frankly, I really don't know what I'm asking. I'm a little confused about what to offer them. . . ."

Mary was like a little kid who wanted to learn to ride a bike but didn't want to take the time to practice on the lawn, where the falls would be less painful. I counseled her to quit worrying about what to offer a seller. That was my job. Her task was to look for sellers who were flexible in price or terms—either someone who'd indicated a willingness to discount price for cash or someone who would carry financing with little or nothing down. When she found that, the hot line staff could tell her what to do next. Things would get clearer to her in time.

"Five days ago I didn't know any of these terms," she said. "And now they're beginning to sound more familiar to me. Maybe in five more days, it'll make some sense."

"It will."

"Your book *Creating Wealth* is really helping me."

"Have you read the chapter on the Lazy Man's System?"

"That's what I read last night before I went to bed. Tom told me to read that. It helped."

"Now, what are your five lines in the water?"

"I'm skimming the daily ads. Sending letters. Passing out fliers. I got in touch with one creative Realtor. He's going to give me expired multiple listings on a daily basis. I'm going to call them personally and see if they might be flexible."

"Excellent. One of my friends is an expert on using expired listings. His standard offer is seventy-five percent of listed price with five percent down and the seller carrying the financing. For every hundred offers he makes, only one is accepted. But that one makes it worth the effort."

"But how do I come up with five percent down? Bring in a partner?"

"Right."

"I've already been doing some partner prospecting—telling people what I'm doing and asking if they'd be interested."

"Good. You might find some partners at the local investment club meetings."

"Yes, I'm going to the meetings this weekend. I've already met the vice-president of one of the groups. He specializes in foreclosures— bought over twenty properties in the last eighteen months. He's going to let me go with him to a foreclosure sale and watch what happens."

"What about your daily routine?"

"It's pretty much established. I wrote it down last night, realizing that sometimes it won't work this way. Two small kids can punch holes in a routine pretty fast. I am getting up every morning at 5:30 and exercising. If Steve is away, like he was last week, I have a memorized hour-long exercise routine that I do. I listen to tapes while I exercise. When Steve is home, I prefer to go jogging. After that, I have a little quiet time. Doing a little bit of reading—usually an inspirational book. I prefer to read the real estate books at night before I go to bed. It sinks in better then. Basically I make calls all morning while the kids play."

"How are you feeling?" I felt she still needed to let loose with some feelings.

"I'm really excited. But yesterday I was feeling a little confused, you know."

"You just have to plow through the confusion until the lights come on."

"I'm not throwing in the towel by any means. When I get to that point, I just sit back, take a deep breath, and try to find out who knows the answer. I look through the books you gave me, *Nothing Down* and *How to Write a Nothing Down Offer* that your brother wrote. It's coming slowly."

Mary hung up the phone partially rejuvenated. She felt reassured that she was on the right track although she still felt lost. In the next few days, her calling proved more fruitful. One home was priced at thirty-one thousand. The seller had an existing loan of fifteen thousand, only wanted seven thousand down and would carry a second mortgage for the balance. Mary even went over to the woman's home to inspect it. The woman's husband wasn't there, but there seemed to be a measure of flexibility that she had not found in calling other sellers. Tom instructed her to make an offer. She excitedly filled it out with his help and dropped it off at the house, anxious for a reply.

And she was getting nibbles on some of her other lines in the water.

"Are your fliers working?" Tom asked her during one afternoon telephone call.

"Yes. But with mixed results. One man called wanting to sell his house for forty-two thousand in an area where I know the houses aren't selling for more than thirty-eight. He thinks it's worth a lot more than it is. I also got a call from a lady who wanted me to come right away and see her house. She said, 'We just want to get rid of it.' So I left the kids with a neighbor and went. It was a real eye-opener for me. I can't believe how some people live. It was a mess. It really needs painting. Outside and inside. The payoff on their loan is twenty-eight five. And all they want is twenty-nine thousand for the place. So they can get into another place. The payment per month is $346 at twelve percent interest."

"What's the house worth?"

"I don't know. If it was painted, fixed up ... maybe thirty-two, thirty-three."

"Only maybe?"

"I'm not sure. It's just in such terrible shape. The weeds were so high. . ."

"Weeding and painting aren't that tough. When I do cosmetic work on a house, I try to keep it under five hundred to seven hundred dollars. Or I won't buy it."

"The basement smelled musty. Now, does that necessarily mean it leaks?"

"No, not necessarily."

"I checked around, and there were some water stains where the sewer had backed up. And it's right next to an apartment complex, so it's not a very desirable location. There's probably not a whole lot of equity in it. As a matter of fact, I've never seen anything so awful."

"Your eyes will be opened."

"A lot more?"

"Yeah."

"Oh, gosh." She wasn't looking forward to that kind of enlightenment.

"Try and keep track of the calls from your ads and fliers. If one works better than the others, we'll put more emphasis on it."

"Thanks, Bob. I just needed some emergency counseling."

"Good luck, Tiger."*

8.

It was time to check in on Philip and Karen. We exchanged greetings, and then I got right down to business. "I tried to reach you several times yesterday," I said, "but you must have been out."

"Yes. I've been working on the Leduc property and a couple of others."

Philip had met someone at the Leduc fourplex the day before who told him he thought the property was worth forty-eight thousand dollars—much higher than the appraisal at the attorney's office. I told Philip to make an all-cash offer of twenty-three thousand dollars with a closing date in the future of at least thirty days.

"Now, about the matter of earnest money. Do you have any savings at all?" I asked.

"I have fifty dollars, and I just borrowed fifty more. So I have a hundred dollars now."

"Okay. Try to tie it up with fifty dollars."

Then I explained how he could find a partner to come up with the necessary cash. Once the property was bought, it could be refinanced for as much as thirty-five thousand dollars, based on its appraisal of forty-eight thousand. The new loan proceeds would pay back the partner and leave at least ten thousand dollars' profit to split after closing costs. "You're onto a good one here," I said. "Don't let it go."

"I've also found another good one," Philip said excitedly. "It's on Maryville in the Century West End. It's an ideal home, priced at twenty thousand dollars—three-story, four bedrooms. I went and looked at it yesterday. The wood floor has been water damaged, but the seller put a new roof on it."

"Why is he selling?"

"He said he just wants out. He says its appraised value is forty thousand dollars. And he wants a price of twenty thousand. I think it's because he's white and this neighborhood is racially mixed. But the neighborhood is coming back. His sister is a real estate saleswoman. And he said I would have to go through her. So she could get the commission."

"How did you find it? Twenty thousand dollars sounds too good to be true."

"Through the paper. I'm getting more confident in my calling. People even seem to help me now when I don't ask the right questions. They correct me."

"How are you feeling about your new profession?"

"People are saying they've seen a change in me. A drastic change. Even Karen has said she's seen a change in me. We're rich now. We just don't have any money."

Philip laughed, and then he said more seriously, "Some of my friends are rooting for me. But some are actually trying to hold me back—as if they're jealous, or something. They've even got jobs and more money now than I do. I haven't figured that out yet. I wonder what they're jealous of?"

I understood immediately. "They can tell that you're going places," I said, "that you're climbing out. If they can hold you down, they'll be justified in saying that there is no way out of mediocrity. But if you make it, Philip, it'll be proof that they can do it, too. You can't let them hold you back. You've got to show them there's a way out."

"You bet I will," he said, letting the thought sink in.

GOD DON'T GIVE YOU NO POINTS FOR DOIN' STUFF
YOU AIN'T AFRAID TO DO.—Robert Blake

ALL I WANT TO DO IS GO THE DISTANCE. IF THAT BELL RINGS
AND I'M STILL STANDING I'M GOING TO KNOW FOR THE FIRST
TIME IN MY LIFE THAT I WASN'T JUST ANOTHER BUM
FROM THE NEIGHBORHOODS.—Rocky

DIGGING IN FOR THE LONG HAUL

1.

Summertime in St. Louis is a season with warm, humid edges and a hot, radiant center. It's not so bad in the suburbs, where each new summer day dawns cool and still. But downtown it's a different story. By noon every time/temperature sign in St. Louis is galloping along toward ninety, and vinyl car seats all over town are busily vulcanizing acres of uncomfortable flesh.

Between the bustling center and the lazy suburbs are pockets of urban decay—the shabby, sometimes burnt-out remains of once-vibrant neighborhoods. In these oldest and most historic parts of St. Louis, each shattered avenue has an oddly endearing name: Chateau, Skinker, Florissant, Delmar, Soulard. To stroll along these crumbling thoroughfares is to observe firsthand the social, political and financial contrasts that have shaped this remarkable city for more than two hundred years.

Fold a street map of the city down the middle, east to west, and the resulting crease—which, incidentally, falls neatly on top of Skinker Avenue—is the Mason-Dixon line of downtown St. Louis. Delmar cuts Skinker at right angles. Walk west on Delmar, and you'll soon appreciate the satirical insight of the unknown street humorist who dubbed it the Africa-Israeli Highway: block by block the crowded tenements, barbecue stands, storefront churches and used-car lots of the inner city quietly yield ground to delicatessens, synagogues and high-dollar condos.

Further west along Delmar, you pass a sign on a stone monument that insists that you are no longer in St. Louis but have arrived at the outskirts of Clayton, Missouri, a uniquely prosperous township that boasts more massive limestone mansions than Monaco and more banks per square foot than downtown Dallas.

In the center of Clayton is the huge urban park through which we jogged so confidently the second morning of training. It's now filled to capacity with happy families taking refuge from the summer heat beneath massive shade trees or splashing happily in the cool, blue Olympic-sized pool.

Mary, Philip and Nora often drove past this park on their appointed rounds but had no time to stop. Their minds fixed on distant dreams, they continued to soldier on through the blistering heat, determined to create something out of nothing, even if it took all summer. And from the looks of things, it very well might.

Philip called me on Saturday, just one week after I had left St. Louis.

It was bad news. His offer on the four-unit apartment building ($23,500 cash in thirty days) had been rejected in favor of another offer of $18,000 cash immediately. He was crushed. So close to a vein of pure gold, and another prospector with a little more money staked his claim first. He sat down to figure up his loss and realized that in one week he had found and lost a property that would have netted him a profit greater than the total income earned by him and his hard-working wife in the past five years!

Frustrated? You bet.

Angry? No. Oddly enough, he experienced an unexpected surge of self-confidence as a direct result of this early failure.

Self-confidence? That's what he claimed, and I was inclined to believe this streetwise realist. True, this one failure cost him and that partner he never found twenty-five thousand dollars in potential profit, but it also provided him with an insight worth ten times that in the long run.

But first he had to get through the short run.

Put yourself in his place: There you stand, an inexperienced fisherman poised on the slippery bank of an unfamiliar pond. You cautiously lean out over the murky waters to spot a fish or two, but you aren't yet experienced enough to see to the bottom of things. And the fish—if indeed there are any—aren't about to make things easy for you. They hide in the shadows. All that stands between you and another hungry night is an old cane pole and some strange-looking bait given to you by a trusted adviser who claims he wants to teach you to fish but refuses to accompany you to the pond.

You feel awkward and uncertain in front of all those veteran fishermen lining the opposite bank. You bait your first hook, and, just as you feared, they all fall down laughing at your bait.

"That there crazy-lookin' bait ain't about to work in these waters, friend," one old codger chuckles, waving a handful of expensive hand-tied flies at you to make his point. "It takes money and lots of it to land the big ones around here."

You decide to keep your line in the water anyway, not only because you're hungry and have no real alternative, but also because you can't afford any other tackle right now. You pass the time trying out a few of the unfamiliar techniques suggested by your trusted adviser—and, lo and behold, you immediately hook into the granddaddy of all time. But somehow you lose him. . . .

Now, according to Philip's line of reasoning, *even if this first one gets away*, it's high time to drop a few more lines in the water and ignore the catcalls of the other fishermen. Why? Because now you know—not "think," not "hope," but know—that there is at least one whopper down there. Just as your adviser said. Got to be another.

"It's out there," Philip stated flatly during a phone call to me the evening he lost the fourplex on Leduc. "Of that I have no doubt. All I need to do now is figure out some way to go out there and get it. My back has not been broken yet. I thought I was tough, but I need to be tougher."

I breathed easier when I heard this. I'd wondered how Philip would react to failure. Now I knew. He had experienced one of the basic truths I had tried so hard to hammer home only two weeks earlier: There is no failure, only feedback.

And he'd gotten good feedback—the bait had worked! Just as I'd told him it would. The whoppers were out there. He had proven to himself that he could hook a "keeper." All he needed was a little more practice reeling it in.

As we rolled into the second week of the ninety-day period, Nora was still struggling. Mary was coming on fast, and Philip had already been close a time or two but had fallen short. Their failure— or should I say their lack of immediate success—was beginning to wear on me as much as on them. My self-appointed role in all of this was to sit by my phone a thousand miles away from the action and fret—reminding myself over and over again that this is a numbers game—nothing more, nothing less. Make a hundred calls, and you'll find a dozen prospects. Write a dozen offers, and you're bound to get three or four nibbles. Follow up enough nibbles, and you'll eventually land a fish. The logic is inescapable.

The problem, of course, is that fish are rarely swayed by logic. They bite when they're good and ready regardless of the bait you use or the hours you put in. That's why faith is so crucial to first-time fishermen like these. It gives them something specific to hang their hopes on until that first big deal tugs at their line.

I warned them all at the outset that the first few weeks might be tough, but another week passed without a serious nibble. It was becoming painfully obvious that the Show Me State was going to be a tough nut to crack. It was enough to shake anyone's self-confidence, even mine. I asked myself over and over again, "Where are all the fish?" But only the fish themselves knew for certain, and, as usual, they weren't talking.

I continued to confer with each intrepid angler every day or so by phone. But as the days passed with little tangible success, my encouragement began to sound like hollow, timeworn platitudes.

"Keep smiling!"

"Chin up. You can do it."

"Keep up the good work."

"Don't die of thirst just inches from the fountain."

"There is no failure, only feedback."

Quite frankly, there wasn't much else I could do except to remind them "to stick to the game plan"—another platitude. They continued to do so, and to report in on a regular basis, but a subtle anxiety began to pervade every conversation. I tried to fan the flickering fires of their Blue-Vase determination but I could feel the initial optimism fading away faster than I could replenish it. The Arch Museum and all its magic seemed like a distant mirage in the desert.

One day, after a particularly frustrating session of phone calls, with the camera crew zeroing in on the action, David Benjamin approached Mary. "How're you feeling?" he asked.

It didn't take much prodding to get her to talk. "Sometimes I feel like a guinea pig, you know. Like an experiment. On display. People watching how I'm going to act and react. Makes me feel very vulnerable. Like I'm taking a risk that I really am not sure I want to take. It's one thing to sign up for a regular Robert Allen seminar, where you're just a face in the crowd. But that's nothing like this fishbowl you have us in."

David nodded, trying to understand and feeling a bit responsible for the pressure she was under.

"It was worse at first," Mary continued. "When you first brought the cameras to my home, I really felt the violation of my privacy. I thought, 'Gee, if I don't learn it, I'm going to look dumb in front of all these people. They're going to see my mistakes.' But, lately, I've begun to feel more comfortable. I know you're not just trying to move me around like a pawn on a chessboard. I finally decided that whatever happens is going to be what I make of it. Bob Allen cannot make me a successful person. The books I read can't make me a successful person. It's going to be a sum total of all these things together. And I alone am responsible."

David was still listening, so Mary kept talking.

"But still, it's such an up-and-down, highs-and-lows kind of thing. Like today, I got all excited and hyped up about a condominium I'd found. In my mind, I already had myself moved in with the kids playing by the pool. And I hadn't even seen it yet!"

She paused, smiling at her impetuosity.

"So I called the hot line and after brainstorming with the financial consultant I could see there was no way I could afford it. So in my mind, I had to move out—and I still hadn't even seen it yet! So, you see, it's exciting and frustrating at the same time. And right now, I guess, I'm feeling pretty frustrated. Bob made it sound simple, but I knew it couldn't be that simple. I'm not saying he misrepresented it, either. He gave us the ABC, one-two-three plan for action, yet he told us all along, it was simple to understand but hard to do. A lot of trial and error. And I'm really beginning to see just how hard it is. I bet I've made a hundred telephone calls in the past three days. Already this morning, I counted thirty phone calls with only two possible 'maybes.' I see something promising and then, all of a sudden, it falls through. I guess I'm just going to have to get used to that."

David nodded, wanting to give her advice, and yet realizing that she was giving herself the best advice of all.

"And then, Monday, Steve went out of town. And so now basically I've been doing it on my own with the two children. Trying to balance being a mother and meeting their needs as well as succeeding at calling people on the phone. It's been very difficult. I'm scared to death. For one thing, I'm still not sure what I'm looking for. Or what to do with it if I find it. I was thinking about it today. It's as if the two-day training period was spent learning how to ride a simple bicycle, but at the end of class we were given a ten-speed bike—and I still haven't figured out how to shift the gears! There are so many areas, so many facets—this language—it's all so foreign to me."

2.

If the Challenge was a horse race, Nora was coming in dead last.

Dr. Lee's description of her the day we selected her was proving to be correct—she wasn't going to break any speed records, but like a tank she'd rumble over her obstacles one by one. But at times, I confess, her unhurried manner haunted me. I just had to bite my tongue and remind myself that she alone among the participants was flying solo—no supportive mate with whom to brave this unknown territory. Besides, as she described herself, she was "basically just a half-Indian farm girl from Kentucky." She needed time to adjust to the fast-paced, high-powered style of high finance she had been taught. Moreover, four of her five daughters were home to spend the summer with their mother. Although I had hoped for faster progress, I constantly wondered how she was able to do what she did.

And even tanks get discouraged.

"You know, you get up one morning and you're happy and everything's great," she observed wryly to David Benjamin one muggy afternoon, shielding her eyes from the noontime glare. "You think you're onto a property that really looks good. Then they say, 'Nah, we won't take this,' and 'Nah, we've gotta have that,' and you just get discouraged. Then you get nervous and upset, and you wonder if you're going to make it."

While I stewed over Nora and Mary, I rarely if ever entertained significant doubts about Philip's ability to make it. Which is strange, because Philip started out a good bit closer to the bottom of the financial barrel than either of the others—never in his life had he owned a home or a late-model car, never had a checking or savings account, never had a bank loan or obtained a major credit card. He was also several years younger than the others—never fully established as a responsible adult in the eyes of his family, much less the rest of the world.

Philip may not have had a house or a car or a spotless reputation like Mary's or a wealth of life experiences that someone like Nora could draw on in a pinch, but he wasn't bankrupt—not by any stretch of the imagination.

He had learned a lot in the years since the juvenile detention home. He also possessed a natural, God-given entrepreneurial talent. Add to that an instinctive understanding of the subtle give-and-take of the negotiation process, a sensitivity to the motivations and expectations of others, plus his drive and ambition mixed with a sense of priorities—a loyalty to his wife and family—and you have the makings of a pretty good businessman.

And he had another thing going for him. Unlike Mary and Nora, who already had comfortable home bases from which to operate, Philip didn't have to fight the creeping complacency that holds most Americans back. He was tired of being poor. And no one had to remind him of it. He had his fears, just like Nora. But he wasn't going to let them get in the way.

With the property on Leduc now out of the picture, Philip began to concentrate on others. The Maryville property, which he had already described to me, was now at the top of his list. Philip had taken Karen to see Maryville the day after he learned of it. They found a well-constructed red brick Victorian home three stories tall—twenty-eight hundred square feet of living space over a full basement—hardwood floors and a large stained glass window and two fancy fireplaces. Also a large, fenced backyard with a modern cement-block garage. They sensed that they had found a diamond in the rough.

"I figure we can rent the place as is for maybe $350 a month—$400 or even $450 if we spruce it up a little," Philip thought out loud as he and Karen raced home to write up an offer. "The seller doesn't owe a dime on it, and the Realtor says he's willing to carry the note for approximately fifteen years with just a thousand dollars down. The payments would be two hundred at the most. That'd leave a nice positive cash flow. But the best part is the price. Only twenty thousand dollars. Got to be worth twice that with a bit of fixup."

With Tom Painter's help, Philip wrote up an offer and submitted it with a thousand-dollar promissory note for earnest money and a request for a thirty-day closing to give him enough time to raise the thousand. If worse came to worse, he and Karen agreed to sell their stereo and the wrecked Audi automobile up on blocks in the backyard.

The real estate agent balked at submitting the offer. The promissory note bothered her. How was Philip going to come up with the down payment, most of which would be commission, if he couldn't even give her a check for earnest money? (If she had only known that Philip didn't even have a bank account!) Although sympathetic, she wouldn't budge. Finally, after much haggling back and forth, they reached a workable compromise—Philip would have to raise at least five hundred dollars and bring her a cashier's check. With this in hand, she would immediately submit the offer—an offer which, she assured him, would be acceptable to the seller, even though it meant his having to pay some modest closing costs out of his own pocket.

During the several phone calls between Tom and Philip about this property, more information was uncovered.

"Tell me more about the twenty-thousand-dollar property," Tom coaxed Philip. "Why is the seller selling?"

"It's been on the market for about two years. He used it as a rental property and had some problems with a tenant. Couldn't stand the hassle. So he just locked it up and let it sit. He still stores a lot of his stuff in the two-car garage. There's a large backyard full of his stuff also."

"And how much do you think it would take to fix it up?"

"I would say about two thousand."

"Have you done any kind of market survey on it to see what the other homes are going for in the area?"

"Not yet. But the woman told me that the last time the house was appraised was a year and a half ago. And it came in at forty. But, myself, I think it's worth about thirty-five."

"OK. Let's say thirty-five thousand. Get out your calculator. If you were to buy it for five hundred down, and then put a new eighty percent loan on it, you'd be looking at a new mortgage for twenty-eight thousand. After closing costs and paying off the seller completely, you would end up with a profit of about five thousand dollars. And you could rent out the house for enough to make your payments on the new loan, and keep the house."

"I like the sound of that," Philip said excitedly.

A day or so later, Philip called a local investor, Bob Coombs, for some advice on what to do. He explained the details and Bob gave him some background on the area and a few pointers.

"That used to be a great neighborhood," Coombs explained. "Then in the early seventies, a lot of the more established people moved out of there and into University City. There were some problems with drugs. I don't know what it's like now. Things might be coming back. I wouldn't buy there myself. Too risky. But you might check with the redevelopment companies and ask them about their plans for the area. Maybe you can sell it to them. And when you make your five grand, you can take me out to dinner with the profit."

"I love it," Philip laughed. "I love it! OK, Bob, thanks for the help. I'll check it out."

After several more calls and conflicting advice from different experts, Philip threw up his hands and called Tom Painter for some more guidance.

"Everybody has a different story. The local expert tells me to forget it. So I stopped thinking about it. I virtually told the real estate agent we weren't interested. And now you want me to make another offer. We go back and forth. Changing our minds. I don't want the Realtor to think that we're just two sucker brains, you know?"

Tom smiled to himself. Sucker brains? "Don't worry about looking like a sucker brain."

"Yeah. Well, the Realtor is a businesswoman, and I'd like to just come to a straight decision and say, 'Yeah, we're going to buy the property, and these are the terms.' Or, 'No, we don't want the property.' So, we're in limbo. But the property's still available."

"How much down would it take?" Tom asked.

"The Realtor told me I have to bring in five hundred dollars in a cashier's check so they know I'm serious."

"Can you get your hands on five hundred?"

"All I got is a hundred."

"Well, we've got to think of some way for you to scrape together some more money."

"I've tried everything I can think of." Just then, Philip had an idea. "Roses!"

"What?" Tom didn't understand.

"I'll call you back, Tom. I've got an idea."

Philip hung up the phone and sat in silence for a moment. A plan was building in his mind.

"Roses! That's the answer."

3.

A few miles away in a modest subdivision named Hollywood Hills by a developer possessed of more advertising flair than honesty, Mary Bonenberger was nervously writing up her first offer on a property she'd discussed with me a couple of days earlier. The house in question was a modestly-priced cookie-cutter tract house in the middle of an older middle-income subdivision that had yet to go to seed. The house would need a small amount of fixup. The seller wanted $31,000 for the property—a fair price, according to Mary—including a $7,000 down payment with the buyer to assume the existing $15,000 first mortgage. The remaining $9,000 could be carried in the form of a second mortgage. His willingness to carry a significant second mortgage with favorable terms suggested that he might be somewhat flexible in other areas as well.

Based on her initial phone conversation with the seller, Mary scored the property a twelve. I felt that her score was accurate and justified an offer. With my help Mary drew up an offer and submitted it to the owner's wife the following day.

Two days later the film crew gathered at Mary's house to film her phone conversation with the seller as he responded to her first offer, carefully written. With Steve looking on and five white hot lights blazing in her eyes, she eyed the whirring camera and sound gear and nervously dialed the seller's home. She swallowed, cleared her throat of emotion and waited as the phone rang once, twice, three times. The seller answered on the fourth ring. Mary got right to the point.

"Hello, Mr. Mehegan, this is Mary Bonenberger. Is your wife home?"

WISDOM FROM THE WISE

Things may come to those who wait, but only the things left by those who hustle.

—Abraham Lincoln.

The best way to be different is to just be yourself.

—Tony Bennett

Maturity of mind is the capacity to endure uncertainty.

—Charles Kettering

Insecurity is the result of trying to be secure.

—Alan Watts

It's never too late to be what you might have been.

—George Eliot

"She's not in right now."

Mary wanted to talk to the wife, with whom she had developed a friendly rapport. She had never met the husband. He sounded much more gruff than the wife. She forged ahead.

"Well, I don't know if she mentioned that I had come by and made an offer on the house. Did you all have a chance to look it over?"

"Yes, we did."

An awkward silence followed. The camera zoomed in for a close-up of Mary's expectant expression as she waited for the seller to continue. When he didn't, she prompted him nervously.

"Did you have any questions or anything?"

"No, we didn't."

"Oh," she sighed.

"That's not acceptable to us."

Mary's face revealed her disappointment, but she remembered my recent advice: Never close any door unnecessarily.

"I see. Do you want to make a counter offer?"

"Just our original offer."

"What exactly was it that you wanted?"

"Well, we wanted to finance nine thousand dollars ourselves with the assumable. The loan balance was fifteen thousand, and then it was seven thousand down."

"Right, but you didn't agree with the way I came up with the seven thousand?"

"No, not where we'd give you two thousand dollars cash."

"That was what I wanted to explain to you."

Mary talked to Mr. Mehegan for several more minutes, but it was obvious to her that nothing she could say at this point would salvage the situation, so she soon thanked him for considering her offer and hung up.

"Back to the drawing board," she reported ruefully to Steve, who had been trying to guess the outcome from his vantage point across the table. "I was really counting on this one to come through. I guess I'll have to learn not to let myself get so excited. How do you feel?"

"How do *I* feel?" Steve thought for a moment. "Not surprised."

"I don't know," Mary said, still confused by the outcome. "The wife seemed to think my offer was OK, but I never had any contact with the husband. Until today...."

She paused to reflect for a moment. There's no failure—only feedback. Next time, she determined to deal with the primary decision maker in the family. In this case, it had been the husband. Unfortunately, Mary had spent all of her energies with the wife.

4.

About three weeks into the Challenge, I discovered that the film crew had started an unofficial betting pool to predict who would be the first to close on a property. Most of the crew favored Philip because of his nose for finding don't-wanters. Some backed Mary, and she didn't disappoint them; she quickly found another promising property to offer on. But Nora was the sentimental favorite. Although I'm not a betting man, I, too, was secretly pulling for Nora— the underdog.

I was proud as a rooster of her efforts to date: handing out hundreds of fliers, running ads in the local newspapers—and getting calls on those ads with remarkable regularity—spending hours on the phone and in the nearby tax assessor's office combing the tax records for absentee landlords anxious to sell. Of the three, Nora had covered the most ground.

That didn't mean, however, that she was making adequate progress. She spent several hours each week talking on the phone with Tom Painter—a key member of my original Mastermind team. He patiently tutored her. She was still petrified of calling sellers on the phone.

As I watched her grope and stumble, it became clear to me how emotional scars from past events color everyone's view of reality, whether we like to admit it or not. Instead of seeing the world as it is, we see it through the colored glasses of our own prejudices, fears and experiences. Thus, every person sees a different world. Would Nora be able to see the new world I had described to her? I wondered if Nora had really grasped the concept that money itself isn't wealth but just the by-product of it. Was she just paying lip service to it in hopes that her money problems would magically disappear?

Although she was doing her best to avoid financial disaster, she began to fall further behind on her own mortgage payments. Was she going to lose her own home to foreclosure? Even those closest to her began to wonder. And a member of the film crew did little to reassure me by observing that Nora seemed to be spending more time dreaming about what to do with her first five hundred thousand dollars than on making that critical first five thousand. My logical left brain warned me to brace myself for Nora's eventual failure; my intuitive right brain disagreed. Nora was a survivor. You could hear it in every word she spoke.

"You wouldn't believe the obstacles I've been up against, but I never was a quitter," she told me early on.

When pressed for examples, she recalled a series of financial setbacks in 1982. She had her car repossessed, a man she owed money to came after her furniture with a U-Haul, and the electric company turned her power off when she couldn't pay her five-hundred-dollar bill.

The blacker things got, the more determined she became.

She dug out an old coal-oil lamp and an old washtub that used to belong to her mother. She set the washtub in her backyard, and every day before she left for work, she would fill it with water so that the sun would heat it. When she returned from work, she would use the sun-warmed water to bathe and wash her clothes. This went on all summer long—no electricity, no hot water, just that coal-oil lamp for light at night. But with September coming and the cold around the corner, she got worried. She had to have electricity.

Finally, in desperation, down to her last two dollars, she drove to the local hardware store and bought a can of silver spray paint for $1.89. She came home, climbed up the trestle in back of her house, pulled herself up on the roof and said a silent prayer.

And then, in big silver letters clear across the roof, she painted out a message that even God couldn't miss. H E L P.

Someone up there must have seen it. Because within a week she had the money to turn her electricity back on.

5.

Then Tom Painter got an urgent message to call Mary.

"Hi, Tom," she said when he called back. "I had a real good thing happen last night." She sounded excited. "I got a call back from a lady whose house I saw on Saturday. And she asked me, 'What do you think about my house? Do you want to buy it?' I couldn't believe it."

"Is she motivated to get out?" Tom asked.

"She seems very motivated. I keep hearing her say things like, 'I have other obligations,' 'I can't afford this house payment,' and this kind of thing: 'I had the house advertised in the paper for three weeks and it didn't sell, so now I've got to do something.' "

"Tell me about the details."

"Well, it's on Dartmore, just a few miles from my house. It's got three bedrooms, one bath and no garage. It's just a bit larger than our house. The seller had an appraisal done on it a year ago at thirty-six thousand dollars. And she owes thirty-two thousand dollars on it. She was asking thirty-five for it in the paper—that was where I saw it. Her husband passed away. She's just had it a year, and she can't afford to keep it anymore. The payments are $395 a month at twelve percent interest. That's with interest and taxes. It's an FHA loan, so I can just walk in and assume it."

"OK." Tom had chased down enough blind alleys as a recent newcomer to real estate investing not to get overly excited. Experience takes the emotion out of decision making—the fear and the thrill. Like a surgeon, you learn not to panic over a little blood or to get overly hopeful when the operation appears successful.

"So, anyway," Mary continued, "in the course of the conversation, she said, 'I really need eight hundred dollars to get into an apartment.' And I said, 'Would you consider an offer of, say, eight hundred dollars or whatever it takes you to get into your new place, plus me walking in and taking over your payments?' I was expecting her to say, 'Absolutely not,' but instead she said, 'Well, I just might do that. I really just can't afford to keep this house any more.' "

Tom broke in. "It's not a very good choice for a rental unit because you won't be able to rent it out to cover the mortgage payments. What do you think you could rent it for?"

"Three-fifty. Maybe three seventy-five."

"Really? Could it go that high?"

"For a three-bedroom? Easily. The payment includes taxes and insurance, so we're pretty close."

"We might have us something here," Tom said. "Since it's priced below market, maybe we can turn around and sell it immediately for a fifteen-hundred- or two-thousand-dollar profit. It's worth an offer."

Tom and Mary went through the process of writing up an offer. It was June 21. They offered to pay five hundred dollars and take over her payments with a closing date of July 30. The offer was also subject to Steve's approval and the right to clean up the property before closing to prepare it for rent or sale.

When they had completed the paperwork, Mary anxiously signed her name, put the offer in an envelope and drove it over to the woman's home. She left the offer in the mailbox. The next day, when there had been no response to her offer, Mary got up the nerve to call the woman on the phone.

"Hello, Miriam," she said. "I know I'm catching you at a bad time. But I wonder if you've had a chance to think over my offer?"

"Yes, I have and I really need more than that. As much as I want to let it go, I just can't let it go at that."

"I see," Mary said, trying to conceal the disappointment in her voice.

"I need at least a thousand."

"Well, if you change your mind, I would appreciate it if you would keep my number. I would like to buy your house, but that's just about the tops I can go. I hope you find somebody to buy it."

"Well, I do too. If I don't, I'll keep you in mind."

Mary hung up the phone. "No, again," she whispered to herself.

Just then, Steve burst through the door returning from a three-day trip to a church summer camp. He entered the room, enthusiastic and refreshed, eager to hear what he hoped would be good news.

"Hi, dear," Mary said less than enthusiastically. "Did you have a good time at camp?" She didn't wait for his reply. "We just got a turn-down on number two. You know, the house on Dartmore?"

"Why?"

"Because she needs a thousand dollars."

"Can't we get her a thousand dollars? That would still be considered a no-money-down deal by Bob's standards—less then five percent down."

"I just don't know if it would appraise at much more than what we would buy it for. If we kept it, there wouldn't be much more than a break-even cash flow. And we couldn't sell it for enough to make five thousand dollars in ninety days."

"But it might be a good little property to keep. Like a little oil well in our backyard pumping out money."

"Well, at least I know what a don't-wanter acts like," Mary said. "She wanted out of that property in the worst way. I really wish I could help her."

They both sat quietly. It was the twenty-second of June. Exactly thirteen days earlier, they had embarked into unknown territory with dreams of reaching their financial promised land. But the weather in the wilderness was brutal. And the natives weren't hospitable. And their supplies were running low.

Oh, Lewis and Clark, where are you when we need you?

6.

It was at a Father's Day barbecue out in the backyard that Philip shared his plan with Karen. "I've got a great idea how we can raise the five hundred dollars for the Maryville deal," he informed her out of the blue. "How about selling roses in Maryland Plaza again? I already talked to Mr. Potter at the greenhouse, and he'll sell me two hundred roses plus baby's breath and everything for a hundred dollars. We could take our savings and the rent money and buy some roses. If you sell fifty roses a night and I sell fifty. . . ."

"Fifty?" Karen said with playful scorn, caught up in the infectious audacity of Phil's plan, "We can each sell a *hundred!* And go back to Mr. Potter for two hundred more."

Phil figured their potential profit in his head. "Let's see, we sell them for two-fifty apiece. Our cost is fifty cents. That's a two dollar profit on each rose. If we could sell 250 roses, we'd have our five hundred dollars."

Their minds awash with visions of the money they could make in just a few short days, Phil and Karen made plans to pick up the roses the next morning.

A more conservative couple might have backed away from risking the rent money on such a plan. Roses have, at best, a twelve-hour life expectancy in the hot summer sun. Not much of a market for wilted, day-old roses. But this thought scarcely passed through their minds as they arose early the next morning to wrap 250 individual roses in bright green florist's paper—each with a small spray of baby's breath to add some extra street appeal—and charged off for Maryland Plaza to earn their five hundred dollars the hard way.

"Roses here!" Philip called out cheerfully. Hundreds of pedestrians thronged the streets of Maryland Plaza—a chic shopping district near Kings Highway. Most of them passed by without a second glance.

Karen worked the crowds, too, but preferred a subtle approach. "Roses for sale. How about a rose, sir? Aren't they beautiful?"

After the first hour or two it became painfully obvious that most of St. Louis' rose lovers were avoiding Maryland Plaza like the plague. In fact, unbelievable as it may sound, Phil and Karen failed to sell a single rose all day long. And as if that wasn't bad enough, a policeman ran them out of the plaza because they couldn't produce a current peddler's license.

"That's what finally convinced me to give up on Maryland Plaza," Phil recalled bitterly. "I guess it just wasn't our day. Karen was all upset and crying and everything, so she went home. I figured I had to get at least a few bucks back out of the roses, so I lowered the price down to a dollar . . . then fifty cents. I finally started hitting these little bars I know. I was selling a dozen roses for a dollar at one point, just trying to get some of the rent money back."

It's easy to say that failure is good for you, but it's hard to live it. It's easy to look at the lives of great men like Edison or Lincoln and attribute their greatness to their willingness to endure the painful shame of failure. It's easy to observe that Babe Ruth set his famous home run records because he wasn't afraid of the stigma of holding the lifetime record for strikeouts as well. But for most of us, it's hard to accept the fact that repeated failure is often the price we must be willing to pay for success. One of the things successful people have in common is their ability to perceive the good in every failure while everyone around them sees only shame.

As they say, "There are only two kinds of investors: The successful ones. And those who give up too soon."

As for Phil and Karen, after using up their savings for the roses, they squeaked by on their rent with less than ten dollars to spare. But Philip still had a five-hundred-dollar problem. Since the rose idea wilted, he tried other ideas: borrowing money from his family, selling parts off his nonfunctional Audi, selling his stereo speakers and various pieces of furniture—all dead ends. He even called me to arrange to sell sets of success sampler tapes on some sort of commission basis to raise the needed five hundred dollars. I nixed that idea. Through all of this failure, he persisted. But to no avail.

His offer on Maryville expired. Reluctantly, he turned his attention to other deals. How frustrating—to be so close to success and to be shackled by an inability to raise a mere five hundred lousy bucks.

A couple of days later Mary called Philip to invite him and Karen to a "debriefing" lunch at her house on June 24. He hitched a ride with the film crew and arrived at Mary's house carrying a dozen long-stemmed roses, a symbolic gift for a group of empty-handed fishermen.

The group, minus Karen, who was working overtime, moved into the kitchen, where Mary had set out a light summer lunch. They took turns talking about the details of the current deals they were pursuing, then got down to brass tacks.

"The plain truth is I've had a lot of misgivings lately," Nora volunteered. "I do fine until people start throwing negative attitudes. And then I start wondering. You can't help wondering at times."

"I don't have as much trouble with other peoples' attitudes, just my own," Mary admitted honestly. "Believing that I can do it."

"Well, long before I met Robert Allen I knew it could be done," Phil interjected. "I just didn't know how. Now I know. I'm finding out that it's got its ups and downs. But when I was out there looking for that job every day, I got the same thing—ups and downs. I like this better because I'm in control."

Phil, Nora and Mary, in three short weeks, had already scanned more classified ads, made more telephone inquiries, inspected more houses and written more offers than most people do in a lifetime. But unlike horseshoe pitching, close doesn't count in real estate.

I wasn't there at the lunch, but David Benjamin gave me a report. My heart ached for them. I had an overpowering urge to fly to St. Louis—to show up unannounced on their doorsteps, to hold their hands, scout out deals for them or perhaps slip them some money on the side so the good deals they'd already found wouldn't disappear down the drain.

But I knew I couldn't do it.

I felt like a veteran football coach in the final quarter of a Super Bowl game, except that this Super Bowl weekend was ninety days long. I found it impossible to avoid agonizing over every fumble, every incomplete pass, every busted play. I wanted to send in a secret play that would win the game for them. But there weren't any secret plays. No shortcuts. This was the only way.

I wanted desperately for them to win in the short run. But I wasn't willing to sacrifice the long run to do it. That was my own personal challenge—to sit tight, patiently watching the struggle. It was one of the hardest things I have ever had to do. The outcome, at this point, was still uncertain. Maybe I was putting them through too much. Should I call it off? Should I let them continue to beat their brains out? Would they come out of this stronger or forever weakened? How could I know?

Then I ran across a story in *Leadership Magazine* that helped me put my decision in perspective:

> A man found a cocoon of the Emperor moth and took it home to watch it emerge. One day a small opening appeared and for several hours the moth struggled but couldn't seem to force its body past a certain point. Deciding something was wrong, the man took scissors and snipped the remaining bit of cocoon. The moth emerged easily, its body large and swollen, the wings small and shriveled. He expected that in a few hours the wings would spread out in their natural beauty, but they did not. Instead of developing into a creature free to fly, the moth spent its life dragging around a swollen body and shriveled wings. The constricting cocoon and the struggle necessary to pass through the tiny opening are God's way of forcing fluid from the body into the wings. The merciful snip was, in reality, cruel. Sometimes the struggle is exactly what we need.

But I wasn't dealing with moths. I was dealing with real people! And saying that struggle is necessary does not make it any easier to live with. Or any less uncertain. The outcome is always in doubt.

I recalled my own struggles as a beginning investor and remembered one bleak month in particular—October 1975. I had just turned twenty-seven and was living in an apartment of single students just a few blocks from the campus of Brigham Young University. I had been investing in real estate for a couple of years and had experienced some success—and a few failures. But lately things had been slow. I was broke. I had to borrow rent money from one of my roommates. That was the final straw. To cover my embarrassment I decided to pack it all in and apply for an administrative job at BYU. I'll never forget the salary they were offering—$10,500 a year. I swallowed my pride and filled out the application, noting my new MBA, my sterling character, and everything else I could think of. I needed that job.

I waited, sweaty-palmed, for their reply.

Luckily, they turned me down.

Luckily? In retrospect, yes; it was lucky. Or maybe providential. Without a steady job, I was forced to keep digging in the real estate mine shaft that I had been working. I tightened my belt. A few weeks later, I hit pay dirt. An option on a piece of land came through, and I deposited thirty thousand dollars in my bank account.

I look back on those black times and chuckle. But it wasn't funny at the time.

Struggle is never fun. Just necessary.

With those thoughts in mind, I continued to monitor the progress of the Challenge team. I felt like a parent sending his child off to college, fully aware that short-term pain of separation was necessary for long-term growth to occur.

At the same time, our impartial judge, former mayor of St. Louis and former FBI agent John Poelker was also monitoring the participants. "I have checked in with each of the three people involved in the Challenge from time to time," he remarked in an interview on June 25, "and they've all had some ups and downs. They knew it wouldn't be easy, that they were like pioneers—there were going to be Indians to fight, rivers to ford, and so on. They're not quite a third of the way along their trek, and truly I feel for them. I know they're all overanxious. But I think they have reached that part of the journey where they can now see that theory and actuality can be somewhat different."

The former mayor paused, puffed on his trademark cigar for a few moments, then continued. "In my career I've made political decisions that were sometimes risky, decisions that I never knew for certain were going to be for the best. But I think if you feel right about it yourself—and these people do—it's easier to brook those little periods of doubt when things aren't going right. It's like a parent teaching his kid to ride a bicycle for the first time. You can't really protect kids from the skinned knees and scrapes and scratches. All you can hope to do is give them enough confidence to go it on their own. And I think that's what Bob Allen is trying to do."

At least, that was the theory behind what I was trying to do. But the real world kept sticking in its ugly nose.

"Sometimes I feel like a total impostor on the phone," Mary complained to me one afternoon. "You know, I say I'm this big investor and the whole time my kids are yelling embarrassing stuff in the background. It's hard sometimes. But then I'll take the kids with me to look at properties and I'll stop and realize how much more time I'm spending with them than I'd be able to do if I worked at a regular nine-to-five job."

Philip, on the other hand, seemed to have gotten back on track, in spite of his earlier setbacks and financial losses. He hooked another big one. This time, the lead came from his ad in the newspaper. A true don't-wanter in the form of a local preacher called wanting to sell a six-room brick home in good condition. Value: $20,000 to $30,000. Loan: $6,000. Down payment required: $4,000. Price: $10,000. Philip couldn't believe what he was hearing! For just $4,000 he could pick up over $20,000 in equity. He rushed over to inspect the property, half-expecting to find either a lousy location or a dilapidated hovel. What he found was very encouraging. He ran a description of the property by me and my staff. We also encouraged him. With this feedback, he wrote up an offer and submitted it, subject to finding a partner. But the preacher didn't want to commit in writing. Instead, he gave Philip his word that he wouldn't sell the property to anyone else if Philip could bring him $4,000 cash in fifteen days. Philip excitedly made the rounds to several small-time investors he had recently uncovered. One of them gave him the green light.

I was excited for him. He seemed on the verge. And then I received a phone call from Mary. "Did you hear about Philip?" she asked. "They sold that house out from under him."

I was stunned. "But the guy was a minister, and he gave his word."

"I know. Poor Philip. Apparently he called the preacher this morning and learned that he had sold it to someone else—even though he had given his word. Philip hung up the phone and went off and cried."

"Oh, that's too bad."

"Philip said it just teaches him that it's important to get things in writing."

When I talked with Philip later that same day he was as low and discouraged as I have ever known him to be. He felt betrayed. He had trusted someone and had walked away with a knife in his back. And to top it off, he had had to call his partner with egg on his face.

But Philip and I weren't finished with that preacher just yet. Together we drafted a letter to send to him, and Philip dropped the letter off at his house the next day. In essence, it said that sooner or later he would have to answer for what he had done.

Philip never received a reply.

Mary, also, was continuing to have her trials.

She and Steve weren't seeing eye to eye. She was the natural entrepreneur, and he proved to be the cautious type. This divergent view of the world caused friction—some of the worst arguments of their marriage. Neither wanted to budge.

Over the years, I have observed a curious thing about many marriage partners: When one is generally positive, the other will most invariably be negative. If one is clearly a left-brain thinker, the other will generally be a right-brain thinker. Where one is strongly conservative, the other seems more risk-oriented. It's almost as if that old truism "Where there's a will there's a way" is subtly altered by the terms of the marriage contract to read, "Where there's a will there's a won't."

"I tend to get extremely panicky where money is involved," Steve confessed to me. "We don't make a lot of money. When you spend down to thirty-eight cents in your checkbook each week, money becomes a pretty serious issue. I tend to be 'safety first' all the time. My wife is thinking a lot bigger than I am right now. We're going to have to make some kind of adjustment in there somewhere."

Mary also had her opinion. "I don't like always being Miss Meek and Mild, and always getting trampled on all the time, always giving in to what other people want me to do."

Fighting over finances is the number one cause of divorce. As I listened to their struggles, I could only hope that I hadn't been the cause of accelerating a breakup between them.

Obviously, their marriage was more important than the Challenge. They were caught in the center of an emotional storm and needed to find a mutually beneficial way through it. Their marriage was like a newly constructed cottage in the path of a hurricane. Like it or not, the storm was going to test the structural integrity of their relationship. This emotional whirlwind had already caused a few

weakened shingles to tear away from the roof, and a few loose
pieces of siding were beginning to rattle. Weathering these storms is
a scary process but something every marriage has to endure. For
many, fortunately, the benefits are long-lasting. When the storm has
passed and the sky clears, the structure that remains can be de-
pended upon to weather future storms. Farmers in Kentucky's Tornado Alley often speak with great affection of ancient oak barns
that have been "tornado tested" over the years. They know that
such barns, like strong marriages, are to be prized above all others.

Mary and Steve were being tornado tested. It was too early to tell
if they would make it through.

Meanwhile, Nora was moving off in a new direction and had
placed another ad in the paper.

> Earn 37% return on your money!
> In prime Missouri real estate.
> Call Nora. 555-1234

It had to work. Nora was on to a good lead, and she would need a
partner pronto.

She recalled her phone conversation of only a few days earlier.

"Good morning. My name is Nora Boles and I would like to talk to
you about foreclosures of property. I've got some money coming,
and I would like to invest in single-family houses."

The banker on the other end of the line gave her a startling reply.
"The only thing we have is in Cuba, Missouri."

Nora had been so conditioned to being rejected that she fumbled
for a minute, not knowing how to proceed. "OK," she continued.
"Would you tell me about it?"

"Yes, it's on an acre and a half. It has a small pond. It's a three-
bedroom frame house with the basement partially set up to finish—
but they didn't finish it."

"Could you tell me what the terms are?" Many days of telephone
calling had taught her to get right to the heart of the matter. For
some reason, she had no fear of talking to a banker as compared to
talking to an average seller.

"Well," he replied, "fifty-five thousand dollars is what the price
will be."

"I see. Well, is that below the market? How much below the market?" Her confidence was showing.

"It was appraised at seventy thousand dollars. We could possibly work out a deal as far as financing. And our interest rate is thirteen percent."

"Thirteen percent," Nora echoed. "And what kind of deal would you consider working out?" Nora's telephone technique had improved markedly. Her constant role-playing with Tom Painter was paying off in a big way.

"If you qualify, we'll take ten percent down and possibly work out a better arrangement on the interest rate."

Nora called me with the details of the Cuba property. I advised her to arrange a tour of the property as soon as possible.

After inspecting it, she phoned Tom immediately. Together, they worked up an offer to present to the bank. Fifty thousand price. Twenty-five hundred down. Balance of the loan carried by the bank at 9.5 percent interest. Nora wondered, as she hand-carried the offer to the bank that afternoon, how any bank could accept such a patently low-ball offer.

"I've been out to the Cuba property," she told the banker as she handed him an envelope. "I'm prepared to make you an offer. I hope it's an offer you can't refuse."

He took the envelope from her.

"Here goes nothing," she thought to herself.

7.

Thirty days of the Challenge blew by like a windstorm. With the Fourth of July just around the corner and thirty days of mass confusion behind them, the Challenge team decided to throw a barbecue at Nora's place to celebrate their own survival. Mayor Poelker was the guest of honor—perhaps the first big-city mayor in the history of American politics ever to set foot in low-income housing in a non-election year.

"This barbecue looks pretty good," the former mayor observed hungrily. "Is it as good as the real estate business, Philip?"

"Right now it's better," Phil confided with a smile, "but I have all the confidence in the world right now. I figure I've made six hundred dollars since I started. That's because I've made six offers and lost 'em all!"

"How about you, Nora?" Mayor Poelker asked as he spotted his hostess coming through the door with a huge bowl of homemade potato salad. "What have you been up to these past few days?"

"Lots of things. I've been working within a fifty-mile radius of here: Pacific, Eureka, Fenton, Valley Park, High Ridge, Cedar Hill, Cuba, all those places."

"Well, that's all fertile territory."

"It sure is," Nora replied. "I've got six offers out right now. I've just got my fingers crossed. We've been at this just exactly one month as of today, and I feel like I'm just starting to get the hang of things."

"How about you, Mary?" Mayor Poelker asked. "I know it hasn't been easy for you with two little ones at home and your husband out of town so much lately. Has your enthusiasm abated any these past few weeks?"

Those who knew something of Mary's inner turmoil awaited her answer with bated breath. "No, not really," she said after a thoughtful pause. "It's been a little rough with the kids and everything, but I've managed to have a lot of baby-sitters, and I've even been taking the kids along to look at properties. It just takes a little creativity. Steve's back in town now, and we found two properties that were all grown up with weeds and sent letters to the owners. One man called us back yesterday. We're going over there tomorrow to make him an offer."

"What keeps them going?" I had asked myself that question a hundred times. It must be that look of determination I spotted that very first morning thirty days before. At this juncture—thirty days into it—I had no way of knowing whether they would succeed or fail. But at least I was certain that they, like Rocky, had the guts to go the distance. Each of them had kept five good lines in the water for thirty days. Each had been "tornado tested" and was still standing. Each had uncovered at least one excellent property and a few more to pursue. Each had a clear sense of just how far they'd come in such a short period of time. Like true blue-vasers, they had done everything asked of them and much, much more.

Didn't they deserve to be financially successful?

Only time would tell.

THINGS TURN OUT BEST FOR THE PEOPLE WHO MAKE
THE BEST OF THE WAY THINGS TURN OUT.—Ty Boyd

15

BEHOLD, A SOWER WENT FORTH TO SOW

1. _____

A great advertising man once remarked that only 50 percent of his advertising budget was effective. He just didn't know which half. So he spent 100 percent of his budget anyway. Had to keep sowing those seeds. No sow, no grow.

"And when he sowed, some seeds fell by the way side, and the fowls came and devoured them up. . . ."

A greater speaker once stated to an audience that over half of them would never achieve their total potential of success for one simple reason: Someone would talk them out of it.

". . . some fell upon stony places, where they had not much earth: and forthwith they sprung up, because they had no deepness of earth: And when the sun was up, they were scorched; and because they had no root, they withered away. . . ."

A great thinker once said that a new idea is delicate. It can be killed by a sneer or a yawn; it can be stabbed to death by a quip and worried to death by a frown on the right man's brow.

. . . and some fell among thorns; and the thorns sprung up, and choked them. . . ."

You never can tell when a casual comment—a seed cast out—will fall on fertile ground. Most of them fall on deaf ears. But every once in while. . . .

". . . others fell into good ground, and brought forth fruit, some an hundredfold, some sixtyfold, some thirtyfold. . . ."

One Sunday, after church, Steve stopped to talk to a young girl in his Sunday school class. He had heard that her parents were moving and that they might need to sell their house. She knew some of the details, the most important of which was that her parents needed a large down payment. Steve shrugged. Obviously, he couldn't afford that! But, out of curiosity, he asked, "Are there any houses on your block that are vacant?"

To his surprise, she described a home in her neighborhood that looked abandoned. A few days later, Steve drove through her neighborhood to see if he could find the house. And sure enough, there it was! The grass was a foot tall, and the property had the appearance of having been forgotten. He checked with the next-door neighbor, an older woman, who informed him that the couple who owned the house hadn't occupied the property for six months. Rumor had it that they were getting a divorce. She was happy to tell Steve all she knew about the former occupants. He sped home to place a call to the husband's place of employment, but he no longer worked there. So Steve went to the post office and paid a dollar to get the forwarding address. Armed with this lead, Steve and Mary sent a letter to the owners offering to buy the house.

"About four or five days later the phone rang," Steve later recalled. "It was the owner. He had gotten our letter and was interested in selling. I made an appointment to meet him at the property the next Saturday at ten o'clock. I waited an hour, but when he didn't show up I went back home and called him. He was still in bed and I woke him up. When the seller finally showed up, he brought two blue letters from the bank. He said to us, 'You open these up. I think I know what they are already.' Just as he thought, the letter stated that he was six months behind in his payments and within the next week, the property would go into foreclosure."

Mary joined in the story. "He was a motivated seller. He had the court, the bank, everybody on his back. I reminded him of the damage a foreclosure can do to a credit rating. He said, 'If you'll just get these people off my back, I'll be glad to sell to you.' So we got to work right away. We checked the neighborhood and found out that the other houses on the block were going for thirty-two to thirty-four thousand. The seller's loan balance was just over nineteen thousand. We figured his back payments would amount to about fifteen hundred dollars. That's when we started to see that this one was glittering pretty good."

"That's when we called you to help us write up an offer," Mary continued. "We offered to make up his back payments and assume the existing financing. This would preserve his and his wife's credit rating and keep them out of court. They both realized the predicament they were in and signed the offer. When we checked with the bank we learned that the back payments were around twenty-one hundred dollars. The existing financing was an FHA fixed-rate assumable loan, 9.75 percent interest. The bank agreed to stall the foreclosure for a few more days.

"Then we hit our first snag. Although he'd already signed the offer to sell, the seller called a few days later to say, 'My lawyer seems to think I ought to get some money out of this deal.' It was a point of indecision for me. I took a deep breath and said, 'We only have enough money to make up your back payments and take over your loan. If you want more than that, then I guess you'll have to find another buyer.' I thought, 'If he turns it down, he turns it down. That's just the name of the game.' And he said, 'Well, OK, that's fine.' I think he was just pushing to see if he could get some extra cash."

Because of the experience of two previous failures, Mary stuck to her guns. Her words had a ring of truth about them. The seller knew that she couldn't go any higher.

So Steve and Mary had finally found an opportunity. Step one complete. The next step was to fund that opportunity. Where were they going to get the money to complete this transaction? They certainly didn't have it. Mary approached her parents, who initially agreed but a few days later called to back out. Although she was disappointed, Mary knew they were having some financial struggles and understood. After several calls they finally located a relative who agreed to share profits with them. The necessary cash was

EIGHT WAYS TO FUND A PROPERTY

There are eight potential sources of money to fund a real estate purchase. Each one of these sources must be considered whenever you are short of money to buy.

1. The seller: The seller may agree to lend you part of the down payment in exchange for higher monthly payments or interest rates, increased security or collateral, a higher price or a balloon payment in the future.

2. The buyer: As a buyer you may have sources of cash you may not have considered, such as borrowing against the cash value of your insurance policy, your own savings and inheritances, your ability to trade your talents and/or skills for a credit against the down payment, your ability to assume some of the seller's debts instead of paying cash or using some of your "dead equities" (cars, boats, stereos, recreational land) in exchange for part or all of the required down payment.

3. The Realtor: Sometimes the Realtor involved may consider lending you all or part of his commission to make a deal.

4. The renters: As a part of a purchase of rental property, the owner receives the rent and deposits of the current tenants. In some states, a buyer can use these funds as a credit toward his down payment to buy the property.

5. The property: In some instances, the furniture, fixtures, assets or excess land in a real estate transaction can be split off and sold for enough to come up with a down payment to buy the remaining property.

6. Hard-money lenders: Banks and other lending institutions can provide all or part of the cash required by a seller.

7. The holders of underlying mortgages: In some rare instances, it can be in the best interests of underlying private mortgage holders (and even future mortgage holders) to cooperate with the buyer of a property in providing funds to purchase the property.

8. Partners: If you don't have it, somebody does! You can always find a partner to lend you cash, credit or a financial statement in exchange for a share of the profits if the deal is right.

deposited at a title company in readiness for the impending closing.

Mary continued, "The bank agreed to hold off the foreclosure till Friday, but the first title company we called told us it would take a minimum of two weeks. That wasn't fast enough. We were discouraged, thinking that we had lost it. But we decided to call some other title companies and finally located one that promised to close by the end of the week.

"Every day was like sitting on pins and needles—just like being on a roller coaster. I was a nervous wreck running papers back and forth between the bank and the title company to make sure we could meet the deadline. [Can you see her Blue-Vase attitude shining through?] All week it was on again, off again, on again, off again! Then, Friday, in spite of all my running around, the title officer told me, 'There is just no way we can have it by today.' So I had to call the bank and buy a little more time. I said, 'Please, I promise you we're going to assume this. We have an investor to put up the money for the back payments. Please, can you hold it off one more day?' And she said, 'We'll hold it off until Monday.' "

Monday came and went. The closing was tentatively set for Tuesday morning.

"I called both the husband and the wife Monday night and told them to prepare for a closing the next day. While I was chatting with the husband, he asked me nonchalantly, 'Say, what is my wife's new phone number? I need to talk to her about the kids.' So I gave it to him. The second I told him, I knew I'd made a terrible mistake. It wasn't until the next day that I found out the extent of the damage.

"The next morning the title company called to tell me that the closing was set for one o'clock in the afternoon. I figured it was in the bag! We had it! I immediately tried to reach the husband, but he didn't answer his phone. I had the operator check to see if the number was working. Still no answer. I was scared to death. I sent Steve over to his apartment. In the meantime, I tried to reach the wife. Her father answered the phone and refused to let me talk to her. He blamed me for giving the new number to the husband. It had caused all sorts of problems. According to the father, the husband had called her and threatened to kill her. So she had gone into hiding. Here it was the day of the closing, and both sellers had disappeared! I was in a panic.

"Finally, Steve called the father and reasoned with him. A few minutes later, the wife called and agreed to sign if we would drive her to the closing. We called the title company and told them we were bringing in the wife but that we couldn't find the husband. The lady at the title company said, 'Oh, he's already been by; he already signed it.' I was about to scream! We jumped into the car and ran over to get the lady and take her to the title company. I really apologized to her for my mistake. I felt so dumb.

"Up until 1:05 that afternoon when everyone finally signed all the papers and the title company lady closed her little manila folder and said, 'Well, where do you want the deed of trust sent to?' I was bracing myself for more bad news. Then I realized that the house was ours! I couldn't believe it!

"The first thing I thought was, 'Gee, now we've got to get over there, clean that thing out; we've got to paint it; we've got a lot of work still to do and a lot of decisions still to make. What are we going to do with it? How are we going to turn it? Are we going to rent it?' You know, all these questions raced through my head. Even the little things like, 'Do I call the utility company this afternoon?' All the little specifics of ownership. Before, it was just an idea! Now it was a reality. We actually had the property! Time to get down to the nitty-gritty. Time to get in there and get some work done."

Steve recalled his feelings after the closing. "I really felt what we did was very up front. We told the sellers right from the start that we didn't have much money to give them. Each one of them was worried that we were giving the other one some money. They found out at the closing that we only had ten dollars earnest money."

Mary agreed. "The seller's husband seemed glad to get it over with. He said, 'Does this mean the bank is finally off my back?' The wife would have liked to keep the house, but she couldn't afford the payments. She also said that, although she was sad about losing the house, part of her life was over and now she could start her life all over again."

On the thirty-seventh day of the ninety-day Challenge, Steve and Mary sat in their living room holding the closing documents to a home they had just bought a few hours earlier. It was July 15. They had found and funded a potential opportunity.

Why do I say 'potential'? Because the third step in the process still lay ahead of them—farming it.

And that is always easier said than done.

2. _____

During this time, Nora was also busy casting out seeds. Mostly, they landed on barren ground.

With my help she drafted a letter to send to a seller who showed don't-wanter tendencies.

Dear Sir:

I am a real estate investor. You are a builder with a property to sell. Since you are in the real estate business and obviously understand the game, I thought that rather than making a formal offer to purchase your property, it would be more productive to write you a letter and show you some alternative ways of selling your property. If one of these alternatives appeals to you, I would be more than happy to sit down with you to put it into writing. Of course, since I am an investor, I need to invest my money into properties that have below-market prices and below-market terms. I am a businessperson and, like you, need to see a way to make a reasonable profit from my efforts.

I am a problem solver. If I understand your situation correctly, you have three problems that need solving:

1. You have property for which you would like to find a buyer.

2. You would like to obtain a down payment of at least $15,000 and would consider carrying the balance.

3. You have recently repossessed this property from a previous buyer and would like to assure yourself that the next buyer is not a flake.

I believe that at least one of the following four solutions will solve these problems if you are flexible.

Solution no. 1. Purchase price to be $65,000 with $15,000 down and balance to be paid at $416.66 per month for 120 months at zero percent interest.

Solution no. 2. Purchase price to be $60,000. Seller to obtain new first mortgage of $25,000 and share $5,000 of proceeds with buyer. Buyer to assume payments on new first mortgage and to execute a new second mortgage to seller for the balance of seller's equity, with payments to be negotiated. Buyer to give additional collateral on another property which has at least $5,000 equity.

Solution no. 3. Purchase price to be $55,000. Seller to obtain a new first mortgage on property for $15,000. Buyer to buy property on a land sales contract with nothing down with monthly payments of $478.68 for thirty years bearing 10 percent interest with a balloon payment in fifteen years.

Solution no. 4. Purchase price to be $45,000, all cash, within sixty days.

There are perhaps other alternatives which you might think of. Feel free to call me and discuss them with me. I am presently looking at several properties to invest in, and my investment funds are limited. Please call me as soon as possible if you are at all interested in pursuing this further.

Thank you for your time.

Sincerely,

Nora Jean Boles

The seller didn't like any of the alternatives.

Nora's seed withered and died in the sun.

3. _____

A few days later Mary called me to brainstorm about what to do with her new acquisition.* She was still excited, but the thrill was wearing off fast.

"I'm so glad that you made it through the first wall of fear," I said. "But you're not into the clear yet. When is your first payment due?"

"In two weeks, the first of August."

"Including the customary fourteen-day grace period, you'll have thirty days to find a renter. Is Steve there?"

"No, he had an emergency. One of our church members is dying in the hospital." There was a pause. Then Mary confided a problem she was having.

"Steve is hung up on security. He's a bit frightened. We both are. But I think I'm more willing to take chances. He understands the benefits of keeping more than he does of selling it. I lean toward selling it and getting some cash to continue our investing. So that's why I'm calling, to get your opinion."

I walked her through a possible scenario for her property. The first step would be to clean the property up in preparation for a new formal appraisal. Then she would contact several lenders to determine the possibility of obtaining a new second mortgage using the property as collateral. On a value of $32,000 and an 80 percent loan-

_____

* Over 500 hours of the Challenge experience have been professionally recorded and edited into a 25-hour home study course. For more information call me at 1-801-852-8700

to-value ratio, she could obtain a maximum loan of $25,600. Since her underlying first mortgage was only $19,650, she should be able to pull $6,000 out of the property through a refinance (25,600 less the current loan of 19,600 = 6,000). The payments on the second mortgage wouldn't be more than $100 per month.

"That would give us $6,000 cash, but what would we do with the property?" Mary wondered.

"You could either keep it or sell it. Let's suppose that you decide to keep it. What would a house like that rent for?"

"I've already done some checking and the range is between $275 and $375 per month."

"Your first mortgage payment is $250 including taxes and insurance. Add to that the payments on the second mortgage of one hundred dollars. You'd have to gross at least $350 to break even. You could probably do this by offering a lease option or an equity-sharing situation."

"How would that work?" Mary asked.

"You could advertise to sell half ownership in your home for nothing down if the new tenants would just make both mortgage payments and pay any maintenance costs. In that way, you'd eliminate negative cash flow entirely. Or you could do the same thing with a renter by offering him the right to buy your property. How do your partners feel about selling or keeping?"

"They don't care, really. They're willing to let us keep rolling with it."

"You could give them a thousand dollars of the refinance money as a return on their investment—to make them feel better—and use the rest to buy more property."

Mary understood immediately.

"So you'd have five thousand in the bank and half-ownership in a rental house. And what other benefits would you have?"

"I'd get a tax write-off."

"Did you pay any taxes last year?" I asked.

"No, we ended with a five-thousand-dollar tax credit. But," she added optimistically, "we're going to make so much money next year that I know I'll need some tax breaks, right?" She laughed happily.

"Now, suppose you decide to sell the property; how would you do it?" I asked, anxious to see if she could tell me the answer.

"I suppose," she said, "that we could just discount the price real low and advertise like a don't-wanter, and try to attract an all-cash buyer."

"Good. You'd run an ad in the paper like this:

Appraisal $32,000. You can steal it for $27,000 with only $1,500 down. Will carry. Take trade for down. Hurry!!"

"Why fifteen hundred dollars?" Mary asked.

"You could give it to your partners to keep them happy. Of course, another alternative would be to exchange your equity for anything of value. After all, you would have already pulled out your cash. The key is to get more lines in the water. But instead of finding sellers, you're looking for buyers."

"I see," Mary said. "It's like I'm fishing in two lakes. In one lake, I'm fishing for trout. And when I catch one I put it in another lake and hope someone else catches it."

"Right!"

"I'm not in first grade anymore. I've graduated. I'm in fourth grade now."

"Have you called Philip and Nora to tell them about your success yet?"

"Yes," she replied, lowering her voice. "That was really kind of hard. Nora's real down. I spent a long time this morning trying to pick her up. Philip's doing great, though. I was pretty worried about him last week, but he's pulling out of it and charging full speed ahead. He's found an investor who wants Philip to show him thirty properties a week. So he's really busting the pavement."

"Great! Listen, I appreciate all the help you're giving the other two. I've been reading a book lately called *Love Is Letting Go of Fear* in which a central teaching is this: 'All that I give is given to myself.' In other words, to give is to receive. And not to give is not to receive. What you're doing to help the others will come right back to you."

"I believe that," Mary said. "Thanks a lot for all your help, Bob. And I'll be getting back to you as soon as we have a nibble."

I didn't hear from her again for more than a week. The next call came on July 24.

"Bob, this is Steve Bonenberger. Mary is on the other line. We have to talk to you."

There was a note of worry in his voice. "What's the problem?" I asked, trying to conceal my concern.

"We've got some real problems with the property we just bought," Steve explained. "I think we made a serious mistake. We've got to dump it fast before it eats us alive."

I listened as Steve poured out a host of problems. Mary did not talk as much as her husband. Whenever she did, it was in more positive terms. She still felt all right about the prospects but was obviously being overruled by her husband. When I pressed him for specifics, there were two major sore points.

"The place is a dog, Bob! I mean, when the city inspector went through the property before we bought it, he overlooked a host of problems. We were so excited to buy it that we didn't look close enough. The basement was a pigsty. I've been over there every night for the last week cleaning out the garbage. I mean, it's awful."

Mary broke in. "So Steve finished the last of the cleanup late last night and sacked all the garbage in bags and set it out on the lawn for the garbage collectors to pick up in the morning. And this morning, when he went over there, he found that scavengers—dogs, cats, whatever—had torn into the sacks and dragged the garbage all over the neighborhood. It was like the last straw."

"Bob," Steve explained, "it was really discouraging. All that work for nothing. I'm not a fixup kind of person. I hate that kind of stuff. I mean, I really detest it. I don't care if I ever see that house again."

"What about you, Mary?" I asked.

"I still think it has potential. But it's going to take more money than we thought to fix it up. We can't rent it until we get a city permit. And we can't get a permit until the work is done."

Steve took up the thread, panic in his voice. "And the mortgage payment is due in seven days. That's $256 . We don't have that kind of money! And if we miss the payment, our hard-earned credit rating goes down the drain."

I smiled inwardly. Buyer's remorse. That was it. I had felt the same way, myself, on many occasions. It's natural to have second thoughts after a major purchase. But there was more to this than just buyer's remorse. Steve was rubbing up against the frontier of his comfort zone, and it was destroying his peace of mind. Like a farmer, he had sown his seed in fruitful ground. But along with the wheat came many weeds. And he was tired of weeding.

In short, *he* had become a don't-wanter!

I tried to explain this to both of them. "Remember what you're feeling right now," I said. "Savor it. Learn from it. You're suffering from a bad case of don't-wanteritis."

"Yeah," Steve agreed, "I'd do anything if someone would come along and take this monster off my hands. I mean, anything!"

"So Mary is right," I thought to myself. "Steve really does panic easily." I recalled a telephone conversation Mary and I had a few days earlier in which she revealed only the tip of a silent iceberg of frustration.

"Steve is still not as comfortable taking risks as I am," she had confided to me. "He's still confusing good debt and bad debt. And he's reluctant to take chances. But we are both working toward a comfortable balance. When we first started the ninety-day Challenge I thought that financial independence would eliminate about 80 percent of our arguments, which all seemed to stem from lack of money. But then I realized that it wasn't the lack of money we were arguing about but our different philosophies on risk. Before, a thousand dollars was a lot of money to us. But as I got into the Challenge, I'd hear myself saying, 'We only need a couple of thousand to get into this great property I just found.' All of a sudden, instead of talking hundreds, I was talking thousands. I wasn't afraid any longer of the bigger numbers. I'd moved up to the next level. I don't even know exactly when it took place. I began to see that we would be able to do things that we never even dreamed possible. But Steve couldn't see it. I'd want to forge ahead; Steve would want to hold back. I was so frustrated. Maybe I'm too impatient, but I don't know how to pull him or push him to the next plateau. He still just worries about everything."

I wondered if some of the friction between them was the result of Steve's uneasy realization that Mary was a butterfly about to launch into a newfound freedom. Steve had been raised in a traditional home. Now the modern world was presenting his wife with different options. Was he just giving lip service to his wife's opportunity for growth while unconsciously trying to sabotage her efforts? If so, he wouldn't be the first modern man to wrestle with the problem. Things that in other generations were taken for granted now have to be negotiated—parental responsibilities, dishes, house-cleaning chores. It would only be natural to have mixed feelings.

I had seen it happen so many times before. Mary was more of a positive thinker. Steve was more of a negative thinker. She was an optimist. He was a pessimist. Who is to say which is better? Perhaps

HOW TO RAISE YOUR THRESHOLD OF RISK

What is a risk threshold? It is the level of risk that you can tolerate and still sleep at night. Some people can handle enormous amounts of risk and uncertainty and sleep soundly, confident in their ability to cope with their problems in the morning. Others toss and turn all night long. Obviously, some people handle risk better than others. If you are serious about improving your situation, you have to learn to live with increasing levels of risk.

The most important step you can take toward gradually increasing your risk threshold is to understand what risk is.

Risk is a scary word until you understand it. Most people spend their lives running from risk. They assume that if they could be perfectly secure (without risk), they would be perfectly happy. Little wonder they are so frustrated! Because there is no way to be perfectly secure in a free-market society. Our economic system is based on individual freedom. But you can't have freedom without risk. And in a free-market society, those who risk the most are also free to reap the greatest rewards. Contrast this with the Communist economic system, in which everyone's security is guaranteed (or where everyone is forced to be secure.) One system has lines of people waiting to get in. The other system has lines of people waiting to get out. Is there any doubt which system you would rather live under? You'll be a lot happier once you stop trying to be secure and start being thankful for the opportunity to risk.

Ask any successful person why they are so successful, and they will answer in two words: good decisions.

But how do you learn to make good decisions? One word: experience.

But how do you get experience? Two words: bad decisions.

Question: Are you willing to risk making enough bad decisions so that you can gain the experience necessary to be able to make good ones?

an ideal mix lies exactly in the middle. Nothing wrong with some healthy skepticism. And optimism, tempered with a grasp of reality, can take a person far.

A negative thinker sees something suspicious on the horizon, immediately imagines the worst and follows things to their logical negative conclusion. Something goes wrong, an unexpected bill, and before you can say "whoops" he is preparing for bankruptcy. No wonder a negative thinker never makes any success happen. He's always too busy battening down the hatches because he thinks the sky is falling down. On the other hand, the optimistic thinker always tries to see things in a positive light—to follow things to their illogical positive conclusion. When he sees a problem on the horizon, he immediately starts trying to find something good with it. If you look hard enough, you know, you can always find something good. No wonder positive thinkers are always smiling.

I ended my telephone conversation with Steve and Mary that July 24 with an exhortation to "let it simmer for a few days"—which was the equivalent of "take two aspirin and call me in the morning."

I knew—or, at least, hoped—that they could work out their problems with time.

4.

Sixty days into the Challenge, Mary and Steve had found their opportunity—but didn't know what to do with it. And both Nora and Philip had yet to find their opportunities. I felt they all needed a morale boost, so I sent each of them a different mailgram, which they were instructed to share with one another. This is the letter I sent Nora:

Dear Nora:

Someone once said that if you throw enough spaghetti against a wall some of it is bound to stick. In other words, if you constantly have five lines in the water, sooner or later you're bound to find a don't-wanter. It's a numbers game. It's not a matter of "if." It is only a matter of "when." As long as you keep searching—blue-vasing— you cannot fail. Quitting now would be like dying of thirst just inches from the water fountain. I would never have asked you to do this if I didn't know that you could be successful. Ponder this and then call the others and relate this message to them in your own words.

Here is the letter I sent Mary:

Dear Mary:

Have you experienced fear today? Have you been afraid to seize an opportunity because of the fear of failure, rejection, or the possibility of appearing not to know what you're doing? Here's how to lose your fear. Whenever you approach someone about buying their property, maintain as your primary attitude the desire to understand and help the seller with his problem. You always win when you help someone. If the seller doesn't wish to reveal his problem, don't be discouraged. He just didn't have a problem he needed to have you help solve. It is not rejection when you try to help someone. Forget about the $5,000 and just concentrate on finding and solving problems and the money will flow to you. Money always flows to a great idea. And helping people to solve their problems is the greatest idea of all. Ponder this and then phone Nora and Philip and share this with them.

This is the letter I sent Philip:

Dear Philip:

I know you're frustrated. You're discovering it's harder than you thought. But how hard is it? Is it any harder here in the new world than in the old world you left behind? Both worlds have their rejections and frustrations. But compare the rewards for success in the two worlds. If you put up with enough rejection in the old world you might be successful and end up with a minimum-wage, dead-end job. Compare that to the rewards for success in the new world where with the same rejection you could end up with thousands of dollars in the bank after a few short months and the ability to be free at last. Isn't that worth the price you pay? Yes! Do you want to go back to an old world where rewards are so small? No! Do you really want to spend your whole life working at a job you hate? Of course not!

So the next time you start thinking how hard it is in the new world, compare that to life in the old world. I never said it was easy to be financially free. But neither is it easy to be in financial bondage.

As I dictated the last letter to Philip, I realized that time was running out. All my positive thoughts still didn't change the fact that the Challenge team was heading into the final period with no points on the board.

COLUMBUS, LOOKING FOR A DIRECT ROUTE TO ASIA,
STUBBED HIS TOE IN AMERICA.—Emerson

16

SERENDIPITY: FALLING INTO GOOD DEALS

Serendipity.

The word was coined in 1754 by Sir Horace Walpole, who derived it from an ancient Persian fable about three princes who lived on the island of Serendip (more recently known as Ceylon and Sri Lanka). According to legend, every time the three princes went on a journey, they stumbled onto valuable things they weren't looking for. Thus, "serendipity" has come to mean finding unexpected treasures.

It's hard to persuade people to go stumbling in the dark in the hope of discovering something valuable. The "grab bag" theory of success doesn't sound too appealing when your life is on the line. It's especially tough when you've been groping in the dark for weeks with little to show for it.

That was the way Philip and Karen felt, especially after they heard that Steve and Mary had closed on the purchase of their first house. Philip felt truly happy for Mary, but he could not deny his own sense of loss. He had always wanted to be first.

He was getting tired of having to pump himself up after every failure, every disappointment. He wondered what his mother would have done. He let his thoughts wander.

There she was, big as life, laughing and carrying on with her children around the dinner table. Eight hungry kids. Philip was the youngest. Just her alone to bear all of the burdens. No husband. Working two jobs to keep the food on the table for the whole family. He could see now what a great woman she was. Only someone great could handle all that without cracking.

The pride swelled up in him about what she had accomplished. Maybe she never governed a nation or discovered a cure for cancer or wrote a great book, but who is to say that she wasn't great? Let the man come forward to deny that she wasn't as successful with what she had to work with as the greatest painter or composer or playwright who ever lived.

It was only now that he was beginning to realize it—now that he himself had a family and had to face the fear of life. Why had he not seen it earlier? All those years of his wild youth when he had never appreciated her. Caused her so much grief.

He could almost see her in his mind, standing over him, that look in her eyes that meant "I love you, son, but you're about to be the death of me!" And she would launch into a tirade about her young son gone wayward.

"What you're doing is wrong, son. Can't keep stealing and selling stolen stuff. I never stole anything. I never sold anything I didn't own. And if I can go out there and work two jobs for eight kids, I know that you can go out there and get one job."

She was right. He knew it. They never had much, but none of those kids ever went without the important things. Philip didn't get a car at sixteen or fancy clothes or a stereo. But wasn't he better off now than all of those rich kids whose parents gave them everything and taught them nothing about life?

"Always keep a little money tucked away," he remembered her telling him. "Always keep some food in the icebox, a roof over your head, and some heat in the house and you'll be happy. Lots of folks don't even have that."

What wisdom! She taught him even more by the way she lived.

All he knew about surviving and surmounting came by observing her. Wasn't that more precious than money? He always knew she loved him. And what's more important than that?

Even when cancer finally got her in 1981, she set the example.

The day she died, Philip went to her apartment to visit her. He tried not to be affected by what he saw. From a robust healthy weight of 165 pounds she had wasted down to 95. He could see her bones protruding. The powerful painkilling drugs often made her incoherent.

Philip stood beside her bed. He looked at her. Deep sadness came over him.

She spoke. Making sense, now. "What're you looking at?" she asked in a weak voice.

He was surprised to hear her talk. "I'm looking at you, old girl," he replied.

"I want to talk to you."

"What do you want to talk about?"

"The same thing I always talk about," she said. "And you better listen. It's going to be hard when I'm gone, but you can make it." Even at the end, she was thinking about others instead of herself. "Just promise me you'll use your head."

"I promise. Besides, you're not going anywhere," he said, trying to cheer her up.

"No, I'm tired," she said. "I can't do it anymore. I'm sorry, but I'm tired, baby."

That was the last thing she said to anyone. About three hours later, she started breathing heavily, and Philip dialed 911. The ambulance came, and Philip went with her to the hospital. There was nothing he could do there but wait, and he returned from the hospital to find Karen and Marcus already asleep on the floor in the living room of the cramped apartment. He joined them and was asleep within minutes.

It wasn't long before he awoke. Or was he awake?

"It was very strange," he remembered, "because I was in a state like I was asleep, but I was really awake. I've never been like that before. I guess it was a dream, but it was so real. I saw my mom. I could see her so close, but I couldn't touch her. She was all in white, and she said to me, 'I'm all right now. I'm fine. I'm doing good. And you're going to be all right, too.' And then she smiled."

At that moment the phone rang and Philip awoke with a start. It was the hospital.

"Hello, Mr. Moore? Your mother just passed away."

It was the memory of his mother that helped keep him going, and as the days droned on, Philip lost count of all the telephone calls. He joked about the calluses he was developing on his index finger and right ear. He seemed to have lost his touch. He heard that Nora was onto a hot lead, a foreclosure. He had nothing promising. He had been close enough to opportunity to smell it, to taste it even. But someone with more money always snatched it from his mouth.

I decided that he needed a shift in strategy. He already knew how to find bargains. He just needed to learn how to fund them. In a long phone conversation, he and I devised a letter to attract potential investment partners. The first line was a grabber.

EARN OVER 100 PERCENT ON YOUR MONEY TAX FREE!!!!!

Everyone knows that if something sounds too good to be true, it probably isn't. And they are usually right. But when it comes to real estate investing, they are absolutely wrong. I am a real estate investor specializing in wholesale properties, and I'd like to show you how you can earn 100 percent on your money tax-free. Let me tell you about two properties I discovered in the last thirty days right here in St. Louis:

Property No. 1: In the paper I located a four-unit apartment building being sold to settle a divorce. The value was $48,000. I offered $23,500, all cash, in thirty days (I needed at least four weeks to arrange financing). Another investor bid $18,500 cash immediately. Because he had cash, his offer was accepted over mine. The property sold for less than fifty cents on the dollar! What will this lucky investor do with the property? If I were him, I'd obtain a new first mortgage of $25,000. This would return his original investment and leave him with an extra $6,500 cash profit (which, by the way, is completely tax-deferred as long as he does not sell the property). Even with the new loan, the property will generate a handsome positive cash flow each month. Because of tax loopholes, this cash flow will be sheltered from taxes. And that's not considering the $20,000 equity he still has in the property. Think about it: he has his money back, $6,500 cash in the bank, a positive cash flow and a $20,000 equity. Why? Because he had *cash! And if that's not 100 percent on his money, I'll eat my hat.*

Property No. 2: I run a regular ad in the St. Louis newspapers that attracts motivated sellers. A few days ago a gentleman called wanting to sell a property worth $30,000. The loan balance was only $6,000. I asked him what he needed out of his property for a quick sale. He replied, $4,000 cash. I couldn't believe my ears. It had to be in the wrong neighborhood. I immediately drove out to inspect it. It was in a good neighborhood. I wrote an offer to give him $4,000 in fifteen days. He wanted the cash immediately. I didn't have it. A few days later I learned that he had sold the property to another buyer. Once again I had lost out.

I know it's hard to believe these stories. Until I started looking for bargains on a full-time basis, I myself was skeptical. But now I know better.

So what does this have to do with you?

I think we need each other. It's that simple.

If I have my guess, you are a professional too busy earning a living to get involved in finding investments like these. What you earn is heavily taxed. You need a way to create tax-sheltered wealth that involves little of your precious time.

That's where I come in.

I am a young investor with a lot of get-up-and-go. I have the time and the expertise to dig up the best real estate bargains. This is all I do. And believe me, it takes a lot of digging through gravel before you find a gold nugget. I have seven or eight sources of flexible sellers that I farm each day. I know how to recognize bargains. And I know how to profit from them quickly. I handle all of the details from start to finish—even to managing the property.

Is this on the level? Yes, it is.

How can you be protected? I want you to check with your attorney and accountant. I am not afraid of scrutiny because I am a totally honest, hard-working individual. Any property we buy together will be thoroughly evaluated. You maintain full control.

What will you be required to contribute to the partnership? You need quick access to at least ten thousand to twenty-five thousand dollars cash plus the ability to qualify for any mortgages. If you don't have this much at present, you may consider obtaining a line of credit at your bank or drawing from your pension and/or profit-sharing plan. I would suggest that your attorney handle all of the paperwork and release the funds with your approval.

What will I contribute? I will handle all of the legwork—everything from finding the bargain to managing it if necessary.

How will profits be split? Fifty-fifty. Of course, you will receive your initial investment back before I receive a cent.

Maybe you're asking yourself, "If this guy is so smart, why isn't he rich enough to come up with four thousand dollars without me?" That's simple. You always run out of money before you run out of good deals.

I can guarantee you this: Within the next few weeks I am going to find a partner or two to profit with me. If it's not you, it'll be someone else. But I thought you'd like an opportunity to say yes.

If you are interested, call me today.

You'll kick yourself if you miss this.

Your friend,
Philip Moore

Philip had a hundred letters prepared at a local print shop and began distributing them at the local hospital. Every doctor received a letter in his mailbox. Out of a hundred letters, how many calls did he need?

One.

How many do you think he got?

One.

Philip picked up his ringing phone about three days after he distributed the letters. An authoritative-sounding man introduced himself. "Mr. Moore? My name is Dr. Williams."

"Yes, sir," Philip replied, his throat tightening.

"I'm curious. How many circulars did you send out—a couple of hundred?"

"No, not that many. I didn't have time to pass out more than seventy-five."

The doctor laughed heartily. "Well, I tell you, your proposition was very well written, very well written. I am interested in real estate. I do have some money that I could put into it. If you do have some very good deals, I'd be interested in talking with you about them."

Philip was stunned. "Okay, then, Mr. Williams," he stammered, forgetting to address his caller properly, "I'd like to know if we could possibly set an appointment to just talk about exactly what I'm doing. I have a couple of properties in mind now that would be excellent for tax shelter and positive cash flow."

"Positive cash flow, fine. As for tax shelter, I'm really not too interested at this stage because . . . excuse me, I have another call."

Philip waited anxiously for the doctor to come back on the line.

HOW TO FIND THE RIGHT PARTNER

You are your wealth. If your wealth is your ideas and creativity, how do you find people to finance your great ideas? Obviously, the partners you choose must be motivated by a desire to make more money than they would in other traditional investments and must not be put off by your own lack of financial resources. You attract such partners in a variety of ways:

1. First, involve those closest to the transaction: the Realtor, the seller, the underlying mortgage holders, the bankers, attorneys and accountants as well as the renters. Those who know the property are obviously more likely to want to invest more money in it.
2. Talk to friends, relatives and business associates and explain your growing expertise in potential money-making opportunities. If they show an interest, you can walk them through the numbers of your latest property.
3. Visit all investors' clubs in your area and pass out your card and/or flier. Tell all interested parties about the bargain properties you have located and what financial resources you are seeking in order to complete your transaction.
4. Advertise in the newspaper. Your ad could read: Earn (include percent figure) in prime (your city) real estate.

People reading the classifieds will see your ad and be attracted by its offering a higher rate of return than other traditional investments. Then, when the calls come, you explain your potential investment. In some states, it is necessary to check with your state department of business regulations, which has rules governing the use of advertising to attract partners.

Another approach might be to advertise a free educational investment seminar in which you extoll the virtues of real estate investments. The attendees can be taught using actual examples of some of the properties you have bought or are considering buying. Interested partners could be given the opportunity to invest if they felt so inclined.

5. Word of mouth: As in all advertising, the best source of future business is a satisfied customer. That is why it is so important to treat all of your partners with fairness and professionalism. A satisfied partner will be happy to share with you the names of his friends who might also benefit from your money-making skills.

He was gone for about a minute. The phone grew slippery in Philip's moist palms.

The doctor came back on the line. "Let's sit down and talk. How about two o'clock tomorrow?"

Philip sucked his breath in. Friday at two. He had a conflict. David Benjamin and the entire film crew were leaving the next afternoon and were planning a big send-off. Once again, the filming was going to get in the way of making money. "Oh, well," he thought to himself. "Better to not appear too anxious anyway."

"Sorry," Philip explained. "I have another appointment."

"Well, let's say two o'clock Monday, then. Can you come to my office?"

"OK, fine."

"I'll look forward to meeting you."

Philip hung up the phone carefully. As soon as he knew the connection was broken, he let out a whoop and jumped high enough to out-rebound Kareem Abdul-Jabbar.

He was on the scent of money.

All weekend long, he practiced his presentation to the doctor. "Yes, sir. I know what I'm doing. No, sir, I don't have any properties yet, but. . . ."

It took forever for Monday afternoon to roll around. Philip borrowed his father-in-law's car and arrived at the doctor's office at precisely two o'clock. He approached the reception desk trying to act professional.

"Hello, my name is Philip Moore. I have a business meeting scheduled with Dr. Williams."

"I'm sorry. The doctor is out for the rest of the day. Are you sure it was for today?"

Philip went numb. "Yes, ma'am. Would you tell him I dropped by." He gave her his number, walked out and stood on the curb. The cars rushed by. He was oblivious to them. Up again, down again. Adrenaline, depression. What would he tell Karen?

Karen took it especially hard. It seemed to be a repeat of the pattern that she and Philip had become so accustomed to during the previous two years. Philip would follow a lead to find a job, and it would crumble into ashes in his hands. The only difference was, this was harder.

As it turned out, Dr. Williams and Philip never did get together. The doctor was more interested in larger transactions. But Philip tried not to let it bother him. He continued to keep putting his lines in the water in spite of the emotional roller coaster he seemed to be on. A few days later, while calling on newspaper classifieds, he got another nibble on a promising property. A woman answered his call and began to tell him about a property located outside St. Louis.

"It's a three-bedroom home on top of a hill overlooking the Mississippi," the woman began. "In fact, I'm sitting here in the dining room now and I can see the river."

"Are you willing to finance it?" Phil asked, getting right to the point.

"Yes. The price is twenty thousand dollars. We don't have any loan on it. We'll take nine thousand dollars down, and carry the rest at about two hundred a month. The interest would be ten percent. That's cheaper than a bank."

Philip was immediately interested. It sounded like an exceptional price. Some flexibility in terms. His heart raced as the woman continued.

"We've got 17½ acres. The barn is big enough for more than six horses."

He couldn't believe it! A house and land for only twenty thousand! He tried to act calm. "Do you have any livestock?"

"There are nine calves we're going to throw in with the place. And there's a little pond stocked with fish. You can even have the tractor."

"Great," Philip exclaimed, unable to hide his delight! "Sounds like my dream house. I'd like to know, do you have any offers at this time?"

"Oh, yes. We've had quite a few offers. At least quite a few people have come and looked at it. One young couple said they would like to have it if they could get the down payment. They're supposed to let us know tomorrow."

"You snooze, you lose," Philip thought to himself as he asked the next question. "Why are you selling?"

"We want to move into town."

"And how was the price determined?"

"Well, we didn't have to go through a real estate agent. That's why we priced it low."

"Okay," Philip stalled as he filled in the blanks of his Bargainfinder. "What are your plans if the properly doesn't sell?"

"We'll just have to stay here if we don't sell."

He made a note that they obviously weren't highly motivated to get out of the property. "How long has this been on the market?" he asked.

"Since Friday. I've had about seventy calls since we advertised it. And about twenty people have looked at it."

"I'm going to talk to my wife and call you back, ma'am. Maybe we'll ride out there and look at it."

He got directions and hung up the phone, feeling more excited than he had in days. It seemed like a dream property. Only twenty thousand for a house, a barn with nine calves, a tractor and 17½ acres. It had to be undervalued. And the terms were great. All he needed was the nine thousand dollars. There had to be a creative way to get that. Only briefly did he wonder why twenty people would look at the property without at least one written offer.

The next morning, he wasted no time in reaching me and quickly told me his story. The facts suggested at least three possible solutions, none of which would work unless the property was underpriced by at least 30 percent.

Alternative number one was to find a partner who would be willing to come up with the $9,000 down payment to buy the property. Then Philip could arrange for a second mortgage using the partner's credit. Assuming a $30,000 value and an 80 percent loan-to-value ratio, they could qualify for a $13,000 second mortgage (80 percent of $30,000 = 24,000, less the seller carry-back financing of $11,000 = $13,000). The partner's initial investment would be returned, leaving $4,000 to split between them. Then the property could be sold, traded or kept for rental. Philip thought he, himself, might like to live there.

Alternative number two was much more creative and tricky. Perhaps Philip could talk to owners of adjacent property and arrange to sell them part or all of the seventeen acres. If the ground was worth a thousand dollars an acre, he might be able to raise almost all of the purchase price from land sales, and just split out enough land for the house and barn. The cost of the house, if all worked out as planned, would then be only $3,000. It was a long shot, but worth checking into.

Alternative number three was to involve the seller in the solution. Philip would propose that the seller place a new fourteen-thousand-dollar first mortgage on the property. The proceeds of this new loan would be split—nine thousand dollars to the seller and five thousand dollars for Philip. The balance of the seller's equity would be secured by a second mortgage against the property. Philip would assume the payments of both mortgages. It was a rather audacious alternative, but not out of the question.

The cleanest solution was to involve a partner. But I encouraged Philip to be careful about becoming emotionally involved with any property. He had to act like a don't-wanter himself—to be cool and detached—or he would blow his advantage in negotiating.

After we finished our phone conversation, Philip began to do his homework. He had found something that glittered, but he still wasn't sure if it was gold. He had to determine if it was undervalued. A few calls to Realtors in the area cast a negative gloom on his optimism. Farmers were falling on hard times, and farmland was selling cheap. He couldn't believe that such a complete package wouldn't be worth two or three times what the sellers were asking. But the Realtors disagreed with him. Just like Mary, he already had himself and his family moved into that little farm, enjoying the view of the mighty Mississippi. And now he had to move out again.

He called me to brainstorm. We decided to make an offer regardless. If the seller would be willing to share some cash with Philip, it wouldn't matter what the Realtors thought. But I could tell that Philip was feeling down. "Karen's been a little bit disappointed," he told me, "because her mother and her father said they were going to give us the money for a couple of pieces of property. But last night everything started crashing in. They told us they didn't have the money."

I hated to hear his discouragement. "I'm beginning to have my doubts about what I've got you into. That's a lot of pressure to put people under."

He disagreed. "I've been livin' under pressure since I was fourteen years old. So, believe me, this is no pressure. This is fun. I'm enjoying this. I just want to protect Karen from too much pressure. But we've lived through tougher times."

"What keeps you going?" I asked.

"I'm scared of being poor. I considered myself a failure practically all my life. Scared to fail. Then you came to town. So many people were betting against me—that I couldn't get a nice piece of property and fix it up. And you were betting your whole reputation that I could. I said to Karen, 'I can't fail at this. I can't be a loser.' "

Hearing Philip talk like this—having so much faith in me—filled me with unbearable guilt. What right did I have to tinker in their lives? Had I raised their hopes so high only to set them up for a crushing defeat? In many ways, they were worse off than when they had met me. How naive I had been! I had actually thought we could wrap it up in thirty days. Now we were approaching the sixtieth day. Sure, Mary and Steve had closed on a property, but there was no guarantee that it would pan out. And even if it did, what about the strain on their marriage? Could either of the two couples survive the pressure?

I was worried about Philip and Karen, too. And Nora. I began to doubt my own philosophy. Could it be that the American dream is *not* available to every American? Is America the land of opportunity for only a few? Is the American dream a cruel hoax, a pot of fool's gold, a pipe dream, a nightmare?

I could just see the headlines: BOASTFUL INVESTOR PROVES THAT AMERICAN DREAM IS A NIGHTMARE!

It was August 7. We were just beginning our third and final month of the Challenge. With only thirty days left to go, I scheduled a conference call with the group. Steve was first.

"Steve, how is your situation going? Have you found a buyer yet?"

"We have two people who are interested. One has made us a lowball offer."

"Like some of the offers you've been making," I joked.

"More ridiculous. Actually, we've been contacted by a local builder who is very interested in buying the house from us. I don't know if we'll sell to him, but he is persistent. Right now, we're just hanging on. Not going to do anything rash. We put a home improvement loan on it—so we've got eight hundred bucks just sitting cool. Our payment's not due for another twelve days. So we've got twelve more days before we start to panic."

I noticed how much different Steve's attitude was compared to that expressed in our last conversation, two weeks earlier. The panic was gone from his voice. He was calm, relaxed, taking things in stride, in control of his emotions. His don't-wanteritis had subsided.

"And even if we don't get the kind of deal that we want," Steve continued, "we're just going to sit on this monster. I don't know how you feel about that, but we're just not going to give it away."

I could sense that he was referring to the fact that this property just might not produce five thousand dollars cash in the next thirty days. He felt an obligation to me to reach the goal we all had set, and yet, at the same time, he could see that our artificial deadline was causing him to make an unwise investment decision. I was glad to hear him rationally weighing his alternatives.

"Well," I said, "I want all three of you to understand that this is just an experiment. We're all learning from it. We're in totally new territory. Sixty days ago, we stood on the banks of the Mississippi looking westward into Indian territory dreaming of owning our own little patch of land by the river. But now that we've been out in the wilderness for sixty days, we have a different perspective."

"My perspective has sure changed," Steve said. "Our position now is that if we can hold this property for six months, fix it up, get a renter in it, get a higher appraisal, it'll be easier to sell and get our five thousand dollars than if we sell now. It's a little money-making machine the way it is."

"Have you found a tenant yet?" I asked.

"We've got twenty thousand people who want it. We get so many calls, it's unbelievable. So that's been an eye-opener. And that's eased the tension."

"Mary," I asked, "what have you learned from this?"

"I know that the possibilities are out there," she said. "But it really does involve a lot of hard work. I've learned a great deal about how to deal—to negotiate. A fellow called to offer me exactly what I had in the house, and I told him we really couldn't accept that. He upped his offer to include paying the closing costs. I still wasn't interested. Kept my cool. I've learned a lot about taking the bull by the horns. Being more assertive. Before, I would have been intimidated."

"Are you getting it down to a system so you can reduce the work?"

"Yes. At first, I ran all over looking at properties. But then I sat back and analyzed my results and realized I should have just stayed home on the phone. I've learned how to cut a lot of corners."

I had warned them of this during our two-day seminar, but experience had taught her another lesson that couldn't be learned in a classroom. "Do you and Steve still have a goal of buying a property a month?" I asked.

"Yes."

"Does that look realistic now?"

"Yes. We wasted a lot of time spinning our wheels on this first deal, but as soon as we tie this one up, we're going to jump right into something else. I wish we could sell it tomorrow. So I'd have that money in the bank to reinvest. I don't even think about spending the money on clothes or things like that."

I noticed that Steve had seemed adamant about hanging onto the property while Mary was talking about selling it. They were still not on the same wavelength. But I knew that the Bonenbergers were well on their way. It was the other two I was worried about. I shifted my attention to Nora. Tom had informed me that Nora had made an offer on the Cuba property. "Has the bank accepted your offer yet?" I asked her.

"They wanted $55,000 with ten percent down," she replied. "I offered them $50,000 with five percent down. They countered with $50,000 and $4,000 down. Closing costs will be about $400. If I accept their counteroffer, I have thirty days to come up with the money."

"And you have an appraisal from the bank manager at seventy thousand dollars?"

"Yes."

"That's great. I can't believe how well you're handling the lingo. Besides that, what do you know now that you didn't know sixty days ago?"

"I know that I'm sufficient through me to do the things I want to do. I know that the opportunities are there. The Cuba property is a symbol to me. Folks have been telling me I can't do it. But I am going to do it. To prove to myself and others that I can. My attitude is doubly better than it was when I started."

"Still haven't put one in the bag, though, have you? Is that discouraging?"

"Yes, it is. But it just makes me work that much harder. And I'm getting better at it."

"Have you received any calls on your ad for partners?"

"Two or three people called, thinking that I already owned property. I just told them that I didn't have any right now. But I got their names and addresses and will be contacting them about the Cuba house. I think I'll be just fine. I'll get a partner. I'm going to keep hanging in there."

"Now, how about you, Philip and Karen? How about your property over by the river? The farm? Have they accepted an offer?"

"Yes, they have," Philip answered, with obvious pride in his voice.

"How many days do you have before you have to bring in a partner?"

"I told them seven."

"When does that time start?"

"It started Sunday. So I have to find a partner sometime this week. I believe I can do it. I also have another property I'd like to run by you."

"Okay."

"Karen's father knows this woman who is a coworker of his, and she told him about a piece of property her grandparents left her. The title is free and clear. But she and her husband don't know what to do with it. So we went and looked at it. There's a lot of work that needs to be done. Water damage, etc. The home has been sitting dormant for two years."

"Better check to see if the insurance will pay for the damage," I suggested. "How much is it worth?"

"In the neighborhood of twenty-eight to thirty thousand."

"How much do they want for it?"

"Five thousand."

"That's all?" I asked in disbelief.

"Yes. And they're willing to wait six to eight months for that. They don't need anything right now. Nothing."

"Well, have you signed it up yet?"

"No. We went and looked at it again. I took a friend of mine who's a contractor. He said it would take at least ten thousand to fix the house up. They haven't turned the water off yet, and it's puddled on the floor. He suggested I offer twenty-five hundred or three thousand cash."

"Maybe you could offer to do the fixup if they'll pay for it. And then you can split the profits."

"They don't want to put a dime more in it. They've been putting thousands of dollars in it. And now they just want out."

"Sounds like you've got a real don't-wanter on your hands."

"Yeah."

"Well," I said, "if you're going to buy it under those kinds of terms, give yourself at least a year. And include a subordination clause that'll give you the right to refinance the property without having to pay them off. Also, a substitution of collateral clause where they'll agree to accept other collateral for their loan if you need it. That'll give you a whole year to do something with the property. If I were you, I'd get over there and tie it up. It can't hurt."

"Okay."

"All right. Good. Hang in there, all of you. And don't forget to involve the Big Man upstairs. Have faith. Sorry for putting you through so much pain. I feel real guilty about it."

"Have faith with us, Bob," Philip said, "because God is not through with us yet."

"I say the same thing," said Nora.

"But when I selected you, I had no idea. . . ."

Philip cut me off in midsentence. His voice took on a tone of authority—as if I were now the pupil and he the teacher. "You didn't select me," he said. "God did. I know that. So what are you worrying about?"

There was silence for a long second. The heavy weight that I had borne for so many weeks lifted. The worry melted. They had passed the test. I didn't care about the ninety-day challenge anymore. I only cared about them.

"I love you," I said impulsively. But I meant it. I loved them. For the first time, with my whole soul, I loved them.

"We love you," Nora said.

And there our conversation ended. After I hung up the phone I thought of Dr. Lee, my trusting adviser. "So this is what he has been trying to teach me," I mused. "Accept them," he had told me over and over again, "That's all they need. Acceptance is harder to give than advice, but infinitely more valuable." I would nod as if I understood. But I had no idea. . . .

"They are the agenda," Dr. Lee advised me again and again. "Go where they are. That's the only place you can reach them. Let them fill their own buckets. You just provide the well."

We had debated this issue for hours. I had argued that I had a task to perform. I needed to ride them until they performed it. Dr. Lee would counter that the people were more important than the task. I told him that wasn't practical. He had just smiled as if to say, "Bobby, Bobby. When will you learn?"

And now, I think I finally had learned—learned to love someone unconditionally, without concern for the outcome. All along I had pretended that I was worried about them—about their welfare. I moaned and groaned, long-faced, about the weight of responsibility

I was carrying. But deep down, I was just worried about me—about what would happen if they failed to reach my trumped-up, artificial, silly deadline. It wasn't the weight of responsibility at all. I had borne the weight of selfishness. *I* didn't want to fail. *I* didn't want to look bad. *I* wanted to look good. What a hypocrite! I thought I had been afraid for them—afraid of what damage I might cause them. But doesn't love cast out all fear? For whom, then, had I feared? For *me!* No wonder I had been so miserable.

With that realization I felt light as a feather. The awareness that I could never really be responsible for them freed me to accept them. And love them.

"Love is so much lighter than selfishness," I thought. And it sure felt better than freedom or self-reliance. Maybe that would be my own next mountain. Curious how it came about. I had been looking for a way to prove the American Dream and had found instead a way to love.

How serendipitous!

I'D RATHER FAIL IN A CAUSE THAT WILL
ULTIMATELY SUCCEED THAN SUCCEED IN A CAUSE
THAT WILL ULTIMATELY FAIL.—Woodrow Wilson

WHEN IT IS DARK ENOUGH,
YOU CAN SEE THE STARS.—Charles A. Beard

17

DOWN FOR THE COUNT

1.

"I'm sorry, Nora," he said. "I'll have to pass on Cuba. I drove out to see it. It's just too far outside the city."

That was Wayne Hessler talking. He was a local contractor who had called on Nora's partner ad. Of all the calls she had received on that ad, she was most excited about Wayne's. He seemed savvy but friendly. He was extremely excited when she described the property to him. He encouraged her to make the offer to the bank—in fact, he had even suggested some changes to make in the offer that would be advantageous to their partnership. But when he drove out to see the property, he cooled immediately. Perhaps he was right. Cuba was a bit far out. Maybe that's why the bank was having a hard time unloading it.

Whether he was right or not, Nora still hated hearing him tell her no. She had done everything she had been told to do. She had found a property that more than glittered—it screamed "Diamond!" But no one would believe her. She fingered the signed offer from the bank as she sat at her desk. "I found it," she muttered, "but I just can't fund it." Without a partner, Nora's offer expired. All that work wasted! She just couldn't seem to get to first base.

Nora wasn't the only one to have an offer expire. Philip's offer on the farmhouse with 17½ acres expired when he couldn't produce a partner either. And then his offer on the Maryville property expired—again. In the past seventy-five days, he had made three separate offers on that same property. All of them were contingent on his raising five hundred dollars for earnest money. He couldn't believe that he hadn't been able to raise five hundred dollars in two hard months of looking!

A dozen times he had put that Maryville property out of his mind to chase after hotter leads. But when those trails went cold, he would return to find that Maryville was still there—just tempting him to buy it. It whispered, "I dare you to figure out a way to own me." It was torture. He just sensed that there was money to be made. The price was right, the terms were right, the location was fine, the seller wanted out. Philip just didn't have the lousy, stinking five hundred dollars! Each time he had tried a different creative twist to his offers. The answer was always the same from the Realtor: "I don't think the seller would accept that."

He could not get Maryville out of his mind. He had walked by it, driven by it, lost sleep over it, dreamed about it, argued over it, everything except forget about it. His subconscious mind was constantly turning it over, churning the details, looking at the different facets of it, seeing it from different angles.

The answer came one hot, muggy day in the middle of August while he was driving his car to an appointment. A question popped into his mind: "Would the seller let you refinance his property?"

It was not a new question. It had been asked before by Tom and others. But Philip had not heard it. He had been too fixed on the obvious, left-brain solution of raising five hundred dollars. But his right brain seemed to be suggesting a new plan. He decided to play along with his hunches. His unfettered thinking was a jumble of questions.

"How much money does the seller need?" his right brain asked.

"Just enough to pay the Realtor's commission and closing costs—

about a thousand dollars." Philip didn't know where the interrogation would lead, but he was curious to find out.

"What if you used the property as collateral to borrow enough for the down payment?" came the next question.

"I don't have the credit to. . . ."

"Answer the question," his right brain shot back.

"I can't get a new loan," Philip said, resisting the flow.

"Turn your left brain off for a minute," the voice commanded. "No negative thoughts allowed. Just pretend that you *could* get a loan. What would this accomplish?"

Philip had a hard time imagining borrowing money from an unfriendly bank when he had not been able to borrow a cent from his own friends and family. "But if I could get a loan," he said, "I would give the proceeds to the seller for his down payment. The property would be mine. And then I would rent it out. The cash flow would cover the payments on the loans."

Philip's left brain muscled into the conversation with a machine-gun burst of questions:

"Who would lend money to a broke, unemployed person?"

"Why would the seller accept such an offer?"

"Why would the Realtor go along with this?"

"You can't do it. You can't do it."

"Don't listen to him," Philip's right brain reassured him. "Put some numbers to it. See what it looks like."

Philip stopped the car. He pulled out his MasterPlanner and calculator. He made some assumptions. The seller would want at least a $2,000 down payment for this new creative twist. Fixup costs would be aound $2,000, maybe more. And as long as he was dreaming, he might just as well throw in $1,000 for himself. Total of $5,000. So the new loan would have to be at least $5,000. That would mean that the seller would have to carry the balance of his equity in the form of a second mortgage above the new loan. The situation would look as shown on page 264.

"It's preposterous!" the left brain exclaimed.

"It's a solution," the right brain corrected. "It could work."

"Too many variables. I can't see it," was the reply.

"Philip," the right brain asked, "are you going to let this gloom-and-doomer talk you out of trying? Are you going to let the idea die right here?"

Philip pictured his bright, fancy idea being strangled to death in a

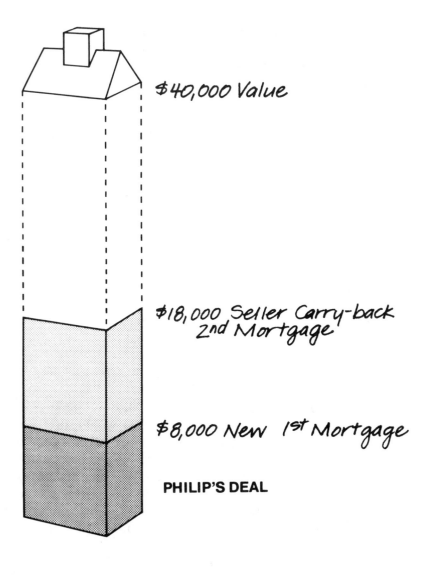

$40,000 Value

$18,000 Seller Carry-back 2nd Mortgage

$8,000 New 1st Mortgage

PHILIP'S DEAL

dark alley by a stranger with two left hands. "It's worth a try," he thought.

"Yes," his right brain nodded, victorious. "Run it by the Realtor. It's worth a try."

The left-brain grouch stomped off to sulk.

That afternoon Philip called the Realtor on the phone. After chit-chatting for a few minutes, he got up the nerve to test the waters with his new idea. "Tell me," he said. "Just between you and me. Do you think that the seller would possibly take out a mortgage on his house for, say, five thousand dollars and lend it to me?"

"Hold on a sec." The Realtor, whose name was Lena, was taken aback by Philip's brash request.

Philip knew he was treading on thin ice but continued, "It was just an idea I had because I don't have any credit."

"No credit is better than bad credit," Lena replied.

"That's true. And I was thinking, you know, I would need about $3,000 to fix the place up. If the seller would take out a $5,000 mortgage on the home, I would give him $2,000 of it and I'd take that $3,000 to fix it up with. And then I could assume the payments on the mortgage. So the seller gets $2,000 and gets rid of his house, and I get $3,000 for fixup costs." It seemed reasonable to Philip but Lena had other ideas.

"So if he put a first on it," she reasoned out loud, "he would have to carry his equity in the form of a second. That would mean he would be paying you to buy his house."

Philip hadn't thought about it that way before. The seller would be paying him to buy his house. "Well," he said, "I would need about two thousand to three thousand to fix it up, and I thought that maybe that was one way I could get it."

In her nicest way, the Realtor was trying to steer Philip away from this alternative. It was going to be just too creative for the seller to accept, she thought. "Why don't you try getting a loan on it after you acquire the property?"

"And I could do that myself?"

"Of course you can do that yourself. Then the seller wouldn't have to have anything to do with it."

Philip could tell she was leading him away from his original idea, but he played along anyway. "I thought I wouldn't be able to get a loan on it. That's good to know. I'll call you back in about half an hour and tell you what I'm going to do."

"I'll be here," she said.

"I told you she wouldn't like it," Philip's left brain said smugly as he hung up the phone.

His right brain shot back, "She didn't say she didn't like it. Write up an offer."

Yes, he decided. What could the seller do? Say no? He could handle another no.

He pulled a purchase offer from his MasterPlanner and began writing up his offer.

It was worth a try.

2. _____

"My, they are resilient," I thought to myself one afternoon toward the middle of August. "True blue-vasers. I wasn't like that when I got started."

Or was I?

I reflected backward through the fat richness of the present to remember leaner times. The first duplex. The seven-unit apartment building. A couple of twelve-unit buildings. Land. A condominium conversion. Nicer and nicer houses for my family to live in. Number one best-sellers. Those were the highlights. Funny how we always seem to remember the good times.

But there were tender spots too. Plenty of them. I counted the failures from which I bounced back. A disastrous subdivision. A forty-unit building gone sour. An eight-unit building I would just as soon forget. Over two hundred thousand dollars down the drain in one year. But I just kept scrambling up from the canvas. Dazed. Punch-drunk. But ready to fight another round.

What drove me then?

I don't know. I must have been crazy. Looking back down the mountain, with perspective, I wondered why I kept coming back for more. I just kept putting one foot in front of the other. Hopeful but ignorant. Always expecting to find success. How was I to know that another failure was lurking just around the corner?

I've often wondered, "If I could have seen the end from the beginning—if I could have know how long it would take, how hard it would be—would I have even dared to take the first step?"

Doubtful.

Maybe that's why we are not allowed to peek into the crystal ball of our future. Hopeful but ignorant, we keep climbing the endless foothills that lead us to the mountains we were born to climb—one step in front of the other. If we really knew that those mountains might still lie a million miles away, we would stop dead in our tracks, overwhelmed. We couldn't bear the pain of all life's lessons combined in one moment.

That's why hope is so important. When hope dies, all progress stops.

My wife and I had attended a piano competition that summer. In the printed program I found an important quote. An agent for one of the pianists had been interviewed and asked what criteria he used for selecting clients to represent. He said simply, "I discourage everyone."

"But why?" someone asked him.

"Because only those who will not be discouraged have a chance."

"How simple," I thought to myself on reading this. "Discourage everyone. What an excellent way to weed out the weak ones. Those who just keep coming back, undaunted, have to be the winners! If even an expert can't discourage them from reaching for their dreams, what else could stand in their way?

So life is designed to be discouraging. Discouragement is a test. Those who refuse to accept discouragement, but march on full of hope, in spite of it, always find their way to the top.

3. _____

If discouragement is a test, Nora was about to be sorely tested. She continued to struggle through the month of August. Her last fifty-five dollar unemployment check came. She forgot about the Cuba property and began focusing on other bank foreclosures. Unfortunately, this time one of them was her own house. She hadn't made a mortgage payment in four months, and the bank was losing patience. It notified her by letter that unless she came up with six hundred dollars by the seventh of September, she would lose her house. Ironically, this date fell on exactly the ninetieth day of the Challenge.

She kept fairly quiet about her predicament. We knew she was under financial pressure, but we had no idea how serious it was. She maintained her daily routine like the others—made her calls, read books, visited properties, wrote offers. She even took time out to tutor another hopeful investor—Joan, the unemployed woman who had sat next to her at the Cheshire Inn on the morning we selected the Challenge participants. They spent a lot of time together, sharing burdens. Even with the weight of her own impending foreclosure, Nora thought of others.

And she still continued to look for that perfect don't-wanter even though she was one herself.

Put yourself in her shoes. Would you have buckled under the pressure, knowing your home was about to be put on the auction block? Or would you continue to plow ahead, stubbornly, like Nora?

"Good morning. This is Nora Boles. I'd like to talk with someone in your foreclosure department."

"What did you want to know?" a woman asked.

"I've got some money coming, and I would like to invest in properties that have a low mortgage balance and you're willing to carry it and be flexible. Like thirty to thirty-five percent below the market."

"We really don't have anything that would come under that heading at the present time."

"Okay, thank you very much."

On to the next call, refusing to be discouraged. This time she was referred to a gentleman named Mike.

"Good morning, Mike. This is Nora Boles. I'm told you're the foreclosure officer for the bank. I like to invest in single-family dwellings. Do you have any on hand?"

"Not right now," Mike said. "What are you looking for—rental property?"

"Yes, or something to fix up, redo and sell. And I'm looking for below-market prices."

"That's the only way you can make money."

"Yes, could I leave my name and number and ask you to give me a call when you have something like that?"

"Sure!"

She made a mental note. "Better give Mike a call back in a week or so. Seems to be knowledgeable, helpful."

Another day, another twenty calls.

With the deadline just a few weeks away, she still hadn't scraped together enough money to stave off foreclosure on her own house.

She was expecting a late income tax refund, but it still hadn't arrived. She was caught in a vise: the bank on one side, the Challenge on the other, both pressuring her to produce. But she just kept plowing forward—one day at a time, one crisis after another, disappointment upon disappointment, hanging onto hope.

Until the twenty-third day of August.

On that day, she had an appointment to see a property on Washington Street. The seller met her and showed her through a neat two-story brick structure that had recently been completely rehabbed. He wanted thirty-seven thousand dollars for it and was not nearly as flexible as his ad had indicated.

Perhaps it was just another wild goose chase. But the accumulated experiences she had passed through the previous weeks were about to coalesce into a powerful insight. Apply enough heat, long enough, steady enough, and the kernel of corn bursts into popcorn. Nora was about ready to pop.

When it was obvious that the seller wasn't flexible, Nora told him about the Challenge and how she was going to buy property with nothing down. She was surprised at his reaction.

"You're crazy. You can't do that," he argued. "Nobody can."

He cut down everything Nora was hoping to achieve, cut her to the bone. She just looked at him without speaking, accepting his anger. But all of a sudden, the lights went on in her head. A pure bolt of insight flooded over her. For the first time, she *knew* she could do it! She was going to be OK. Hadn't she found the Cuba property? Hadn't she tied it up, just inches from buying it? Who was he to tell her that she couldn't do what she had already done? From that moment on she began to pay less attention to what other people said and to have confidence in her own judgment. She was wealthy!

She ran out to her car and began to write down the experience before the light faded.

"All my hard times and everything that has happened to me were all for a reason," she wrote. "There was a purpose for it!"

Old memories accosted her. Painful memories. Her childhood. The poverty. Her hard life. Jeffrey. The divorce. Up until that moment she had ached with no reason, no purpose to support her. Up until that moment she had just bowed her head and borne the senseless pain, like Job.

LEARNING TO TRUST YOURSELF

When will you learn to trust yourself? When will you come to the realization that your answers are just as good, if not better, than those of anyone else? When will you stop passing the buck for your life and assume control? When will you stop making excuses and start making progress? When will you allow negative feedback to roll off you like water off a duck? When will you learn to trust yourself?

When? Why not today? Why not now?

Because just as soon as you decide to take charge, to stop being dependent, to be the master of your own destiny, you will begin to notice a new power, a new energy come into your life. It may not happen overnight, but you'll begin to notice a new aliveness overtake you. You will be more creative, happier, more confident, more at peace. People will notice it. Instead of a quiet desperation, you'll exude a quiet power.

That's what happens when you learn to trust yourself. You watch.

Try it. You'll like it.

But, in one moment, everything made sense. Even the pain. Especially the pain. Even the pain of losing a son.

June 10, 1968. Would she ever forget that day, the day she lost her son?

The day before had been a Sunday, and she and her husband, Max, and the girls and four-year-old Jeffrey had gone to a church picnic. It was a beautiful day. They spent the afternoon singing old country gospel songs, laughing, playing baseball, drinking cold Pepsis from a big old picnic cooler sweating condensation in the sun. When they returned home at about 6:00 P.M., they poured the iced water out of the cooler and set it down at the foot of the basement steps to dry out. After church that evening, Nora had to go to work—the graveyard shift at the cotton plant.

By the time she returned home the next morning, Max had already left for work. The sun was up. She fed the kids and sent them out into the backyard to play. A little while later, while talking to the preacher's wife on the phone, she looked out the kitchen window. She could see the girls but not Jeffrey.

She called out the window, "Girls, where's Jeff?" They didn't know. She hung up and went searching all through the house. She called the neighbors. No Jeffrey. She looked and hollered outside, around the house, growing more worried. Nothing.

An hour and a half went by. The preacher's wife came over to help. Nora called Max at work. By the time he arrived home, she was frantic. The whole neighborhood was out looking for Jeffrey. Then after hours of fruitless searching, one of the neighbor women, running down the basement steps, bumped the old picnic cooler. The lid flew open. And there he was. Suffocated.

Nora heard the scream and knew in an instant what had happened.

"Oh, my God. My baby! My baby!" she cried.

What good could come from all the bad things that had happened to her? Nora had asked herself that question a thousand times. Now she was beginning to see an answer. As she sat there, that hot August afternoon, the pieces were beginning to fall together. She wrote furiously in her notebook.

"How can I teach someone else to pull themselves out of hard times unless I've been down there myself and pulled myself out. I know it from my heart that if they took my house today, if they took my car today, I'd just go get another one! I would! And if I can make it through, anyone can. Thank you, Lord. Make me big enough for the job."

Nora drove home a different woman. Head up. Growing in confidence.

None of us, not even Nora, would learn until the final day whether she would lose her house or not.

But it didn't matter anymore.

THERE'S NO SUCH THING AS AN UNREALISTIC GOAL.
JUST AN UNREALISTIC TIME FRAME.—Don Hutson

IN THE DEPTH OF WINTER I FINALLY LEARNED THAT
THERE WAS IN ME AN INVINCIBLE SUMMER.—Albert Camus

18

TIME'S UP!

1. _____

Hurrying through St. Louis International Airport, I passed beneath a full-scale replica of Charles Lindbergh's famous *Spirit of St. Louis*. Ninety days before, when I'd first spotted that silver monoplane, I'd been about to face the greatest challenge of my career. Like Lindbergh, I had dared to dream an extravagant dream. I, too, had embarked on a flight of discovery. But now it was time to touch down.

The Challenge was over, and the group was meeting at the Cheshire Inn. The drive from the airport took twenty minutes. I climbed out of the car and surveyed the mock-Tudor facade of the inn as if for the first time. My eyes seemed to be playing tricks on me. Had I really spent an entire day here just three months earlier? In place of the quaint country inn I vaguely remembered, I found instead a large complex of American buildings dressed up to look English. The gabled roof, heavy stucco and half-timbered walls and leaded glass windows seemed oddly out of place on a building in St. Louis in much the same way that a McDonald's must seem out of place in London. It all had the appearance of charm but not the heart of it. Even the authentic red double-decker bus parked in front seemed insincere.

"You can't fake charm," I thought. "You can't add it on like a facade—like makeup. Charm is created from the inside out—in buildings as well as in people."

I entered through one of the side buildings and climbed the narrow staircase leading to the second-floor conference room we had rented. I took a deep breath. This is where it had all started. Where would it end? I had no idea what to expect. I hadn't seen any of the group for ninety days. How would they look and act? Or feel?

Footsteps on the stairs jarred me from my thoughts. Excited words exploded on the landing. Mary Bonenberger burst through the door with Steve a step behind. "We did it!" she exclaimed proudly, waving a tiny white rectangle of paper overhead like a victory pennant.

I glanced at the cashier's check in Mary's hand.

"We closed today! We did it!" she exclaimed again.

After exchanging congratulatory hugs, Mary and I stood back to look at each other. My recollection of her had been of a young mother, struggling albeit competent. Now before me, stood a different woman. Her countenance radiated an energy that was greater than the excitement of the moment. She exuded the quiet peace of someone who had just conquered a very high mountain.

I motioned for them to sit opposite me. Steve spoke first.

"Ninety days ago we didn't have any money. I mean, literally no money. Zero dollars," he said. "What's happened in ninety days? First, we purchased a house. We found an investor willing to put up the money. Then we sold it. We closed on it this morning—the ninetieth day of the Challenge."

"We just closed our sale a couple of hours ago," Mary added. "It's been a tough three months, but this suddenly makes it all worthwhile."

Mary handed me the check and in bold red letters on a crisp cashier's check was the sum Three Thousand Nine Hundred and Seventy Five Dollars and Twenty Cents. Add to that the money left over from the home improvement loan of approximately eighteen hundred dollars, and the Bonenbergers actually had over five thousand dollars in the bank as of the ninetieth day of the Challenge.

They had done it! The financial requirements of the Challenge had been met.

Mary quickly filled me in on what had happened. They had sold their first house to a fixup expert. The offer to sell had been signed on August 21st. The closing had been set for September 1, then September 3, and finally, after much nail biting, it closed on the morning of September 7.

"I feel like I've been on a journey to Oz," Mary said. "But unlike Oz, this really happened. I was searching for a magical formula to make me happy. But I discovered I had the key all along. I now have a whole new level to my life. Before the Challenge, my home was my little fortress to keep me safe from the world. I was afraid. I still am afraid. But now I understand the risks. I'm confident I can handle the surprises, take things in stride without falling to pieces. I understand the total picture better. I've experienced the rewards of my hard work. But it wasn't easy. Some of the highest peaks and lowest valleys in our married life happened during the last 90 days. But Steve and I have grown, been strengthened and learned a lot more about each other. And that's exciting!"

I interrupted her. "Would you have learned these things without experiencing them?"

"No," she answered. "None of the information made sense to me until I'd lived it. It's just like having your first baby. You can read every book in the world on the subject, but it's nothing like the real thing. But once you've done it, a lot of the fear is gone."

"Fear holds a lot of people back. What would you say to them?"

"Put aside your fears and your doubts and just do it. Don't let anyone talk you out of your dreams. Believe in yourself. Believe that you have a task on this earth to do that is bigger than yourself. Write it down, say it to yourself every day. Then never give up, never say die. Don't let anyone discourage you."

"Did any of your friends try to discourage you?"

"Did? They still do. I even discouraged myself. But through all of this, I've come to grips with who I am. I used to try to fit into the image of what I thought an investor should be. Then one day, I just came home in tears. I thought, 'The banker must think I'm a joke.

One day I'm in his office all dressed up, saying I'm an investor, and the next day he sees me in the bank dressed in shorts wrestling with my kids.' Steve helped me realize that there is really no standard investor image. I can be myself—a mother with two toddlers—and be successful at investing too. Once I realized this, things got a lot better."

I changed the subject. "Today you're excited. But only a few weeks ago, you were ready to throw in the towel."

Mary nodded, remembering our telephone call of July 24. "It was pretty bad. I hope I never have to feel like that again."

"Yeah," Steve added. "Now the Challenge is over, we're going to slow down to a steady stride—remove the sense of panic. I'm beginning to develop a feeling of expectancy, like good things are just around the corner—this sense that the things that I've been preparing for all my life are beginning to come together. I think there's a German word for it, *Zeitgeist*. The idea is that when a person takes responsibility for his life and chooses a path, certain unknown spiritual forces begin to erupt around him. That's how I'm feeling right now."

Steve looked at Mary and continued, "We've established a goal for this year—one that we feel is realistic, attainable and challenging—to buy at least one property a month for the next twelve months. From each property, we plan to pull at least two thousand dollars net profit plus a fifty-dollar-a-month positive cash flow. Like Robert Schuller says, if you just set a goal, ten times that amount eventually comes your way."

I couldn't help smiling as I listened to their story. I glanced around at David Benjamin and the audio technicians. They were enjoying it as much as I.

"This hasn't been a piece of cake," Mary said, "a get-rich-quick scheme. The approach you taught us works, but it doesn't happen overnight."

"But," Steve said, "if you can take people like us with zero cash and teach us a workable plan to make thousands of dollars in ninety days, that's really something. There are millions of folks like us who can do the same thing."

"Do you feel wealthy?" I asked.

"Yes. In my own way," Mary answered. "I don't think I'll ever gauge my wealth in terms of material possessions."

I turned to Steve to ask my next question. "What are some of the unexpected lessons you've learned from that experience?"

"Being a pastor of a church, I don't make a lot of money. When a bunch of preachers get together, there's always one topic that comes up. 'They don't pay us enough.' We have a hard time feeding our families. But I'm beginning to see a way out of that. And that feeling of freedom is something I didn't expect."

"Which of the books and tapes you read was the most helpful?"

"That Earl Nightingale tape was pretty important for me," Steve answered.

Mary agreed. "I bet I listened to that tape twenty times while jogging. For the first two months I lived with earphones on my head. The motivational tapes were like dessert. The real estate tapes were the meat and potatoes."

"How about books?"

"Your brother's book," Mary responded, *How to Write a Nothing Down Offer.* That's my bible. I'm constantly using it."

"Your parents were rather skeptical at first. Has that changed?"

"It sure has," Mary said. "Steve's mother is now so excited, she is just beside herself. She keeps finding properties to buy and calls me up to bounce them off me."

"What changed her mind?"

"She saw that it was working for us. Even Steve's dad has taken an interest. This has really been a relationship builder for Steve and his dad. Before, they didn't see eye to eye. His dad called him 'Moses' and told him to go on his way. Now at least they have some common ground."

"What are some of the other benefits?" I asked.

"Buying and selling this house has been a real learning experience," Mary replied. "Steve and I didn't always see eye to eye on financial matters. He's a lot more conservative than I am. More red flags come up for him than for me. So that was the cause of a lot of creative conflict. It's lucky we have a good, strong marriage. We didn't agree on hardly anything at first and it got pretty tense. Finally, we had to sit down and iron things out. After that, things calmed down. We've learned to listen to each other."

"So what's next?"

"We're ready to reinvest in another property," Mary said, "and I'm really excited about that. It feels good to have some money in the bank—to be operating from a position of strength this time. This time I'll probably be a little calmer, a little more cautious. I won't feel the pressure of a ninety-day deadline."

2.

When the interview with Steve and Mary drew to a close, we stood and walked out into the hall. There, we saw Nora talking excitedly on the pay phone. David let me in on the excitement. Nora had gotten an offer accepted on a property that I had never heard about.

I walked back into the interview room and waited for her to finish. A few moments later, she walked in. Since I had only seen the back of her head at the pay phone, I was surprised to see the way she looked. She had dyed her hair a lighter blond color, and it did wonders for her appearance. The last time I had seen her was at the end of a grueling two-day training session in which all of us were weary and overloaded. Now, instead of looking five years older than her age, she appeared five years younger. I offered her a seat, and the cameras started to roll as I asked her about her experiences. "You've had some rough days through all of this, haven't you, Nora?"

"Yes," she said, "but I wrote my favorite Scriptures on the wall and read them every day: 'If you have faith as a grain of mustard seed you can say unto this mountain, be removed to yonder place and it should be.' "

"You look more peaceful now than the last time I saw you."

"I am. I solved a big problem this morning."

"What happened?"

"I scraped together five hundred dollars and took it to the FHA to stop my own house from going into foreclosure. Talk about ironic! I'm out trying to acquire a home through foreclosure, and my own home just about gets foreclosed."

We both laughed.

"But I pulled it out. I worked hard on my part-time job and saved every penny these past three weeks and pulled together five hundred dollars. This morning I marched into the banker and handed him a cashier's check to stop the foreclosure."

I shook my head. Once again, Nora had bounced back.

"It's kind of crazy, isn't it?" she continued. "I can talk to foreclosure officers, and it doesn't bother me. But when I get on the phone with normal, ordinary sellers, it bugs me and I feel like I am prying."

"So you developed your own style. Something that is comfortable for you."

"I guess so. I'm more comfortable with foreclosures. Just yesterday, I found a glittering one. It just needed some minor repairs— odds and ends and little things. The bank wanted their money out of the property—only eighteen thousand dollars. It's in a mixed neighborhood. Property values are thirty to forty thousand dollars. So I figured that eighteen thousand dollars would be a pretty good deal. I went back and wrote up a contract just the way Tom showed me. I offered them a thousand dollars down, with them carrying the balance at 9.5 percent interest for 84 months with a balloon and a 20-year amortization. The Realtor lady told me she didn't believe the bank would take it, but I told her to present it anyway."

Nora explained that before she heard from the Realtor, she called her partner, Wayne, and told him about the property. Wayne agreed to supply the credit and the thousand-dollar down payment. Nora would do all the work. And they'd split fifty/fifty.

"I was getting ready to go to work on my regular job at five o'clock last night when the Realtor lady called. She said, 'I've got some good news for you. The bank accepted your offer.' I was so happy. Believe it or not, I sat down and cried."

"What will you do with the property?"

"Well, first I'll clean it up. Then I'll advertise to sell it. I want to turn over this first one and pull some cash out of it. The value is at least thirty-six thousand dollars, and I'll sell for thirty-two thousand. My partner and I will split the profit. I have a goal to have at least ten properties in two years."

"Now," I said, "you're talking pretty high finance, but on the home front, things haven't been going so well, have they?"

"No. Everybody told me I was crazy. They had a point because my own house was up for foreclosure. But I just couldn't sit at home and feel sorry for myself. It was either sink or swim, and I decided to swim. I don't want people to help me because they feel sorry for me. I don't want people to give me anything. I don't want to be on welfare. I want to pay my own way like everybody else. And I will!"

"How soon do you think you'll close on that property?"

"The twenty-third of September. I'll work on it on the weekends. Give me two or three weekends at the most and it'll be fixed."

I interrupted her story. "I can't believe it. Not just what you've done but the way you're talking about it. Your confidence is just fantastic!"

"It hasn't been easy. There were times when that phone was a dread. I'd procrastinate, get scared, quit, and start over again. I was taking two steps back and one forward. It took me a long time to realize that it was really a numbers game. I thought that if I called two or three sellers I was going to find at least one good property. But that wasn't enough. So instead of five calls a day, I made ten and fifteen. That's when I started taking two steps forward and one back."

She paused before she continued. "At first I couldn't see any way out of the bad times. But I've been listening to a tape by Robert Schuller called *Tough Times Never Last But Tough People Do,* and it inspired me to see that there are two sides to every coin. I was just looking at the bad side. The positive side was that I had some assets—an identity, a brain, a plan. And I began to like myself."

HOW TO DEVELOP THE SKILL OF GRACE UNDER PRESSURE

When you find yourself in a stressful situation (i.e., a closing that is coming up, an especially important negotiation) you may discover that your normal cool is replaced with panic. With practice, you can learn to handle these situations with grace and poise. Here are some points to consider:

1. Step back and see the big picture. Almost invariably, when you find yourself losing your cool it is because you fail to see things in perspective. Look back ten years from where you have come. See the progress you have made. View your present situation as just another stepping-stone in your long-term progression. Ask yourself where you are going to be in ten years. The stress you feel in your present circumstances will diminish when viewed in this context.

2. Review your goals. Hannah More wrote, "Obstacles are those frightful things you see when you take your eyes off the goal." Keep your eyes on the goal, and you won't have time to lose your cool.

3. Realize that stress is caused by fear. Fear is not a thing. It's

just a thought. It can't stop you. Only you can stop you. So get out of your own way. Quit thinking fear thoughts. Start thinking success thoughts.

4. Give yourself a pep talk with phrases like these: Inch by inch, anything's a cinch. No pain, no gain. It's always darkest before the dawn. Who am I doing this for? My family. Is their long-term success more important to me than this momentary stress that seems to be holding me back? Yes. Is there any other way? No. Then do it.

5. Do it now. Develop the habit of doing what you need to do when the thought comes to you. Don't put it off. Your habit of procrastination is really just another camouflaged form of fear. You must face it. Do it now.

The ability to exude grace under pressure is the result of passing through many positive and negative experiences in which you finally see that you can handle whatever gets thrown at you. Things are rarely all or nothing, make or break, do or die. Regardless of the outcome, the sun still comes up in the morning. Life teaches that things are never as good as they seem or as bad as you imagine. Even the failures often turn out to be the best answer in the long run. There are good things in bad situations and bad things in good situations. There are just as few reasons to be overly excited about something as there are to be overly despondent. Wisdom dictates that you learn to be more even-tempered. Moderation in all things, and from this comes grace.

"When did that happen?"

"Two and a half months ago. I was reading my Bible, and it dawned on me that it's just like planting a seed in the ground. If you plant corn, you're not going to get apples. You're going to get corn. And whatever you plant in your life, you're going to get back. I began to realize that I'd been planting bad attitudes, and the fruit I was getting back proved it."

"Suppose you had an opportunity to speak to everybody in the United States for five minutes," I asked her. "What would you say?"

"I'd look the world straight in the eye and say: 'Hey, you can do it! I did it! Before, I didn't see any hope—just total hard times. Now I do. I have command of me. What you do and how you do it is totally up to you. You can make it if you want to.' "

3. ───────────────────────────────

When Philip and Karen entered the room, they too looked different. Enthusiastic. I knew that they had been working on two hot properties, and I was eager to know what had happened in their lives. "Ninety days ago we started on an adventure together. Tell me what it's been like."

"Well," Philip began, "I learned a lot. I thought it would be a little bit easier—just one, two, three and people would open their doors for me. But it didn't come that way. I'm glad it didn't because I wouldn't have appreciated it if it had come too easy. We had to go out and hustle to find what we needed by ourselves. And it paid off. Now we have more in the bank than we did ninety days ago—five hundred dollars. We've also established some credit. So that's an accomplishment." Although his offer on the Maryville property was still up in the air, Philip went on to describe how he had bought and closed on his first investment property—the five-thousand-dollar house. The seller had accepted a five-thousand-dollar unsecured, interest-free note for the entire purchase price. The note was due in nine months with the understanding that the property would revert back to the seller if Philip hadn't been able to sell it within nine months. It wasn't five thousand dollars in the bank, but, nonetheless, Philip was now a property owner. And conservatively, his net worth had increased by at least ten thousand dollars.

"It was a win/win situation," Philip explained. "The owner had a property that she didn't want. It needed some fixup, and I needed a property at the time to start me off. There are several ways we can profit from it: We can fix it up for two to three thousand and rent it for nine months to get our money back; we could rent it as is with an option to buy; or we could sell it as a fixup, handyman property. One of those ways has got to work."

"What's the one lesson you've learned from this experience?" I asked.

"If I had known six months ago what I know now, we would have a lot more than we have now. Not to say that we would have great wealth, but what is wealth anyway? Knowledge is great wealth. We have great wealth now. People are calling us to help them find property. And you won't believe this, but I have actually had several job offers during the past ninety days. I guess they could see I was a go-getter. It's the first time I ever turned down a job offer. But I'm into a whole new world. And I'm not turning back."

"How are you feeling, Karen?" I asked.

"I feel great! We've really come a long way. I feel totally different from how I did the first time we were in this room having an interview. Then, I had the jitters and I was wondering, 'What are we getting ourselves into? We're already broke; we're going to be broker.' But now I can see the progress that we've made. We don't have five thousand dollars in the bank as of yet, but it's coming."

"Karen is even starting to find properties to buy," Philip said. "Tell Bob about that."

She told me of a two-family flat that one of her coworkers was selling for fifteen thousand dollars. All she wanted was one thousand down and she would carry the balance of the financing at 10 percent interest.

Karen was animated telling her story. "So we're going to take a look at it tomorrow. We're going to take a purchase offer along with us, and maybe we can negotiate."

"But you don't have any money," I said. "How can you make an offer on a property?"

"We've scraped together five hundred dollars," Philip said. "She only wants a thousand dollars down. I was thinking of giving her a five-hundred-dollar promissory note and five hundred dollars cash. Once we tie the property up, we would then go out and find a partner."

"So you're on your way," I summarized.

"I'm sure we are," Karen said. "Having this wealth of knowledge is unbelievable. I feel within myself that I've changed drastically. I have grown. It has definitely brought us closer as a family unit. We've learned to block out the negative and concentrate on the positive."

"But what about the negative?" I asked, playing devil's advocate. "There are people starving in America today. What about them? When you block out all the negatives, don't you insulate yourself from the real world?"

"No," Karen stated flatly. "Sure, there are problems—we still have problems ourselves. But you deal with them, not dwell on them. Then you can move on to more positive things. That's basically how I see it."

"What about you, Philip? What would you tell the people of this country if you had them for five minutes on national TV?"

"I would tell America that 'you can do it.' This is a land of opportunity. Here in America, if you really want something and it's within the law, you can achieve it if you work for it. Keep knocking on those doors, and one of them is bound to open. Go for it."

"But," I countered, "not everyone who goes for it is going to make it. Some of them are going to fall off the mountain. The obstacles will be too great. There will be casualties."

"That's life. But you come out better if you tackle the obstacles than if you run from them. Even if you fail a hundred times, you still have to say, 'My back has not been broken yet.' Nothing came to me free—nothing. Nothing! I wouldn't appreciate it otherwise. I don't want anything free—with strings attached. Let me work for it. Then I know I've earned it. I have a personal goal that I haven't told too many people about. I'd like to set an example for the people in the community where I grew up. They know me and Karen—that we have something that's together. So I want to buy real estate in that community, make it a better place. If people in that community don't do it, no one else will."

Philip turned to Karen, and they looked at each other. They were together in this goal as in everything else. She would support him.

"How do you feel," I asked, "about the fact that Mary and Steve were first to complete the Challenge?"

"It's not who's first but who crosses the line," Philip said. "I'll never forget watching the women's marathon during the 1984 Summer Olympics. As the winner jogged into the Coliseum for the final lap, the crowd cheered her on to the finish line. After her, thirty or forty others completed the race. Then, a hush came over the crowd as a lone woman staggered onto the track for her last lap. She was in obvious pain, but she was determined to finish. The doctors ran onto the track, concerned about her health, but she waved them away, knowing that if they touched her, she would be disqualified from the race. The crowd, moved by this display of sheer willpower, shouted encouragement as she staggered and weaved the final few yards. When she crossed the line, the crowd cheered more for her than for the woman who had finished first. It gave me chill bumps all inside. That's how I feel about this Challenge. I know I didn't come in first. But I'm going to cross that line. I don't care what it takes."

4. _____

That evening, we sat around a big table in an upper room of the Cheshire Inn and reminisced about the experience.

"I was wondering about the Wealth Secrets," Mary asked. "You only taught us eleven of them. What's the twelfth one?"

All eyes turned to me as if to say, "Yeah, what about it?"

"What do you think the twelfth secret is?" I asked, returning her question with another question.

"I don't know."

"What have you learned in the last ninety days about wealth that is still a secret to the average American?"

She thought for a moment. "The average American doesn't know that it can be done."

"And can it?"

"Sure it can. I did it!"

I nodded knowingly and waited for the question I knew she would ask.

"So is that the twelfth wealth secret?" she asked, "that anyone can do it?"

"What is a secret?" I asked, trying to lead her to her own answer.

"Something that's hidden from common understanding," she replied.

"Hidden?" I continued to question her. "Did I teach you anything that was hidden from anyone? No. It was all plain, simple common sense, available freely to any person who will simply put it into action. And that is the final secret."

WEALTH SECRET NO. 12: THERE ARE NO WEALTH SECRETS. COMMON SENSE PLUS ACTION EQUALS POWER.

(For a free handsome scroll of the 12 Secrets of Wealth see my website at www.Robert Allen.com.

While they were debating the issue of the twelfth secret, I slipped away and walked down to the lobby of the hotel. I was looking for a gift—something to give Mary and Steve, Philip and Karen, and Nora to remind them of our journey together. In the gift shop I found the perfect souvenir and bought each of them a red baseball jacket with the crest of the Cheshire Inn—an old English lion—emblazoned on the back.

I came back up to the interview room and pulled David Benjamin, the filmmaker, aside. "I've been thinking, David," I said. "I've put these people through a lot in these ninety days—camera crews intruding on their lives, phone taps, interviews, everyone peeking into their fishbowl. I want to give them something."

I showed him the jackets I had just bought.

"But," I continued, "I don't think a jacket is enough. I'd like to give them some money—just a small amount to repay them for all they've done. What do you think?"

He pondered for a moment.

I asked, "Do you think it would compromise the Challenge if I gave them each a thousand dollars?"

He broke into a broad smile. He knew what they had been through as well as I. In fact, he had grown so close to each of them during ninety days, living their pains and failures, that he had lost his usual filmmaker's skeptical objectivity, becoming their most ardent cheerleader on the sidelines.

"I don't think Mayor Poelker would care," he said, referring to our watchdog. "It's the least you can do."

19

GETTING AHEAD

1. _____

On October 23, Philip wrote another offer to buy the property in
Maryville. And, miraculously, it was accepted. In a nutshell, the
Maryville offer looked like this:

Price:	$20,000	
Down:	$ 2,000	
New first mortgage:	$ 8,000	at 13.5 percent for fifteen years with three-year review with payments of $103.08
Second mortgage to seller:	$18,000	at 10 percent for fifteen years with payments of $193.43
Cash to Philip:	$ 6,000!	

The seller agreed to let Philip place a new first mortgage on the property and to carry back a second mortgage for the balance of his equity. Ever since the depression, parents have taught their children that a first mortgage is safer than a second. Then why would this seller even consider Philip's offer? It boils down to one simple reason. The seller was a don't-wanter.

With an accepted offer in hand, Philip set about funding it. After several phone calls he linked up with a banker who seemed interested in making a loan. The bank appraiser inspected the property and agreed with Philip that it was substantially undervalued. The bank's eight-thousand-dollar loan would be well secured. The paperwork was started. The ball was rolling.

At this point Philip had to make a tough decision: Should he wait for the property to close before beginning to fix it up, or should he get a headstart and begin immediately? He decided on the latter. With the seller's permission he began fixing up the property. It would need new paint in all eleven rooms, new carpet, repairs to the toilets and some windows replaced—not a small job. With little thought of what would happen if the bank loan failed to go through, Philip and Karen began the tedious job.

Every morning he and Karen rose at about five o'clock. At six he'd walk Karen to the bus stop so she could catch a bus to work. He didn't dare let her walk alone in their neighborhood. After Marcus left for school at eight, Philip would take a bus to the Maryville property. With the transfer, it took about forty-five minutes to get there. It was frustrating, but he had no other form of transportation. He'd work till 2:30 and then come home so as to be there when Marcus got home from school. Karen would arrive at around 3:30. Then Philip would go back to Maryville till eleven or twelve at night. Lots of work to do. At least a month of this routine before he could relax.

He patched and painted walls, fixed the plumbing, cleaned out the junk—all by himself. Nobody cared about that property the way he cared about it. In fact, he became so obsessed with the notion of doing everything by himself that it started to affect his relationship with Karen. They quarreled, until she made clear that she wanted to be in on the action too.

The events leading to the closing on the Maryville house flew by in a blur. It turned out that Philip needed a cosigner for his loan. He turned to Steve and Mary Bonenberger and offered them one thousand dollars cash for their creditworthiness. They consented. Then Philip rented out the Maryville house, even before he closed on it. The deposit plus rent came to over a thousand dollars. The tenants were so anxious that they moved in before the fixup was completed.

After numerous delays, the closing date was set for November 28. At the closing, the seller got two thousand dollars from the loan proceeds and paid the Realtor her commission. The closing officer handed Philip a cashier's check for six thousand dollars. He had to peel himself off the ceiling. He and Karen had never been in possession of so large a lump sum. Philip marched right down to a bank and opened up his first bank account.

Buying Maryville was the beginning of many good things for Philip and Karen Moore. Bank accounts, four major credit cards, a van for transportation, people calling for advice. Philip's celebrity spread. A local accountant with substantial assets heard about Philip's story and called him to form a partnership. He and his partner have now bought several more properties.

Within a year, Philip and Karen moved out of their cramped duplex on Leduc and into the spacious quarters of the Maryville house. The small five-thousand-dollar house that Philip bought for nothing down with a nine-month balloon was deeded to him by the former owners at the end of the nine months. Philip is now looking to dispose of it. His latest acquisition is a twenty-thousand-dollar house, which he bought for fourteen thousand dollars with absolutely nothing down—and without partner assistance.

In a few short months Philip's entire economic and philosophic perspective changed.

A few days after closing on the Maryville property, he drove me over to the group home where he had spent many months paying for his misspent youth. We pulled up in front of a tall two-story structure about ten blocks from his former Leduc apartment. On the steps of the group home, he spoke of his vision.

"When I was here, there were eight of us. Me and seven other guys. I was the youngest and the smallest." Then he told me of the fate of his seven fellow group home friends. Two had been murdered. Two were in prison, two others had gone straight. One had dropped out of sight, but was most likely into drugs.

"I feel lucky," he said. "And I've got to tell the kids who are here today what I had to learn the hard way. I've got to show them an alternative. Karen tells me that I can't save the whole world. But if I could just help one person. . . ."

We walked inside the home. To the right in an open room that used to be the living room of the house were four tables at which seven or eight young black boys were gathered for lunch.

"Hi," Philip said. "My name is Philip Moore. I was in here six or seven years ago. Just came by to look over the old place. It hasn't changed much. Cooking still good?"

A few of the boys nodded suspiciously.

"What was your problem, Mr. Moore?" one of the boys asked.

"I had a lot of problems. But the biggest problem was me. I got into a lot of trouble thinking I deserved a free ride in this world . . . that other people should give me what I wanted. Then I finally figured out I had to do it for myself. I just came by here today to tell you that once you get out of here, you can make it if you want to."

"What do you do now, Mr. Moore?" another boy asked.

"I'm a real estate investor," he replied.

2.

On October 26, Nora and her partner, Wayne, closed on the foreclosure house. That day was one of the happiest of her life. She felt that she'd finally arrived—that she was not a failure. She could hold her head up high again.

But euphoria lasted only a few weeks.

On Thanksgiving Day, she and her daughters, Jennifer and Sylvia, spent the day working on the house with Wayne and his wife, Judy. That evening she built a fire in the fireplace, and they all sat around the fire eating turkey sandwiches, laughing and reveling in a day of work well done. Then, someone accidentally spilled gas near the fire. Seconds later, flames engulfed the room. Nora grabbed her Challenge jacket—the one with the Cheshire lion on the back—and used it to beat out the flames. But the damage was done. The living room was gutted, the carpet ruined, the drapes charred. Even the Challenge jacket was destroyed.

Don't ask me why these things happen. A black cloud has seemed to follow Nora all of her life. And yet a more loving, caring, helpful person I have not met. When the chips were down for someone else, she was the first one at the scene. When someone was hurting, she went to them and hurt with them.

How long will she have to wait for her ship to come in? I don't know. Will she ever have her resort on those 975 acres in the woods of Missouri? Maybe. Maybe not. Her crystal ball is still unclear.

But one thing is certain. Nora will keep on trying until she gets what she wants. No matter how long it takes.

Life doesn't give us many answers. But for some strange reason, whenever I think of Nora, I always think of a story told to me by Charlie Jarvis.

A missionary was sent to Africa, where he spent many long, faithful years in selfless service. Finally he was called home. He booked his passage on the next boat to America. Because he couldn't afford regular passage, he went in steerage. It was a long, rough voyage. When the boat docked in New York, the passengers disembarked to the greetings of friends and families. There was celebration in the air. But when the missionary came down the gangplank, no one was there to meet him.

He stood on the dock, alone and discouraged. Finally, he looked heavenward and said, "Lord, twenty-five years I've served, and when I come home, not even one soul comes to greet me."

Suddenly the air became still, and from the clouds he heard a small but piercing voice.

"Son," said the voice. "You're not home yet."

Some people feel that this life is just one brief spark amid a dark, lonely, endless night. How we get things twisted around! Isn't it just the opposite? A brief eclipsing darkness amid a bright, eternal day.

So remember, Nora: You're not home yet.

3. _____

Mary and Steve felt vast relief when the ninety-day period was over.

They had made it! Squeaked under the wire.

The giant cloud of pressure evaporated. But along with it vanished the excitement. The constant attention and reinforcement from the camera crew and my headquarters subsided. They were left on their own. Filling this void, however, was the renewed attention of friends and family who were just beginning to recognize some of the subtler benefits of the Challenge. One afternoon, Mary received an unexpected call.

"Hello, Mary? It's Mark."

Mary was surprised. Mark was the husband of her best friend, Deena. He had an MBA degree—a corporate man on his way to the top in a well-paying job. In his hotshot way he had ridiculed Mary for investing in real estate. Even though he'd lost a fair amount of money himself in the stock market, he still couldn't see the potential of real estate. Maybe Mark felt that Mary was having a bad influence on Deena. Whatever the reason, he had been very negative about the Challenge from the outset.

"Mary," Mark continued, "I've called to apologize. I'm really sorry I've been acting the way I have."

Mary was floored. She hardly knew what to say.

"That's all right, Mark," she stammered. "I ..."

He cut her off. "I realize I've been negative. I thought you were both crazy. But now I see that what you're doing makes a lot of sense."

Mary felt such a glorious sense of vindication on hearing his words. After all Deena was the only friend to really support her during the Challenge. With Deena, Mary didn't have to be Mary The Preacher's Wife or Mary-I've-Got-It-Together. She could let her hair down and just be Mary-I'm-Going-Crazy. To Deena, Mary had poured her heart out about the overwhelming need to expand her horizons—to do something with her life. Now she was doing something with her life. She was glad that other people were able to see it.

Deena had also been the first to notice the change that had transpired in Mary. She knew how miserable Mary had been in pre-Challenge days—how bogged down she had felt, how finances used to frustrate her. Deena marveled at how different Mary had become. More capable. Confident. Happy.

Deena told her, "You're doing more now than you ever did before. I'm amazed how you juggle everything: your real estate, our friendship and your kids."

Others were also sitting up and taking notice—the same people who just weeks ago had told her that she was expecting too much out of life, that she couldn't have the best of both worlds, that she couldn't have both money and time with her kids and self-respect. She had dared to break with the herd, and they had shunned her like a leper. Now, they were coming to her and Steve for advice—hounding them for information. How ironic!

Negative comments now rolled off her back like water off a duck. She knew better now. She and Steve began to pay off old bills and to climb out of financial bondage. Instead of leaving her children with baby-sitters, Mary took them with her to look through houses and help her count the rooms. Mary made a game of it. "Katie, let's see if this house has a laundry chute." Katie, now four, began to learn that work doesn't have to be something you hate.

The benefits were also being felt in Steve's life. "Before the Challenge I was always afraid that I couldn't support my family," he told me. "Now, I've lost that fear. If they take my job I can still minister. There are a lot of rumblings in me. I'm not going to lose my faith in God or anything. But I want to have the freedom to think my own thoughts. I don't want to color somebody else's picture anymore. I want to have the freedom to draw outside the lines. I don't want to draw circles that fence people out. I want to draw circles that include everyone. I'm moving toward another dimension of the ministry. It might sound weird, but I can see myself being some kind of a motivational speaker. Isn't that just another dimension of the ministry? I like the 'me' that's emerging, though. I really do."

"I've grown too," Mary added. "I may be a little colder, a little tougher, when it comes to negotiating a business transaction. But I'm a lot warmer on a personal level. I can give so much more to people now than I ever could before. When something impossible comes up, I just take a deep breath, step back, and say, 'Somewhere in here I've got the strength to do it.' I've learned two valuable lessons. One is: Don't give up, just try another source, another direction. That's the Blue Vase concept, I guess. It comes to mind time and time again. The other lesson is: Always check with an expert, but remember that experts don't know everything. I'll always remember your mountain-climbing story. That story really stuck. I still get the feeling that I'm on a journey, an adventure to someplace that I've never been before. Every once in a while I wonder if this is too crazy for me. But then I start thinking about what it was like before, and that's when I know I never want to go back. This is working. Why would I want to go back to something that wasn't working? I'm no longer the classic nagging wife always harping on her husband about what she could have done if she hadn't sacrificed so much for him. I can have it all. I even think within ten years Steve and I can actually be millionaires."

In November Steve and Mary bought and moved into their second property—a forty-seven-thousand-dollar three-bedroom home with a garage, located in a better neighborhood. The down payment was less than a thousand dollars. Steve's mother overheard someone talking about the house at the donut shop and passed the lead on to Mary. They moved out of their two-bedroom house, never to be cramped that way again, and rented it to a couple in their church.

Incidentally, their first investment house, which they bought and sold during the ninety-day Challenge, was resold again by the gentleman who had bought it from them. He spent two thousand dollars and two months' worth of evening labor—and came out ten thousand dollars ahead.

In a few months, Mary and Steve had acquired four properties generating several hundred dollars a month in cash flow, growing equities and cash in the bank. Within a year, Mary went on to sell a million dollars' worth of real estate as a licensed agent. Steve eventually resigned his pastor's position in St. Louis in preparation for starting a new church. And he and Mary moved their family to West County, to a beautiful condominium worth three times as much as their first home.

By then, Mary was on the lecture circuit herself.

WHEN YOU BREAK OUT OF PRISON BE SURE
TO LEAVE THE KEYS BEHIND.—Robert G. Allen

20

AFTERWORD: THE CHALLENGE NEVER ENDS

The runway disappeared in a burst of power as TWA flight 347 bound from St. Louis to San Antonio lifted off into the crystal cold of a Missouri blue sky.

Mary pressed her nose against the chilled windowpane and watched as the plane rose and banked over the gleaming buildings of downtown St. Louis and the Gateway Monument. She reflected back to the day she had spent at the Arch Museum with the Challenge team. It seemed impossible that six months had blown by so quickly.

She tingled all over. For the first time, flying high over the arch, she fully understood that she would never have been in that airplane—not in a hundred lifetimes—if she hadn't stepped out across the frontier to embrace the risks of the unknown. She was a pioneer now. She had tasted of the fruits of it. And they had been sweet.

This brought into focus her next frontier—the reason for her plane trip. As the Boeing 727 leveled out its southwesterly trajectory, Mary reflected on her assignment. It was a tough one, almost a Mission Impossible. . . .

to fly to San Antonio, Texas—a city in which she had never before set foot—choose three individuals with limited financial resources and investment experience. Teach these individuals in two days the secrets of wealth. Give them a Challenge to lift themselves into financial self-reliance.

What was she doing?!

She was actually on a plane to San Antonio! Six months before she had never heard of a wealth secret. And in twenty-four hours she'd be teaching them to three strangers!

Was she nuts!? She wasn't an expert. She was just Mary Bonenberger—housewife/investor. How could she have let herself be talked into this? She just knew that she was going to fall flat on her face!

She was met at the San Antonio airport by Lupe Lloyd, a local Realtor and president of the San Antonio Real Estate Investment Group, who had volunteered to chauffeur Mary about the city to give her a feeling for the market. Mary liked Lupe immediately. She was creative, on the ball. "A real blue-vaser," Mary thought. "If I were an investor in San Antonio and had her for a friend, the possibilities would be endless."

With the help of Tom Painter, Dr. Blaine Lee and David Benjamin and under the watchful eye of Marie Laynn Natoralva, executive director of United Way, San Antonio, Mary selected three San Antonio residents for the Challenge training. Instead of going to the unemployment lines, she chose average people with jobs and small bank accounts.

The first couple chosen was Joseph Gutierrez and his wife, Cheva. They were of Mexican descent. Joseph was thirty-eight years old and worked at Southwestern Bell as a telephone repairman. Cheva also worked for the phone company, and both of them had aspirations to be financially secure.

Next was Jean Scott, an eight-year resident of San Antonio employed as a commercial insurance salesperson. Jean's financial goal was to be able to put her two daughters through college.

The final members of the San Antonio Challenge team were Larry

Dyer and his wife, Penny. They had recently sold a tobacco store, which they had owned for ten years. Their savings were down to ten thousand dollars, and they were anxious to find another opportunity.

As Mary began the two-day training at 8:00 A.M. the next morning she hesitated momentarily as the fear welled up inside her. Then she took a deep breath and stepped out across another frontier.

"Good morning. My name is Mary Bonenberger, and I'm here to show you how to start on the road to financial independence. It's a road I started down myself only six months ago. You can duplicate what I have done in the past six months—even more so. And it will change your life, just like it changed mine...."

The next two days flew by. As Mary finished her instruction, she gave them a final challenge.

"When Bob came to St. Louis in June, he taught us an old Chinese proverb: 'Give a man a fish, and you feed him for a day. Teach a man to fish, and you feed him for a lifetime.' Bob taught us how to fish. All he asked in return was that we teach three other people what we had been taught. I agreed to do that, and I want you to do it too. If each of you would just teach three others, and so on, the message would spread and bless many lives. Will you accept my challenge?"

They nodded and with that, the seminar was over. Mary had done it! The cycle was complete. The dream was alive. The ripples were beginning to spread.

Except this time, the ripples turned into waves.

Within ninety days, Jean Scott bought one property with a contract on a second one, soon to be followed by a third. Her first property—an $80,000 duplex with a detached third apartment on the back—was purchased by borrowing a $3,000 down payment from her personal house equity. She financed the balance with very creative seller financing allowing her to end up with a positive cash flow of over $500 per month for the first year. After $7,500 in fixup costs (which was borrowed from a home improvement loan) the property appraised for over $100,000. This property became the showplace for the neighborhood prompting other neighbors to renovate. She has a waiting list of tenants.

Within a year, Jean became the owner of an insurance agency, which she bought with a partner. Instead of selling insurance as an employee, Jean is now the boss. As she knows, there is a world of difference. Both of Jean's daughters are in college. One of them has become interested in real estate investing and has made indications of following in her mother's footsteps.

Joe and Cheva Gutierrez started out very conservatively. They searched carefully for their first investment property—a small home bought 30 percent below market—within the ninety-day deadline. Within the next few months they bought four other properties, all 15 to 30 percent below market—the cheapest being forty-five thousand dollars and the most expensive being seventy thousand—all with positive cash flows. Cheva quit her job to spend full time on their investments, and both she and Joe are bubbling over with excitement about their newfound career.

Larry and Penny Dyer also wasted no time after the training. Their first deal, ironically, was one that conservative Joe and Cheva passed up. A don't-wanter owner of two duplexes needed a quick sale. They were each worth ninety-five thousand dollars. Larry and Penny offered eighty-five using a five-thousand-dollar promissory note as the down payment. The seller readily agreed. He had owned the duplexes for several years and had a nice built-in profit. The closing date was set for sixty days in the future. But before that time had elapsed, Larry and Penny found a buyer for the duplexes. When the smoke cleared, the Dyers walked out of the closing with ten thousand dollars cash—without ever having owned the property!

Within the next twelve months, the Dyers went on to buy over $1 million in property and to put over $170,000 cash in their pockets from their real estate investments.

And while these three were tasting the fruits of success, Mary, their teacher, was just coming into her own. Mary and Steve Bonenberger formed an investment group that now controls over several million in real estate.

But that's another story.

Dear Reader,

Your success is important to me. You too, like the people in this book, can learn to become more successful in all areas of your like. And I would love to help you make your dreams come true. If I can help people from an unemployment line to make dramatic progress in only 90 days, just think of what you and I could do together.

Currently I am looking for a small group of people to prove more of my financial strategies work. I am in the process of finishing my latest book in which I reveal financial techniques and strategies for earning high returns on your money. I will also show you how to earn as much as $1,000 a day right from your own home. In addition I will reveal new Real Estate strategies for the next decade.

For this new book I need success stories, just like those in the "Road to Wealth". If you would like to be one of those success stories let's work together. Call me now at 801-852-8700 or visit my website at www.RobertAllen.com.

I wish you a happy, healthy, and abundant future.

Your Friend,

Robert G. Allen

Robert G. Allen

ABOUT THE AUTHOR

Robert G. Allen, the famous Author, lecturer, and millionaire has had graduates of his popular nationwide seminars successfully apply his highly profitable techniques and philosophy in all 50 states and Canada. Today there are literally thousands of real estate millionaires nationwide who attribute their success to their contact with Mr. Allen. He is a popular television and radio guest, appearing on hundreds of radio and television programs, including *Good Morning America, The Regis Philbin Show* and *Larry King Live*. Articles have been written about him and his ideas in publications nationwide including the *Wall Street Journal*, *Newsweek, Barons's Money* magazine and *The Reader's Digest* to name just a few.

Robert Allen's blockbuster best-sellers, Nothing Down and Creating Wealth, have inspired and helped more than one and a half million hardcover readers seeking financial success and independence. Now, in The Road to Wealth, Allen takes a giant leap forward by proving that any reasonably intelligent American can drastically improve his or her financial situation in only 90 days. To this Mr Allen made the challenge – "Send me to any unemployment line. Let me select someone who is broke, out of work, discouraged. Let me teach him in two day's time the secrets of wealth. And in 90 days he'll be back on his feet, with $5,000 cash in the bank, never to set foot in an unemployment line again..."

Everywhere, skeptics came out of the woodwork to say it couldn't be done and that putting his reputation on the line was too risky. Nevertheless, under the watchful eye of former St. Louis Mayor John Poelker, Robert Allen selected not one but three individuals. You are going to be amazed by their stories.

In one of the most inspiring–and practical–books you'll ever read, The Road to Wealth tells just how he did it, using the actual names and true stories of the people involved.

The Road to Wealth is much more than a book about several unemployed people who overcame their fear of failure and learned the strategy of winning. It is really about you–your dreams, your goals, what you want out of life. And in addition to detailing these specific case studies, Allen provides special self-help guidelines throughout the book to give you the knowledge and motivation to make the leap to real rewards. He shows you exactly how his techniques were successfully applied as he guides you through every step of the process.

Once you begin reading this book you won't put it down, for it reads with all the drama and drive of a good novel; yet every word of it is absolutely true. Here's a book filled with advice that anyone can follow to succeed. If you have desire, determination and persistence, the rest is all here in the pages of this book.

Dear Wealth Seeker:

Would you like to make an extra $50,000 to $100,000 a year for life?

Because of your interest in Making Money. I want to work with you on a personal basis to help you reach your financial goals.

My name is Robert Allen. I'm the author of two of the largest selling financial books in history; both #1 New York Times best sellers—read my millions of people in the past 20 years.

My current best-selling audio program from Nightingale/Conant is entitled Multiple Streams of Income: How to Generate a Lifetime of Unlimited Wealth.

103,000 people attended my $500 weekend investment seminars in the 80's.

20,000 people attended my $5,000 week long Wealth Training in the 90's.

Thousands of them are now financially free.

I'm now in the process of finishing my latest book in which I reveal many little known financial techniques and strategies for earning 18%, 36% and as high as 50% on your money. All guaranteed by the government! Plus 6 other ways of earning as much as $1,000 a day right from your own home.

Every time I write a new best seller I do a challenge to prove that the new techniques can be profitably applied by anyone.

When I wrote my first book I said:

"Send me to any city in America, take away my wallet, Give me $100 for living expenses and in 72 hours I will buy you an excellent property, all with none of my own money."

The Los Angeles Times took me up on my challenge. They flew me to San Francisco with an L.A. times Reporter. In 57 hours I had purchased 7 properties worth $722,000. Today those assets are worth almost triple that amount.

For my next #1 best seller, I did the St. Louis Challenge. I said:

"Send me to any unemployment line. Let me select someone who is broke, out of work, discouraged. Let me teach him in two day's time the secrets of wealth. And in 90 days he'll be back on his feet, with $5,000 cash in the bank, never to set foot in an unemployment line again..."

I selected a young couple from the unemployment lines of St. Louis, Missouri. Ninety days later they had earned $5,000 using one of my techniques.

In the next 12 months they had earned over $100,000. To celebrate, I took them on Good Morning America with me.

To publicize my next book, I accepted an invitation to appear on the Regis Philbin Show. From the studio audience, I selected a woman named Pat Watson.

90 days later, Pat and I were back on the show with an incredible story to tell. Starting from scratch, using my system, she had earned over $20,000.

I've been working on my latest book for the past 8 years. I'm, now, ready for my next challenge. I call it the Multiple Streams of Income Challenge.

"Send me a group of people who want to become financially independent. Let me teach them my strategies for Creating Wealth. In 90 days, they will have developed multiple streams of income. Eventually these streams of income will give them the freedom to do what ever they want for the rest of their lives."

What's the bottom line? I need success stories. I'm looking for a group of people who are willing to follow my advice and make money with my strategies

Interested?

I'm in the process of selecting a group of people to work with me on a personal basis. We go into depth in three areas.

#1 Real Estate (Nothing Down and Foreclosures)

#2 Info-Preneuring (Information and Internet)

#3 Financial (Stock Market and Asset Protection)

Our Goals are simple:

#1 Buy an excellent piece of Real Estate at a bargain price.

#2 Start on the road to make a $1,000 a day on the Internet.

#3 Make money in the Stock Market. Set up your Financial Fortress with Corporations, Limited Partnerships and Trusts.

Read the Road to Wealth. If your intuition tells you that it's appropriate to work with me, give my office a call at **1-801-852-8700. Or visit my website at www.multiplestreamsofincome.com**

Good Luck

Robert G Allen